ECONOMIC BACKWARDNESS AND ECONOMIC GROWTH

ECONOMIC BACKWARDNESS

Studies in the Theory

One of a series of books from the research program of the Institute of Industrial Relations, University of California

AND ECONOMIC GROWTH

of Economic Development

HARVEY LEIBENSTEIN

Associate Professor of Economics
University of California, Berkeley

NEW YORK · JOHN WILEY & SONS, INC.
LONDON ·

THIRD PRINTING, SEPTEMBER, 1962

Library of Congress Catalog Card Number 57-12296
Printed in the United States of America

To my parents

Preface

A preface provides a writer with an opportunity to express to the reader the sort of things he might say to a friend about to pick up his manuscript. These may include reflections about the nature of his work, perhaps a capsule summary of the contents, some incidental information of a background nature, and, in an effort to avoid misunderstandings (an effort that is not always successful), some statements about the limits and boundaries of the work. I will begin with the capsule summary.

The first three chapters, introductory in character, outline the nature of the problem, and set forth my modus operandi. The heart of the book, to be found in chapters 4 to 13, may be divided roughly into two parts. In the first of these, the state of economic backwardness is analyzed. The characteristics usually found in densely populated underdeveloped economies are examined, discussed, and, in part, explained. The broad aim here is to show that these characteristics are part of a pattern, that they are of a piece, so to speak, and that they generally help to reinforce each other. The basic notion is that the simultaneous concurrence of these conditions can be best understood in terms of the "quasi-equilibrium" that underlies the state of economic backwardness. The second part deals, in one way or another, with the possible escape from economic backwardness, with the factors that underlie the transition to sustained economic growth when certain limiting conditions are met. The last two chapters are of an applied nature: Statistical and other data are presented in chapter 14 to suggest the relative magnitudes of the main variables involved in the earlier theoretical sections. Chapter

15 looks at some of the investment policies that have been suggested from time to time in the light of the theory developed in earlier portions of the book.

Throughout the writing of this book my aim has been explanation and understanding—*not prescription.* I hasten to emphasize this point in the hope of avoiding inferences on the part of any reader about specific remedies. None is intended. Nothing in this book should be taken to be in support of any measure, especially specific control measures such as government investment or control of industry, to achieve development. I doubt that any specific course of action for backward economies could be charted on the basis of a general analysis of the problem. Prescriptions would have to take into account the unique aspects of and differences among backward economies. Furthermore, one can hardly advocate specific means without taking into account and deciding upon the "correct" social goals, ethical norms, moral restraints, and political values. These are very important matters, but they are not considered in this volume.

Any book in the economic development field must be incomplete. The field itself is exceedingly broad and has often been characterized as being underdeveloped. Its boundaries, professional or otherwise, are still undefined and certainly debatable. Most variables that economists deal with, and many that they do not consider, can in some way be connected with development problems. Considering that the scope of the field is still unsettled and that many of the issues are still hotly debated, it seems unlikely that a *complete* scheme of analysis applicable to these problems can be developed at this stage. The most that one can hope for is to make a contribution toward such a development. I hope, of course, that this book, or parts of it, may turn out to be helpful in this connection.

Many of the concepts and ideas that we usually employ are part of our professional equipment and come as a result of professional training. However, some ideas, and these are difficult to acknowledge specifically, we may borrow almost imperceptibly from the intellectual climate in which we live and work. We do so almost without knowing it, often in the process of "talking shop." In view of this it is impossible to acknowledge one's total intellectual indebtedness, or even to acknowledge the most important instances, for these may well be the instances of imperceptible borrowing. If, in the course of my work, I have borrowed in this manner, this paragraph should be taken as its acknowledgment.

On a formal level I began the research that resulted in this volume sometime in 1952 under the stimulus of the late Lloyd Fisher, and through the encouragement of Chancellor Clark Kerr. The research was carried out mostly during the years 1952–1954. Most of the ideas were developed during that period. A complete draft was written during the academic year 1954–1955. Revisions of a stylistic nature were carried out during the year that followed. Throughout this period my work was supported, in part, by the Inter-University Study of Labor Problems in Economic Development. I am indebted to the coordinating board of the Inter-University Study, Clark Kerr, Frederick H. Harbison, John T. Dunlop, and Charles A. Meyers, for the help that made it possible for me to carry through the research.

In the course of preparing this book several individuals were helpful in various ways. I am indebted to Alec P. Alexander, Glen Cane, John Conroy, Mrs. Greta Heinz, and Barry Siegel, for research assistance at various stages of the work. Mr. Richard Gamble, a graduate student in sociology, read the manuscript from the viewpoint of a non-economist and made a number of helpful suggestions that improved the exposition. Mrs. Jeanette Podvin typed the final version of the manuscript and handled a number of details in a most efficient manner.

Dr. Margaret Gordon and Professors C. M. Li, A. G. Papandreou, and P. S. Steiner read the manuscript critically and made a number of useful suggestions for improvement. Some sections of the last chapter are, in part, an outgrowth of work carried out jointly by Walter Galenson and myself. Last but not least I am indebted to my wife, Margaret Libnic Leibenstein, for help in many ways, not all of which can be adequately acknowledged in a preface. Of course, none of those that I have mentioned, including the last mentioned, should be presumed necessarily to share any of the views found in this volume or to be responsible for errors or omissions that it may contain.

I also want to take this opportunity to express my gratitude to the *Journal of Political Economy* for permission to reprint, in somewhat different form, my article, "The Theory of Underemployment in Backward Economies."

HARVEY LEIBENSTEIN

May, 1957

Contents

CHAPTER 1

The World's Inequalities

The Need for an Explanation

It is probable that never before have the differences in the levels of living among average persons in different countries been as great as they are today. Although it may be impossible to prove this assertion in view of the lack of statistical information for many historical periods, there can be little doubt about the vast disparities that exist between the inhabitants of the highly developed countries and those that live in the backward economies that comprise over two-thirds of the world's population. A glance at any of the recent computations of per capita income comparisons among different countries suggests the enormity of the gap. (Compare, for example, the United States per capita income of $1453.00 in 1949 with that of Indonesia of $25.00 as computed by the United Nations. The same set of computations also reveals that in 1949 some 54 per cent of the world population lived in countries with less than $100.00 per capita income while only 7 per cent lived in a country with over $1000.00 per capita income.)[1] Even more striking must be the differences in the rates of change among different countries. Given the current disparities in per capita income, and if it is known that a country like the United States has enjoyed a rate of

[1] Statistical Office of the United Nations, "National and Per Capita Incomes Seventy Countries—1949," *Statistical Papers Series E, No. 1,* New York, October 1950, pp. 14–16, and p. 29.

growth of something like 3 per cent per year over the last 130 years, it must be clear that by comparison the rate of increase in income per head for the countries with lowest incomes must have been slow indeed over the last century and a half. Indeed, for some countries any improvement over a former age is in considerable doubt. Although it may be true that the problems inherent in income measurement, and the statistical conventions employed, lead to results that exaggerate the extent of the differences, there can be little doubt about their existence. Perhaps the thirty- or fortyfold differences in per capita incomes between the most advanced and the least advanced countries do not quite give an accurate reflection of relative standards, but surely it is correct to infer that the disparities are exceedingly large.

Despite such striking facts, and despite the usual humanistic concern with trying to understand why some should live perpetually on the brink of starvation, it is of interest that until this last decade modern economists have done very little in trying to fathom this dilemma. In part this neglect has been due to the fact that economic research, like other aspects of life, is subject to fashion. In part it may also have been due to the fact that the problem is inherently exceedingly difficult. Whatever the reason for the recent upsurge of interest in what has become known as "the underdeveloped areas problem," it can hardly be because the problem is readily understood, or because the elements of the problem especially lend themselves to the type of theorizing customary among economists. The upsurge of interest, if it can be explained at all, probably arises because of some feelings about the intrinsic significance of the issues, as well as an urgent need for solutions.

We can hardly exaggerate the "felt" urgency of the problem if we consider such diverse influences as the widespread interest in the alleviation of poverty, the fact that in many countries "economic development" has become a matter of public policy, also the fact that in recent years vast international institutions have been created precisely for this purpose, the observation that there seems to be a steady increase in the number of national and international plans for development and growth (indeed "development planning" seems to have become a political byword and catch-phrase denoting a virtuous activity that few civic-minded people would dare suggest that we do without), the increasing number of countries being subjected to rather hurried studies in order to determine their "development possibilities," and, finally, the increasing tempo with which these activities are being undertaken.

And yet much of this activity is carried on in the absence of what would generally be recognized as a theory of economic growth. Indeed, if we may be permitted to speculate on the matter, we suspect that the urgency of the problem and the almost frenzied nature of some of these activities militate against the development of theory. Where there is a sense of urgency there is usually little room for seemingly idle and disinterested speculation, especially the type of "free-wheeling" speculation in which there is neither a commitment to nor any overt concern with the practical aspects of the problem. Yet it is often this kind of speculative exercise, divorced from practicality or reality, in the narrow sense, that leads to formulations that can serve as an integrating device for the study of "the facts" and for the evaluation of practical policies. Excessive concern with urgent practical issues forces us to consider the problem in all its multifarious complexities, and eventually results either in our being bogged down by our inability to cope with a mass of detail or in compromising by limiting our consideration to a narrow aspect of the problem.

An alternative approach, and the one that we shall employ, is to look at the matter as a purely intellectual problem, quite unconcerned with the need for immediate solutions or the requirement of immediate empirical verification. This approach may lead not only to a formulation in highly abstract terms but also to one that abstracts the intellectual problem from its broader social and political setting.

The abstract, non-empirical, and non-historical approach is especially congenial to the individual worker who is interested in the development problem as a whole. The problem of explaining the present disparities in per capita income is an historical as well as an analytical one. Anyone hoping to come up with a really detailed explanation would have to possess an amazing complex of talents. He would probably require a complete knowledge of the economic history of each of the countries under consideration and of the other countries with which the country under scrutiny has or has had economic dealings, a capacity to manipulate vast amounts of statistical data, and, finally, a capacity to concoct an adequate theory so that he could explain not only why certain events transpired but also why some alternative sequence of events did not occur. Obviously it is impossible for any individual to acquire such knowledge. In view of the framework of ignorance within which we are forced to work, it would certainly be convenient if we could frame our problem in such a way as to take the intellectual question out of its historical context. This objective, of course, need not prevent us from presenting, from time to time, statistical or historical data either as examples of possible situations or as a means of illuminating certain issues.

The Abstract Problem

The nature of the abstract problem can be outlined in the following terms: (1) We begin with a set of economies (or countries), each "enjoying" an equally *low* standard of living at the outset. (2) Over a relatively long period of time (say, a century or two) some of these countries increase their output per head considerably whereas others do not. (3) Furthermore, apart from cyclical fluctuations that may arise, the gap in per capita output between the advancing countries and the stagnant ones steadily increases. (4) We treat as a matter of secondary importance the question of whether or not the backward countries remain at their initial position or merely advance exceedingly slowly, although we do give this question a limited amount of attention. Now our problem is to formulate an hypothesis (or theory, if the reader prefers that word) that explains "in the general case" why some countries should have developed while others remain more or less stagnant, or why some countries remain economically backward while others experience sustained secular advance.

The words "in the general case" call for explanation. Why should we limit ourselves to the general case? One of the major difficulties, as Haavelmo's[2] study illustrates, is that the abstract problem really admits of too many solutions. There are far too many possible models that can be invented in which certain values of the parameters will lead to the type of per capita income disparities we have mentioned. In other words, if the problem remains completely unrestricted, it becomes all too easy to think of a large group of hypotheses that would lead to the type of per capita income disparities we want to consider. Therefore, we have to restrict our problem.

It seems reasonable to do so by requiring that our model of the economic process and the related explanatory hypotheses should fit the general case of growing and backward economies as these have been observed over the last two centuries or so. In other words, we want a theory that is not inconsistent with the *commonly observed characteristics* of backward economies. Also, we want a theory that can account for those characteristics commonly found in advanced economies that are absent in the backward ones. Following this requirement, we shall, in chapter 4, present a list of some of the more or less common characteristics of backward economies and discuss, in chapters 4, 5, and 6, explanations for the simultaneous occurrence of these

[2] Trygve Haavelmo, *A Study in the Theory of Economic Evolution* (Contributions to Economic Analysis 3), Amsterdam, North Holland Publishing Company, 1954.

characteristics. Throughout the writing of these chapters we have tried to keep such characteristics in mind. Furthermore, at one stage of the research we attempted to work up several sets of characteristics of both backward and advanced economies on the basis of much of the literature bearing on the subject, some of it written by first-hand observers. Although the characteristics that make up a list obtained in this manner are not always mutually consistent, and although many of them are stated in broad and rather vague terms, they, nevertheless, form a basis of choosing some relationships and weeding out others. In this way we are able to avoid the consideration and presentation of an almost infinite variety of possible theories.

Introduction to the Chapters That Follow

The chapters that follow are intended as a *contribution* to the theory of development. The contents are more in the nature of a series of closely related essays with a central theme than a full-blown treatise. The general problem is so broad and the possible elements so numerous that there is almost no end to the aspects of the problem that can be selected for consideration. Since the investigation of one element leads to another and each, in turn, leads to a third, there is almost an infinite regression of suitable topics that can be picked for detailed investigation. Clearly a choice has to be made, and to some extent the choice must be arbitrary.

Yet, all in all, the chapters that follow seem to add up to at least a "partial" theory of economic development—"partial" only in the sense that certain aspects of the problem are not considered explicitly. For example, the monetary and banking aspects of the problem as well as the international trade aspects are left out. However, the treatment is sufficiently general so that the net result is the development of hypotheses that can serve as an explanation of the disparities considered.

It is, at best, a moot point whether anything that we may call a theory of economic development, in the sense that we have conceived the development problem, exists today. At the same time, it would probably be equally untrue to assert that there is a complete void in this sphere. Certainly the concepts of conventional micro- and macroeconomics are applicable to some aspects of the problem. In addition, some elements of business cycle theory offer insights and parallels that are useful. Furthermore, the models presented by Professor Haavelmo, as well as the less formalized speculations of a number of other writers (including the classical economists who often had much to say on this problem), yield a number of possible alternative hypotheses on various aspects. Surely no writer on the subject need begin with a *tabula rasa,* or in any sense *de novo,* as it were. Yet theorizing on the subject is still in a sufficiently early stage so that nothing very much seems to have jelled. There is still considerable doubt as to what aspects of received theory are really useful here and what aspects have to be thought through again, reworked, and fitted into a framework more suitable for the problem at hand.

A number of possible pitfalls seem to face us when we work on the theoretical aspects of economic development. Since most of us value, to some extent, the current reservoir of economic theories, concepts, and ideas, there is the danger of being so slavishly attached to this set of hypotheses and concepts, framed initially with different problems in mind, that they form blinders to aspects of the problem that may turn out to be of importance if seen in the light of a different conceptual framework. At the opposite pole there is the danger of trying to see the problem in so original a fashion that we discard much that may be valuable in the existing conceptual reservoir. In the chapters that follow, we have tried to steer some sort of middle course—to see the overall problem in the light of a central hypothesis that may be called "the critical minimum effort principle"[3] (see Chapter 8 and later chapters)—but much, though not all, of the supporting edifice utilizes conventional notions common to present-day economics.

A warning to the reader may be in order before he has invested too much of his time in perusing these pages. This book is, quite frankly, a venture in the art of speculation. The reader should not be misled by the fact that at various junctures in the argument statistical or other empirical information is presented either to bolster the argument or to suggest the importance of some of the variables. It is not an empirical book. Adequate factual evidence is most probably unavailable either to "prove" all the propositions that are suggested or to support all the generalizations that are made. In many respects the phenomena with which we have to deal are amorphous, ambiguous, and mercurial in the extreme. Indeed, at some points merely defining the variables that may be of significance is a very difficult matter. But if some of the entities that we shall consider appear to lack sufficient concreteness, it is probably because this is the price we have to pay if we wish to treat the problem as a whole. Despite such difficulties we hope that we shall succeed in what is really our major concern—to paint a picture of the development process in such a way as to see something of the essence of the problem even if we miss much of the detail.

---

[3] Harvey Leibenstein, *A Theory of Economic Demographic Development,* Princeton, Princeton University Press, 1954, Chapters IV, V, and VI.

CHAPTER 2

Per Capita Output as an Index of Development[1]

Introduction

In the chapters that follow we shall utilize per capita output or per capita income as our index of development. Although this is not a novel idea, it is one that is not universally accepted. Some writers appear to take it for granted, for example, the group that wrote the United Nations report, "Measures for the Economic Development of Underdeveloped Countries,"[2] whereas others, for example, Viner,[3] are somewhat uneasy and equivocal about its use, while still others, for example, Professor Frankel,[4] are unquestionably opposed to viewing per capita income as either an index, criterion, or goal of development.[5] It is incumbent upon us to defend the use of such a measure.

---

[1] The reader who is convinced at the outset that per capita output is a good index of economic growth may skip this chapter.

[2] United Nations, Department of Economic Affairs, *Economic Development Studies,* New York, 1951. See also W. A. Lewis, *The Theory of Economic Growth,* London, George Allen and Unwin, 1955, pp. 420 ff.

[3] Jacob Viner, *International Trade and Economic Development;* Lectures delivered at the National University of Brazil, Oxford, The Clarendon Press, 1953, pp. 125 ff.

[4] S. H. Frankel, *The Economic Impact on Underdeveloped Societies;* Essays in International Investment and Social Change, Oxford, Blackwell, 1953.

[5] It is of interest to note that Norman S. Buchanan and Howard S. Ellis, in

There is no traditionally established and clear cut notion as to what is meant by economic development. Ideas of change, growth, and betterment are obviously involved. But what kinds of changes represent growth rather than regression? This is a difficult question to answer without some model of an ideal growth pattern. Economic activity involves many dimensions. Therefore, many patterns of change are possible. If there existed a constant pattern of change and its direction were determinable our problem would be solved. But this is not the case. Although we must beware lest we imply that no uniformities whatsoever exist, it certainly appears reasonable to believe that there are many patterns of change, hence we cannot compare any existing pattern with some norm or ideal and determine the extent of growth.

The problem is especially difficult because not all the variables move in the same direction. For example, aggregate national income may increase while per capita income declines. Does this represent growth or retardation? It would appear that we must choose an index derived from a set of variables and employ it as a criterion. The basis on which the index is to be chosen depends on the problem we have in mind. But this may imply an extent of arbitrariness that is misleading. Economic variables are closely related and many of them will generally move in the same direction.

Another difficulty arises from the fact that all macro-economic variables involve the difficulties inherent in the aggregation of heterogeneous entities. Concepts like income, productivity, investment, etc. involve a very high degree of aggregation and, as a consequence, a problem of translating the individual entities into some common value unit. There exists considerable literature on this matter and we shall refrain from adding to the volume of controversy and speculation. In principle, there is no solution that will satisfy the purist.

But we cannot take a perfectionist view. If we did our efforts would stop at the very outset. We may have to go on with other problems before we completely solve the ones with which we start. Progress in economics, as well as in other fields, did not proceed through the finding of solutions to each conceptual problem before continuing on to the next one. At some point in our researches we decide that we have done about as well as we can; we make a temporary, albeit to some extent arbitrary, decision and proceed to the next step. In other words, we do not climb

---

their recent study, *Approaches to Economic Development,* The Twentieth Century Fund, New York, 1955, take the view that ". . . development means developing the real income potentialities of the underdeveloped areas by using investment to effect those changes and to augment those productive resources which promise to raise real income per person" (pp. 21–22).

from one intellectual victory to the next but we plow ahead despite the fact that the problem we have left behind has not been cleaned up entirely. The alternative is not to proceed at all. For example, economists have developed a useful theory of income and employment determination despite the fact that many of the concepts possess or conceal methodological shortcomings. It is, therefore, not convincing to be told that our index of economic growth does not imply everything it should for all conceivable problems. It must be taken for granted that an index of any sort is only a bench mark or a sign of something and not a substitute for the complete vision and understanding of everything that may interest us.

One of the sources of considerable confusion and idle controversy is the failure to distinguish between an index of observation and a goal determined on welfare grounds. By an index of observation we mean something that we employ to judge the picture as a whole when it is either impossible, impracticable, or inconvenient to consider all of the aspects of the problem simultaneously. Although the index may be a variable of some sort, we do impute to or see behind it more than just changes in the value of this specific variable. In other words, we have some notion, one that need not be stated explicitly, as to how other variables are linked or likely to behave in relation to our index. Thus, in knowing the value of one we do have some notion as to what happens to the others, although the relationships between the variables need not be of an exact or cardinal nature. It is simply that we cannot bother to try to observe or keep in mind at one time the changes in all of the variables that may be of significance. We use one to imply something about all the others but not necessarily everything. Thus, if per capita output increases, this has certain implications for changes in aggregate output, in per capita consumption, in the probable rate of investment, *in the possibility of the community to attain a certain standard of life,* as well as the possibility to achieve a certain expectation of life, etc. Parenthetically, we may observe that the last few phrases indicate the nature of our argument, namely, that our index of development implies a set of *possibilities of achievement* that rise and fall as our index rises and falls.

An index of observation is bereft of welfare implications. It implies neither the desirability nor the undesirability of the index rising, falling, or staying put. This is not to imply that it is always illegitimate to attach or couple ethical or value connotations to these concepts. It is simply that the value meaning and the descriptive meaning of these categories are clearly separable. Thus, if we use average output as an index of observation for economic growth or development we need not imply that increases in output and in the concomitant changes in the structure of the economy are necessarily good. We need not settle the "value meaning" of these concepts in order to use them in their descriptive senses.

Viner, in his essay on economic development, argues that, ". . . the primary emphasis . . . properly belongs, on per capita levels of living, on the issue of poverty and prosperity, although it leaves room for secondary emphasis on quantity of population."[6] A few pages later Viner seems to insist "that the reduction of mass poverty be made the crucial test of the realization of economic development."[7] Finally, he says, "I use the term [economic development] to signify not merely economic growth, but economic growth with which is associated either rising per capita levels of income or the maintenance of existing high levels of income."[8] Although Viner's final position is not entirely clear we can glean certain conclusions from it. These are: first, that mere aggregates are not a test of development; second, that the ultimate realization of development must be higher levels of consumption for the masses of the populace. At one point, he appears to accept per capita income as an index of development, but elsewhere in the paper he appears to have qualms about the acceptance of a mere average as an index. He appears to insist at least on the side condition that the level of living of the bulk of the people not decline.[9]

For a closed economy, per capita income and per capita output are identical but there may be considerable deviation between per capita output and the per capita level of consumption. In the short run raising per capita output and raising per capita consumption are antithetical to each other. For the rate of capital accumulation will depend, in part, on the extent to which increases in output are not followed by equal increases in consumption. Although increasing per capita consumption levels may be, and perhaps must be, an ultimate goal, the concentration on maximizing consumption at the outset may result in the ultimate goal never being achieved.

The basic and significant difference between backward and developed countries lies in their vastly differing *capacities* to produce goods and services per capita, be they all consumption goods, all capital goods, or some mix of the two. Therefore, development implies the enhancement of an economy's power to produce goods and services per capita, for such enhancement is the prerequisite to raising levels of living. It is from this

[6] Viner, *op. cit.*, p. 125.

[7] *Ibid.*, p. 127.

[8] *Ibid.*, p. 129.

[9] *Ibid.*

point of view that per capita output can be looked upon as an index of development.[10]

At this point something should be said in defense of our use of an aggregate as an index of economic growth. What about the distributive aspects? Is it not possible for almost everyone's position to be worsened and only one man's position to be improved sufficiently so that the average rises? The answer to such questions depends on how our index is interpreted. If we interpret our index as a reflection of a necessary increase of actual welfare or happiness then our use of such an index is certainly subject to the criticism. But this is not the interpretation we should give to such an index. The accurate interpretation and the assumptions underlying it require that we make a number of distinctions. The two main distinctions are: (1) the separation of the distributive aspects from the problem of maximizing the aggregate, and (2) the separation of the possible satisfaction that can be achieved with a larger aggregate from the actual satisfaction that occurs. In other words, our argument is based on the notion that with a larger aggregate output there is some redistribution of goods that is possible that will enable the recipients to have a larger utility than with a smaller aggregate.

The "possible achievement" approach[11] to the interpretation of an aggregate involves two types of conceivable redistributions. It implies something about the possible redistribution of the factors of production as well as the possible redistribution of the final product. In other words, if we call aggregate A larger than aggregate B then we imply two things: first, that it is possible to redistribute the factors used in the production

---

[10] Ultimately, of course any argument for the use of maximizing per capita income as a goal for an economy must rest on values or ethical preconceptions that, to some extent at least, have to be accepted without a complete proof. Specifically, maximizing average income plus abiding by certain constraints, such as not worsening the distribution of income nor increasing the rate of capital accumulation to a greater extent than the proportional increase in income, will imply rising living standards. Beyond that point we cannot argue without implicitly postulating some ultimate value system. To the extent that mankind values increasing the material aspects of living, to that extent can we be persuasive. Values that rest on some form of asceticism will diminish or nullify the persuasiveness of our argument. Also, values based on non-material aspects of desire or existence coupled with the empirical demonstration that increases in the material aspects of life dull or diminish non-material or spiritual aspects would equally do violence to our argument. We cannot enter into a discussion of the validity, persuasiveness or virtue of such ultimate values.

[11] This is consistent with the argument of Lewis that economic growth is desirable because "it gives man greater control over his environment, and thereby increases his freedom." *Op. cit.*, p. 421.

of *A* in such a way as to produce at least the same quantity of every commodity in *B* and then some; second, that it is possible to redistribute the final product produced under the redistribution of the factors of production utilized to produce *A* so that everyone has at least as much of each commodity as he enjoyed under *B* and then some. The extent to which such an approach is valid will depend on whether such redistributions can actually be carried out. In situation *A* the nature of the resources may be such that it may be impossible to redistribute and transform them in such a way as to produce the bundle of goods under *B*, even though in value terms *A* is larger than *B*. For very small differences in the values of *A* and *B* this is a conceivable situation, namely, that there is no redistribution of resources in either situation that will permit the production of that bundle of goods produced in the other set of circumstances. However, it seems reasonable to suppose that the greater the difference in value between *A* and *B* the greater the likelihood that such transformations can actually be carried out. Thus, we might conclude that above some minimum difference in the values of *A* and *B*, the value aggregates do have ordinal significance. In other words, let d be the necessary minimum difference. If *A* is greater than $B + d$ then we can say that the aggregate in *A*, be it income, consumption, or output per capita, is larger than in *B*. And if situation *A* occurs after *B* then we can assume that economic growth has taken place.

In other words, we suggest that by the statement that the country in time period *A* is more developed than in time period *B*, we mean that in *A* we have an economic state in which it is reasonable to assume that, in proportion to population, it could, if it wanted to do so, produce the goods produced in time *B*, while in *B* it is unreasonable to infer that the economy at that state could have produced all the goods at time *A*. The main point is that we want an index that will enable us to distinguish sustained development from a lack of development *for the same country* (that is, we are not primarily concerned with being able to say that country *A* is more developed than country *B*).[12] For the purpose of gauging the state of development within a country, per capita income is likely to work out quite well as an index. For if the calculated per capita income level continues to rise, it is likely that a point will be reached at

[12] The problems that arise when we try to compare relative states of development or relative standards of living between countries often disappear, or their force is diminished, when we compare only different time points within a country. Comparisons between countries often involve vast differences in tastes, climate, cultural setting, etc., that somehow have to be taken into account. On these and related issues see United Nations, *Report on International Definition, and Measurement of Standards and Levels of Living,* New York, 1954.

which the calculated level is sufficiently above some initial level so that the test mentioned in this and in the previous paragraph can be met.

There are several related issues which we have touched upon into which it may be well to go a little more deeply. Broadly speaking, the issues we have in mind concern the choice of average output as our index of observation versus alternative indices. At the outset we have to admit that for some problems the use of some aggregate variable would be superior to an average. For example, if we are concerned with the question of gauging the developing potential military might of a nation, indices like total output or total capacity in some branch of industry may be more revealing than the changes in per capita consumption standards. Indeed, it is quite likely that the aggregate power of a nation might increase while at the same time per capita consumption levels decline. Of course, even in such cases some knowledge of per capita indices is not without interest but if we must choose a single central variable as the focus around which to build our model, then the aggregate might be a more strategic choice. Whenever the problem is such that the point of interest is the behavior of the total economy rather than the effect of total behavior on individuals, it follows that some aggregate would be a superior index to some average.

But, of course, our interest here is just the opposite. We are seeking to develop a model that will attempt to explain what it is that prevents the level of living of the majority of the people from rising. But, it may be argued, would not a theory that determines aggregate output do as well? We would have to agree that this would certainly be the case if changes in population size did not play a crucial role in the determination of average output and in the level of living. But we hope to show that the effects of population growth may be such that aggregate output and levels of living move in opposite directions. Indeed, we can go further than that. For the range of problems we have in mind, we can assume that increases in average output will always imply increases in aggregate output. But not vice versa. It is this lack of symmetry in the causal sequence that persuades us to choose the average rather than the aggregate. The reason for this is that in most cases, if not in all, the neo-Malthusian conditions to be found in many of the underdeveloped areas are such that increases in per capita output will be accompanied by population increases while increases in aggregate output may be accompanied by such large increases in population as to depress the average from its former level. It is, of course, true that on the purely general, theoretical plane the nature of the implication may go in any direction but the practical problems we have in mind are such as to eliminate the possibility of increases in average output being accompanied by decreases in the aggregate. From this point of view it would appear that the per capita measure is by far a more strategic variable since a knowledge of the direction of the per capita measure implies the direction of the aggregate but not vice versa.

Another possible index is the per capita level of consumption. At first blush this would appear to be a more strategic variable to look at than per capita output if the object of our interest is really the level of living of the people. Although this is unquestionably true at any point in time, it happens that it is not true if our interest lies in gauging the *growth* of living levels and the development of the economy. In other words, if we are interested in the time process of development then per capita consumption will be somewhat less revealing than per capita output. It is clear that it is per capita output that controls the maximum consumption standard at any time and not vice versa. Furthermore, per capita consumption tells us much less about that other crucial variable, the level of investment, than does per capita output.

Yet, in a sense, it is the level of consumption, rather than per capita output, that can be more nearly equated with what we usually refer to as the level of living. And it is possible to have increasing per capita output, increasing aggregate output, and yet have the level of consumption not rise at all or even decline. For example, some claim that for a considerable period of time the economic history of the Soviet Union represents precisely such a case. But we should note that if we focus our entire attention on per capita consumption in the case just mentioned, then we might conclude that no development has taken place. This last would certainly be dangerously misleading. Furthermore, and especially if we are interested in gauging the ability of an economy to provide a certain standard of living, change in per capita output is certainly a more revealing index than the actual level of consumption since to a considerable extent much of the previous allocation of resources to investment can usually be shifted to the production of consumption goods. In any event, it is quite a simple calculation to deduce from our knowledge of per capita income and the level of investment the actual per capita level of consumption. Thus, nothing is really lost in choosing average output as our index of development, and much is gained.

CHAPTER 3

Economic Backwardness as a Quasi-Stable Equilibrium System

The Four Main Hypotheses

A knowledge of the general framework of ideas within which we plan to develop our more detailed arguments and investigations should help us to proceed in an orderly and connected manner. Therefore, we shall present in this chapter a short outline of the general theory that will form the foundation of many of our subsequent discussions. Broadly stated, this involves the notion that it is convenient and useful to look at backward economies (or underdeveloped economies, if the reader prefers that term) as equilibrium systems in which the equilibrium state possesses some degree of stability, and to see advanced economies in terms of disequilibrium systems.[1] This distinction should enable us, from the very

[1] For a specific model of this type, see Leibenstein, *A Theory of Economic Demographic Development,* Princeton, Princeton University Press, 1954, Chapter IV. See also Richard R. Nelson, "A Theory of the Low Level Equilibrium Trap in Underdeveloped Economies," *American Economic Review,* December 1956, pp. 894–908. See also Robert Solow, "A Contribution to the Theory of Economic Growth," *Quarterly Journal of Economics,* February 1956, pp. 90–91. The pioneer article by P. N. Rosenstein-Rodan, "Problems of Industrialization of Eastern and South-Eastern Europe," *Economic Journal,* Vol. 53 (June 1943), is of great interest in this connection.

beginning, to focus our attention on what is at the root of the problem, namely, the question of determining the conditions under which a transition from one system to the other can be obtained.

A word of caution may be in order at this point. We shall not try to defend all the notions to be advanced here. It is left to the subsequent chapters either to demonstrate or at least suggest the reasonableness of the major propositions. Here we intend mostly to indicate some of the more probable "models," or ways of looking at the problem.

The general theory to be developed depends on four main hypotheses. The exact meaning of and reasons for these hypotheses will be examined later but it may be easier to see the logical structure behind some of the ideas if we indicate the nature of these four hypotheses now without elaboration or defense. These are:

(1) It is useful to characterize a backward economy as an equilibrium system whose equilibrium state (or states) possesses a degree of "quasi-stability" with respect to per capita income, but that advanced economies cannot usefully or accurately be described in such terms.

(2) If the equilibrium of a backward economy is disturbed, the forces or influences that tend to raise per capita incomes set in motion, directly or indirectly, forces that have the effect of depressing per capita income.

(3) In the disequilibrium state (in the backward economy), for at least the lower incomes above the equilibrium level, the effects of the income-depressing forces are greater than the effects of the income-raising forces.

(4) During any period there is some absolute maximum to the effects of the income-depressing forces, but the absolute maximum (if there is one) of the effects of the per capita income-creating forces is greater than that.

On the basis of these four hypotheses we can deduce one of our basic ideas, namely, what we shall refer to as "the critical minimum effort" thesis (see chapter 8). Briefly, it is that in order to achieve the transition from the state of backwardness to the more developed state where we can expect steady secular growth it is a necessary, though not always sufficient, condition that at some point, or during some period, the economy should receive a stimulus to growth that is greater than a certain critical minimum size. These basic ideas, and others, are to be elaborated in the pages that follow.

Some Basic Definitions and Distinctions

To set the stage for our discussion we must indicate at the outset how we intend to use certain terms and to draw certain distinctions. Words like equilibrium and disequilibrium, stability and instability, are concepts that are closely related to the highly developed conceptual schemes with which economists are familiar. They are like old friends about whose characteristics and family background we know quite a bit, and their appropriate employment may tell us something about the nature of a problem even if the setting is unfamiliar. Thus, if we can show that it is proper to view economic backwardness in terms of a special kind of equilibrium state and to see development as an "explosive disequilibrium path," this will suggest something of the essence of the problem, which is to find out how to upset permanently the initial equilibrium.

There is now a large and growing literature on the meaning and nature of such terms as equilibrium, stability, disequilibrium, and their relation to static and dynamic systems. The intricacies involved in the use of such concepts can be found elsewhere.[2] For our purposes it will suffice if we indicate briefly what we have in mind when we use certain terms.

(*a*) The distinction between a *state* and a *system:* By a *system* we mean a set of relations (or equations) between various specified entities (or values of these entities) by which we describe the economic process under certain circumstances.[3] By a *state* we mean only one specific set of

---

[2] See W. C. Hood, "Some Aspects of the Treatment of Time in Economic Theory," *The Canadian Journal of Economics and Political Science,* Vol. 14, No. 4 (November 1948), pp. 453–468. See also the following: P. A. Samuelson, *Foundations of Economic Analysis,* Cambridge, Harvard University Press, 1947, Chapters 9, 10, and 11. J. M. Clark, *Preface to Social Economics,* New York, Farrar and Rinehart, Inc., 1936, pp. 196–228. Frank Knight, *The Ethics of Competition,* New York, Harper and Brothers, 1935, Chapter 6. J. R. Hicks, *Value and Capital,* Oxford, The Clarendon Press, 1939, pp. 115–127. R. Frisch, "On the Notion of Equilibrium and Disequilibrium," *Review of Economic Studies,* Vol. 3, No. 2 (February 1936), pp. 100–105. Erik Lindahl, *Studies in the Theory of Money and Capital,* London, Allen (1939), Part I: "The Dynamic Approach to Economic Theory." Jan Tinbergen, *The Dynamics of Business Cycles,* Chicago, University of Chicago Press, 1950, Chapter 9.

[3] Strictly speaking, we may be using the notion of a system in a more restrictive sense than is usual. For we have in mind the additional restriction that the relationships are in some sense "bounded." That is to say, the description of behavior characterized by such relationships is meant to apply only under certain conditions, if either the initial conditions or the values of the variables are within certain bounds. Perhaps we should use the term "sub-system" for what we have in mind. We could visualize a very general scheme that describes economic behavior and events under all possible circumstances. Now, given the initial conditions the path of the economy is determined. We divide all the possible initial conditions into two groups: one group of sets of initial conditions that will lead to an ultimate equilibrium state and a group that does not. We can visualize each group of initial conditions and the equations that describe the economic processes as a sub-system of the larger system. There seems to be little point in adding to our terminology at this stage, hence we shall look at them as two separate systems.

values of the variables. By an *equilibrium system* we refer to one that has at least one equilibrium state, that is, that there exists for this system at least one set of values for the variables which, once attained, would repeat themselves period after period. Or, put slightly differently, we might say that an equilibrium system is one in which there is a set of magnitudes of the "stocks" in the system that remain invariant period after period.

(*b*) Distinction between *stability* and *quasi-stability:*[4] If an equilibrium is stable then all the variables return to their equilibrium values after any disturbance of the equilibrium position. By a quasi-stable equilibrium we refer to a condition where only *some* aspects of the system are stable. That is, after the initial disturbance of the equilibrium position the system will not settle down to the same equilibrium values as before but only *some* of the variables will return to their initial values. Hence, in describing a system as a quasi-equilibrium system, we have in mind a system where, if the initial condition is an equilibrium state then the variables remain in that position, but if the initial condition is a disequilibrium state then the variables will eventually approach a state in which only *some* of them always return to their previous equilibrium values. Of course, in the quasi-stable case we have to specify the variable or variables that are stable.

(*c*) Distinction between a disequilibrium state and a disequilibrium system: Just a word or so is needed on this distinction. A disequilibrium state is simply a state when the economy is not in equilibrium, a state that is transitory since the economy (or more accurately the values of the variables that describe the state) is moving to new positions. This type of state may exist either in an equilibrium or a disequilibrium system. Of course, by definition, all states in the disequilibrium system are disequilibrium states. Although the path of such a system may have a specific direction, the economy is not moving toward any state of rest.

Definitions of concepts appear exceedingly barren until they are used. Some examples in this and the next section may help to clarify the types of models we have in mind for the underdeveloped economy.

First consider this non-economic example: Imagine a situation in which an attempt is made to increase the flow of traffic on a certain country's roads where the roads are very narrow to begin with. Now suppose that the flow of traffic depends only on the width of the road (the

---

[4] The term "quasi-equilibrium" is borrowed from Trygve Haavelmo, *A Study in the Theory of Economic Evolution* (Contributions to Economic Analysis 3), Amsterdam, North Holland Publishing Company, 1954. For a technical definition of what we mean by a quasi-equilibrium system see the brief appendix to this chapter.

number of lanes that are possible, the width of each lane, etc.) and the width of the cars. At the outset the cars are also exceptionally narrow so that their employment may be safe and feasible on the narrow roads. The authorities decide to widen the roads in order to increase the flow of traffic. But as soon as some of the roads are widened, car manufacturers produce wider cars in response to consumer demand. The new ratio of car width to road width is soon the same as before, and the average traffic flow is also the same as before. Here we have a quasi-stable equilibrium system. The absolute magnitudes of both cars and roads increase. But road width per car width remains the same, and the consequent traffic flow remains the same.

Of course, such a system is likely to be only "stable in the small."[5] That is, for *small* increases in the width of the road, the width of cars would soon increase proportionately, but for really large increases this would not be the case since there is some maximum to the width of cars that consumers desire. Hence, if the authorities increased the width of the road very rapidly and they continued to do so beyond some point, the increasing width of cars would never catch up to the widening road.

Illustrations of Quasi-Stable Equilibrium Systems

One of the difficulties in tackling the underdeveloped areas problem is that of determining how to begin. So many aspects proliferate that at first one may find it very difficult to know just how and where to "enter the problem," so to speak. By beginning on a very general level we reduce the number of possible approaches. The graphical illustrations that follow, though not exhaustive, serve to illustrate some of the alternate ways of viewing the state of backwardness. We shall see examples of systems that are unstable and others that are completely stable. The more interesting examples, as well as the ones that seem to have the greatest promise for further development, are those in which the system possesses only a quasi-stable equilibrium with respect to per capita income. The graphs and the surrounding discussions that follow will illustrate the fact that two fundamental questions are intimately related. These are: (1) How do we visualize the condition of economic backwardness? and (2) How can we achieve development? We shall see that the second question is meaningless without the answer to the first.

Suppose we decide to look at backwardness as a quasi-stable state. If we determine that this is a reasonable approach, we have an entrée into our problem. For this suggests a number of questions which in turn suggest others whose answers suggest still others. For example, to what

[5] See Samuelson, *op. cit.*, pp. 260 ff.

extent is the equilibrium stable? What factors or influences maintain the equilibrium income level? Is escape from the underdevelopment equilibrium level possible? Which are the stabilizing and which are the destabilizing forces in the system? And so on. Thus picking what looks like a reasonable, though very general, abstract model at the outset can serve as the seed out of which an endlessly proliferating and multi-branched conceptual tree can grow.

With this last in mind we consider now a simple system that comes much closer to the heart of the underdeveloped areas problem, the type of economy often visualized by the classical theorists.[6] Utilizing the traditional approach to this problem, we visualize the factors of production in terms of land, capital, and labor that combine to produce commodities. For our purposes it is best to combine capital and land and talk of them as "resources." Now, the commodity flow in any period is either consumed or becomes part of the capital resources of the subsequent period. To the extent that consumption is less than current output, the resources will be augmented and the productive capacity of the economy will increase. If the labor force were constant, the equilibrium position would be reached only at the point at which additions of capital would not add anything to output (that is, where the marginal productivity of capital would become zero). Of course, the labor force and the population will not only grow simultaneously but will grow because of the increasing resources and consequent increased output.

This growth will occur for one of two reasons. Either the growth in incomes will be transformed into consumption that is conducive to the reduction of mortality rates, or there may be secular changes that lead to improved knowledge, sanitation, or other public health measures, that in turn reduce mortality rates. In any event, the consequence of the operation of these forces will be an increase in the population size and, assuming decreasing returns with respect to increases in labor, a consequent reduction of per capita income. If the system is stable, the reductions in per capita incomes will proceed apace until per capita income reaches a "subsistence equilibrium level." That is to say, a level where the economy finds it possible just to replace those resources that wear out during the period, and just to maintain the population. This, in brief, is a description of a system that possesses a stable equilibrium with respect to average income. The system permits the occurrence of

---

[6] Compare: Adam Smith, *The Wealth of Nations* (Editor, Cannon), Modern Library, New York, Chapter 8; David Ricardo, *Principles of Political Economy and Taxation* (Everyman Edition), E. P. Dutton and Company, New York, 1911, Chapter 5; and J. S. Mill, *Principles of Political Economy*, Longman Green and Company, London, 1904, Book I, Chapter 10; Book II, Chapter 11; among others.

outside events the initial effect of which may be to increase resources per head, but eventually there is a return to the initial equilibrium per capita income while other magnitudes remain at their expanded level.

With the aid of graphical methods we now turn to an examination of this system and of a number of its more complicated variants.

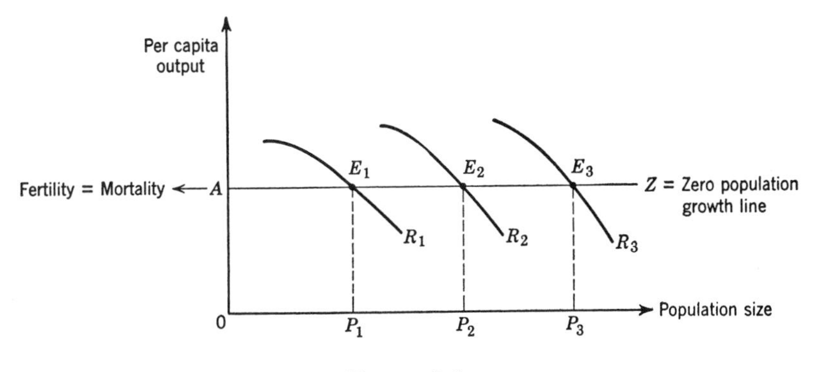

FIGURE 3–1

EXAMPLE 1. In figure 3–1 we illustrate a system in which the following relations hold. Output depends on two variables—resources and population size. The greater the resources and/or the greater the population, the greater the output. But output is subject to diminishing marginal (and average) returns with respect to population. The curve R_1 represents the alternate per capita outputs that could be obtained from the given resource base (R_1) at alternate population sizes. Population growth is a function of per capita output. Note especially that above a certain per capita output, OA, population growth is positive, and below OA it is negative. R_2 and R_3 show the per capita output-resource relations if resources are R_2 and R_3, respectively. Now, suppose that all goods except those necessary for capital replacement are consumed. Consumption above the OA level reduces mortality and as a consequence the population grows. Fertility is assumed to be constant. The line marked Z we shall call the zero population growth line. When resources are R_1 the equilibrium per capita income is E_1. Since there is no investment from within the system, all additions to resources are assumed to be autonomous rather than induced. Thus, if in some way resources were augmented so that the resource level rose to R_2, the immediate effect would be to raise per capita income above OA. The rate of population growth would be positive and it would continue to grow until it reached P_2 where a new equilibrium at E_2 would be established. This system clearly possesses quasi-stability with respect to per capita income. Neither population nor resources return to their initial equilibrium position, but the system settles down eventually to its previous per capita income level.

EXAMPLE 2. In figure 3–2 the relationships are exactly the same as in figure 3–1, except that we have added an investment function. The rate of net investment is a function of per capita income. At some level of per capita income, say OA, the capital goods produced are just sufficient for the replacement of the capital that wears out, and net investment is zero. Hence the line X is a zero investment line. Here we note especially that above X net investment is positive, and below it net investment is negative. The reader will also note that in this figure the zero investment line and the zero population growth lines coincide. We consider later other variants of the zero investment line and the zero population growth line. Now, E_1

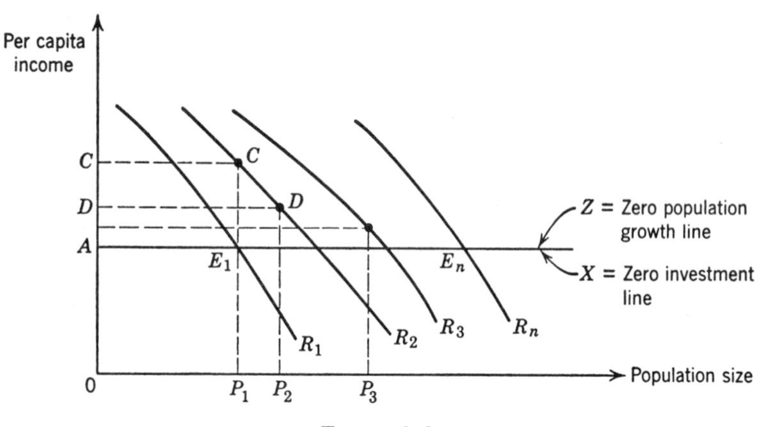

FIGURE 3–2

is the initial stationary equilibrium position. In the interest of brevity we consider only those disturbances that initially increase per capita income, that is, those displacements that are initial stimulants to growth. We can trace three possible sequences of events set in motion by such a disturbance, that is, by a change whose impact at the outset is to increase per capita income from OA to OC.

Possibility I. The first possibility is that for every disturbance, no matter how large, the long-run effects of population growth will be more significant than the effects of the induced investment. The result in this case is that the equilibrium will retain its quasi-stable property. For suppose that induced investment raises resources to R_2, but that population growth increases population to OP_2; then income falls from its initial disequilibrium level of OC to OD. We can visualize a continuing sequence of this sort which results in the eventual return to the equilibrium income level of OA. More complicated sequences are, of course, possible (e.g., fluctuations around a secular trend leading to OA, or fluctuations around OA, and the eventual coming to rest at OA), but exact details need not detain us here. At this point we are primarily interested in pointing to that class of possibilities that involve paths leading to an eventual return to the initial equilibrium income, but not to the initial population size and resource base. Thus the final resting place may be E_n, with a larger population size and resource base than the initial one.

Possibility II. The second possibility is that the system is quasi-stable for small displacements but not for large ones. In other words, the second possibility is that there exist stimulants to growth sufficiently large, which if they occurred, would set in motion a pattern of persistent growth. In other words, for small disturbances, the effects of population growth in reducing incomes per head are more significant than the effects of induced investment in raising incomes, but for large stimulants to growth, the marginal effects

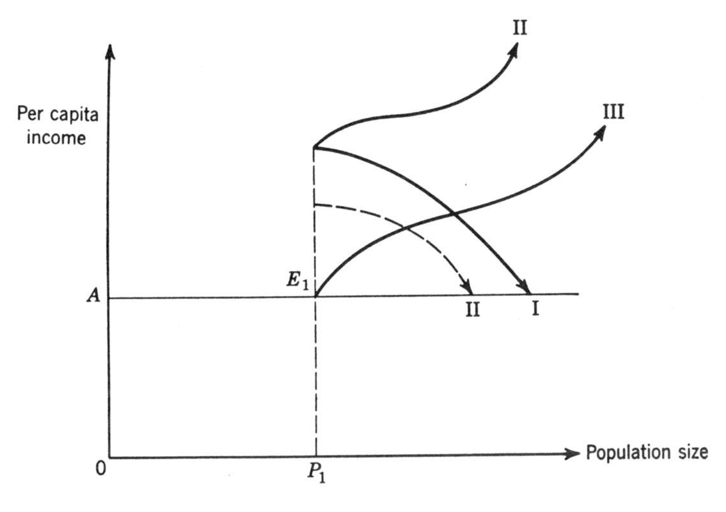

FIGURE 3–3

of population growth in reducing incomes become progressively less significant, while the effects of the induced investments either do not decline or their rate of decline is less significant than that of population growth. In any event, it is not too difficult to visualize some conditions under which the equilibrium possesses quasi-stability for small displacements from equilibrium—but not for large or perhaps very large ones. (The three possibilities are illustrated in figure 3–3; I illustrates the path of income and population changes if the system possesses perfect quasi-stability; II illustrates the paths where the system is quasi-stable for *small* displacements only; and III illustrates the case where the equilibrium is completely unstable.)

Possibility III. The third possibility is, of course, that the equilibrium is unstable to begin with. This implies that any change, no matter how small, that results in an initial increase in per capita income will set in motion a series of induced investments, period after period, that will always raise per capita income to a greater extent than the induced rate of population growth will reduce it. We will indicate later our reasons for not taking this third possibility very seriously and why we shall concentrate our considerations on a model of the second type, although a much more elaborate one.

EXAMPLE 3. *Models where the zero-population and the zero investment lines do not coincide:* The reader may have felt that it is surely arbitrary to assume that the zero-population growth line and the zero-investment line will necessarily coincide. Why should they? And what if they do not? We illustrate such possibilities in figures 3–4, 3–5, 3–6, 3–7, and 3–9.

In figure 3–4, the relationships are of the same type as in figure 3–2, except that the zero-investment line is above the zero-population growth line. *The result in this case is that there can be no equilibrium position to begin with.* Let us start with a population of P_1 and a per capita income of OA. Since per capita income is below OB there must be disinvestment and the resources curve shifts to R_2. This must result in a decline in per capita income below OA which in turn leads to a reduction in population. If the population decline does not raise per capita income above OA temporarily, we have a sequence of alternating disinvestments and population declines until both the population and the economic resources disappear. If the effect of population growth does not raise incomes above OB at any time then there must be continuous disinvestment until the economy disappears. It would seem

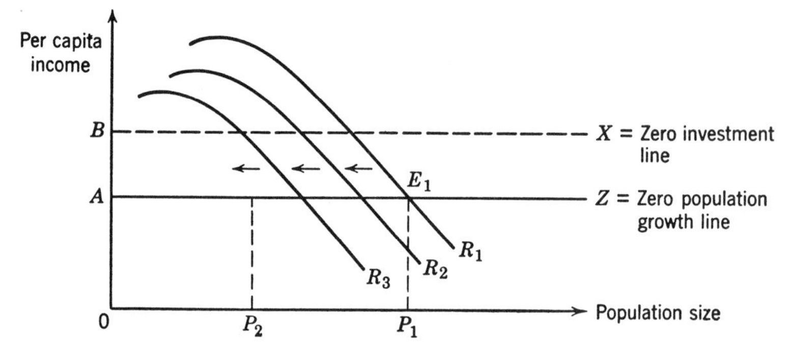

FIGURE 3–4

that as long as the initial position is one of income below OB the economy is doomed. For, with income between OA and OB both disinvestment and population growth have the simultaneous effects of reducing incomes still more. This implies that additional people are created at the expense of the capital stock. Thus, if we begin with a point between A and B, income must fall toward OA as long as the population continues to grow. At OA population ceases to grow but resources decline. Below OA disinvestment continues and resources must continue to decline. For although it is possible that population decline (in the OA interval) may arrest the income decline temporarily, income cannot stay very long above the OA level, for as soon as income gets above the OA level both influences operate to depress it below that level while resources continue to dwindle.

The other possibility is for us to start with an income above OB. Here, as in figure 3–2, two paths are possible. The influences on per capita income work simultaneously in opposite directions—net investment raises income while population growth depresses it. If at some income above OB the long run investment effects outweigh the population growth effects, the system enters a state of steady growth. If the population growth effects predominate then income will eventually decline to OA and enter the area between A and B. Once there, resources dwindle eventually to zero. Hence, we see that in this model we have the curious situation of a system in which either income is at the outset high enough and the investment effects great enough so that the economy can grow or it will disappear. Such an economy must either grow or die but it is not one that can persist in a semi-stagnant low income state. There is no mechanism for survival when incomes are low unless we introduce some factor or influence that causes X and Z to coincide at some point. As is, this type of model represents an unstable system, and one that would not appear to be especially useful if we want to explain the long run persistence of poverty accompanied by simultaneous growth in population and resources.

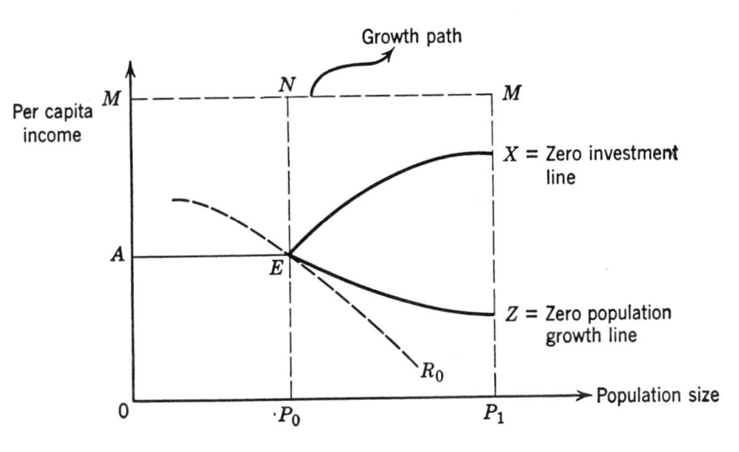

FIGURE 3–5

We now consider briefly two possible variations of the situation depicted in figure 3–4. These are shown in figures 3–5 and 3–6. An examination of figure 3–5 will reveal that E represents a stable equilibrium state with respect to displacements that involve no initial reduction in population. Let the line MM indicate the minimum income line above which sustained growth occurs, i.e., if incomes somehow get above OM sustained income growth takes place. Now, suppose that the initial disequilibrium position is a point in the area EXZ. In this case both the forces of disinvestment and population growth operate toward depressing per capita incomes. Per capita incomes must fall below points on the line EZ. Below EZ population will decline and disinvestment will continue until eventually a point of rest is reached at the point E, since at E there is no longer any tendency towards investment, disinvestment, population growth, or population decline. It can readily be seen that if we begin with an initial disequilibrium point within the area P_0EZP_1 there will be an eventual return to the point E since population declines and disinvestment take place simultaneously. Similarly for initial disequilibrium points within the area $EXMN$ there must be an eventual return to the point E, since by the construction and definition of the line M we imply that the population growth effects are eventually more significant in reducing incomes than the investment effects are in raising incomes. This means that at some point incomes will be forced below a point on the line EX and from there on, as we have seen, there must be an eventual return to the point E. Hence, we see that in the case of sufficiently small displacements involving a population no less than the initial population, the system is fully stable and not simply quasi-stable. For displacements involving a population less than P_0 the system may be only quasi-stable for reasons considered in our discussion of figure 3–2.

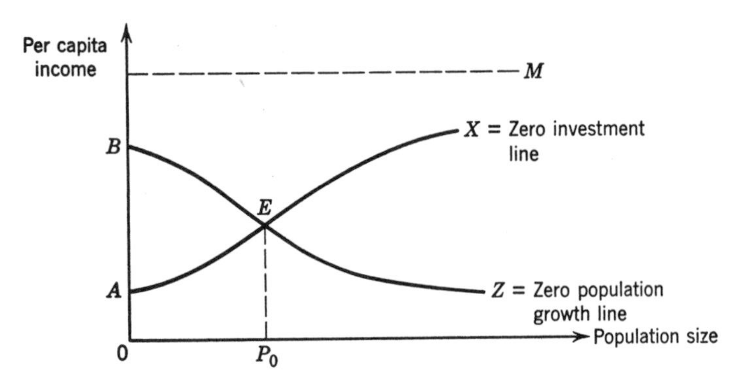

FIGURE 3–6

In figure 3–6, *AX* and *BZ* are the zero investment line and the zero population growth line, respectively. By similar reasoning to that considered in figure 3–5 it can be seen that *E* can be, *but need not be,* a stable equilibrium point for small displacements regardless of whether the initial displacement increases or decreases the equilibrium population size. The reason it need not be a completely stable equilibrium point is that in this case it is possible that for some initial displacement points that fall in the area *AEB,* the rate of population decline may be so rapid that the population disappears before per capita income is raised to a point above the points on *BE.* Although this last possibility is an interesting theoretical curiosity, it is probably not especially relevant to our general problem.

EXAMPLE 4. Now, suppose that the zero population growth line is above the zero investment line. This possibility is depicted in figure 3–7. In this case the economy is increasing its investment even at those levels of per capita income where it cannot maintain its population. The interesting segment of the income range is that between *OB* and *OA,* for here both the population effect and the investment effect work simultaneously toward raising per capita incomes at least to the level *OA.* Above *OA* the population effects and the investment effects work in opposite directions, investment tending to raise per capita incomes and population growth tending to diminish them. Now let us suppose for a moment that for some range of incomes above *OA* the population effects are more significant than the investment effects—what then? Let the line *M* reflect the upper bound of the range where the population effects are greater than the investment effects. In this case we have a very interesting model in which the line *Z* operates as a type of quasi-stable moving equilibrium line. With incomes above *OB* both the population effect and the investment effect force incomes toward *OA,* but above *OA* (but not above *OM*) the population effects are sufficient to eventually depress incomes to the *OA* level. Thus *OA* operates as a floor above which incomes may fluctuate and at which investment is always positive. Both capital and population will grow but there will always be a tendency for per capita income to be pulled toward the *OA* level.

We should note, however, that here too we have to admit the theoretical possibility that for some initial positions between *OA* and *OB* the rate of population decline may be so rapid that the population disappears before income is raised above the *OA* level. We mention this for the sake of completeness and not because this is likely to be an important possibility.

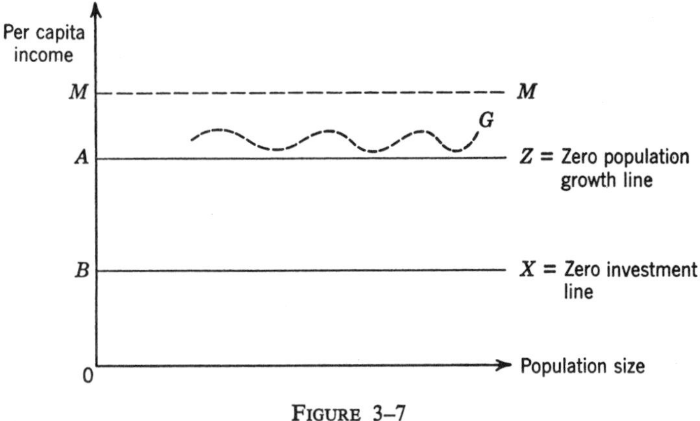

FIGURE 3–7

Of course, the system is not stable for large displacements given the existence of the postulated line *M*. If a positive displacement is somehow strong enough to lift per capita income above *OM* then a path of persistent growth is set in motion. Once again we have the familiar case of a system that is quasi-stable for small displacements but not for large ones. There is a strong similarity between such a system and the one depicted in figure 3–3, possibility II. The difference between the two are, however, worth noting. In figure 3–7 the expansion of resources and population is induced, it comes entirely from within the system while in figure 3–2 the expansion of resources and population is the result of an exogenous displacement. There will be more on this point later.

EXAMPLE 5. "MOVING" EQUILIBRIUM SYSTEMS. An important set of possibilities occurs where the paths of change involve movements from one equilibrium to another if the initial equilibrium is disturbed. Such possibilities are depicted in figures 3–8 and 3–9.

Of course, we note at the outset that all of the possibilities of stability and instability considered in connection with figure 3–2 are also possibilities here. But for the present it is sufficient to consider only the case in which the system is "non-explosive" with respect to per capita income, that is, the case where above the *Z* line the population growth effects are greater in the long run than the investment effects. In figure 3–8 we observe that both the population growth line and the investment line rise simultaneously for larger alternative population sizes. This means that if we are given an exogenous increase in resources the system will eventually settle down to a new equilibrium position, say at E_n. The shape of the Z line implies that either the mortality rates rise as population increases or birth rates decline. Similarly, a moving equilibrium system would exist if the Z and X lines were negatively inclined. We need not go into reasons for either possibility at this juncture since at present we are only interested in showing some of

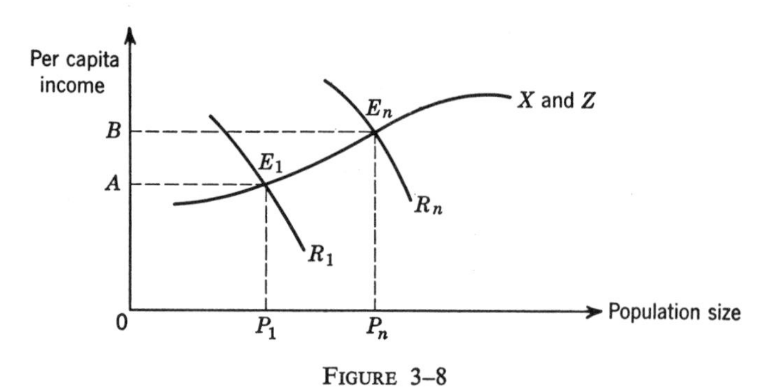

FIGURE 3–8

the variations on our initial simple quasi-equilibrium system. In figure 3–9 only the population growth line rises as the population size increases. As we have seen in our discussion of figure 3–7, once per capita income is raised above the initial equilibrium level at E_1, the system can follow an expansive path something like the one followed by the broken line marked

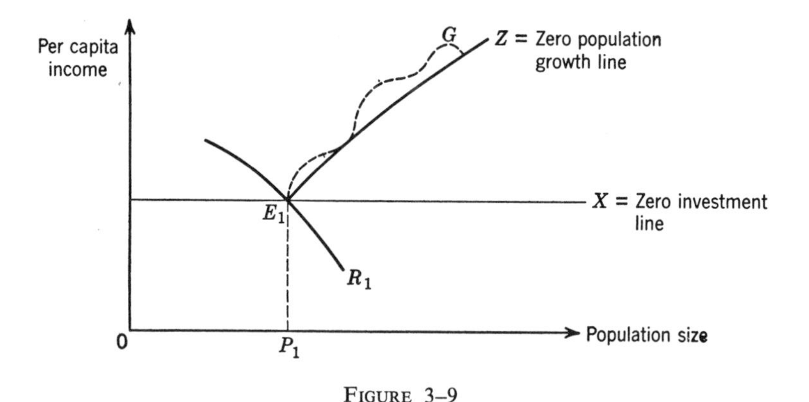

FIGURE 3–9

G. It is of interest that in neither of the cases depicted in figures 3–8 and 3–9 does the initial equilibrium position possess, strictly speaking, what might be called quasi-stability. Yet in both systems there are equilibrating forces. Although a displacement from the equilibrium position does not result in a return to the equilibrium values of any of the variables, there is always a tendency toward a return to an equilibrium position or toward a given locus of per capita income values (the line EZ in figure 3–9). In other words, we visualize an equilibrium locus of per capita incomes and we picture the economy as one in which actual per capita income is always moving toward this locus if the occasional outside forces to which the economy is subjected are not large.

Before leaving our graphical illustrations, we should perhaps pause and raise the question: What purpose do they serve? It must be self-evident that the real problem of economic development involves more than merely the two variables of investment per capita and population growth.

Although it seems preferable, for expository purposes, to speak in terms of the effects of investment *versus* the effects of population growth, in actual fact the models could have been developed on a more general plane. We could, for example, have considered an X-function and a Z-function, where X represented those forces that were monotonic increasing functions of per capita income which, above some income level, tended to raise incomes further, and below some per capita income level tended to reduce them, while the Z forces reduced incomes, when incomes were above some specified level and raised them below that level.[7] This procedure would have made the analysis appear more general. We could in this way have considered not only investment but also an amalgam of such factors as innovations, increased energy of the labor force, superior organization and management, and any other influences that may, in part, be functions of the per capita income level. Similarly, we could read into the Z-function a host of factors that would tend to inhibit further growth. *But the main point, of course, is that these abstract and simple models enable us to see the process of economic change as one in which the outcome depends on a struggle between conflicting forces that operate simultaneously,* and, further, to see some of the variations in outcomes that are possible even when considered on so general a level. From what we know about the empirical aspects of the situation it seems to be reasonably clear that the development process is one in which forces that can promote growth do, in fact, have to overcome forces that inhibit it.

Nature and Stability of the Low Income Equilibrium

Since our view of the problem is very much broader than that suggested by our graphical illustrations, it may be well to describe briefly some of the relationships and processes we have in mind. And although what follows is of an elementary nature, it is probably desirable to present these ideas if only to indicate the wide range of the elements that must

[7] The Z-forces would probably have to be a function of both per capita income and population size.

be considered and to emphasize the fact that in dwelling on development problems we really must have in mind a range of phenomena that is unusual in conventional economic analysis.

Beginning with elementary notions this is our general picture. At any point in time the economy can be described by a set of stocks. The stocks represent a snapshot of the economy at an instant. During a time interval the economy can be described by the flows that occur. These are the results of the activities that take place, the activities in which the stocks are involved. Stocks and flows are related in a number of ways. Generally, the stocks in any period are equal to the stocks of the previous period plus the *net* flows during the period. The flows during any period are determined by the nature of the stocks at the beginning of the period. Thus, any given set of flows implies a set of stocks at the beginning of the period. And, a set of equilibrium flows may be said to imply a set of equilibrium stocks. By equilibrium flows we refer to that set of flows that maintain the stocks at the same level, period after period.

The specific stocks that we have in mind include, of course, those usually considered in economics; namely, the usual fixed and augmentable resources of any economy: land, capital, inventories, and labor. But we must go beyond this list and include not only the labor power involved in the population but also other characteristics or powers inherent in that population. Hence, we have to include such properties or qualities as skills, the technical knowledge that exists, as well as the mores, traditions, and goals, etc. Although this last group of "stocks" that inhere in the population are intangible and amorphous and of a type that it would be impossible to treat numerically, they are, nonetheless, exceedingly significant "stocks" from the point of view of the determinants of development.[8]

Now, during any period the stocks that we have mentioned combine with each other in various ways in order to engage in activities that result in the flows of the system. These activities can be subsumed under three general processes: (1) the production process, (2) the reproductive process, and (3) the educative process.

The production process involves those activities in which tangible resources are combined with labor power to produce a flow of consumer

---

[8] See Buchanan and Ellis, *Approaches to Economic Development,* The Twentieth Century Fund, New York, 1955, Chapter 4, also p. 407 where the authors contend "that the really substantive barriers to development are non-economic . . . ," that is, of a cultural and sociological nature. See also, United Nations, *Processes and Problems of Industrialization in Underdeveloped Areas,* New York, 1955, pp. 15–25, for similar arguments and examples.

goods (including services) and capital goods. In equilibrium the capital goods are only for replacement of the resources that wear out.

The reproductive process involves those activities that maintain the population, that is, consumption for subsistence, and those relating to the birth and nurturing of offspring, thus replacing that portion of the population that dies. In other words, in this process we consider all those activities concerned with the maintenance and augmentation of the population stock.

The educative process involves those activities that to some extent may utilize capital and labor power to maintain the level of knowledge and skills of the population, and to determine or maintain the mores, traditions, and general modes of behavior of the population. (Further sub-classification of each process is, of course, possible but unnecessary at present.)

These processes occur simultaneously and feed upon each other. During the period some stocks wear out, are discarded, and some members of the population die. In the static equilibrium state the three processes imply activities that result in the augmentation of the stocks so that the initial levels of all stocks are maintained. Thus, resources and labor combine to produce the consumption goods that nourish the population and to produce the capital necessary to replace discarded and worn out resources. The members of the human population combine into family units in order to nourish the young, maintain themselves by consumption, and to produce offspring to replace those that die. The processes must interact not only to maintain the non-human resources and the population stock but also to maintain the qualities and characteristics of the population as well. The importance of this last to the development problem cannot be overstressed. It is related to the view that it is the non-economic factors that are the significant obstacles to development. By this writers usually mean that the mores, traditions, institutions, and goals of underdeveloped countries are of a kind that is a hindrance to change and progress.[9] If development is to take place, drastic changes in the mores, beliefs, goals, and modes of behavior of large segments of the populace must occur. Obviously, such mores and traditions are not innate. They are learned and it is the educative process that maintains them. It may be argued that the reason they are maintained is that they have had, at some time in the past, a survival value for the population in question. Societies with less stable mores have disappeared. We can see that part of the equilibrating process must be in the educative process, that is, activities which result in the "teaching" or

[9] *Ibid.*

in the acquisition by the young of the values, goals, and mores of their elders so that the constellation of mores and traditions subscribed to by the population at large is somehow maintained.

In our mention of the equilibrium state we did not say anything to suggest that this is a state in which incomes per capita are exceptionally low. Some additional properties have to be indicated in order for us to deduce an equilibrium in which incomes are low.

For example, will a flow of consumer goods that just maintain the population necessarily imply a low income equilibrium? The answer is "no" if the birth rate is low. For, if the birth rate is low then the equilibrium mortality rate must also be low, which in turn normally implies a fairly high income equilibrium. Therefore, if the equilibrium income level is to be low, traditions and practices that determine the nature of the reproductive activities must be of a kind that sustains a high birth rate. This last implies something about the educative process in backward economies. Here one of the conditions is probably that the values, mores, and traditions passed from generation to generation are essentially conservative, tradition-bound, non-explorative, and non-innovating in nature. This means that the initial "stock" of mores and traditions must not only be conducive to high fertility rates, but they must also be of such a nature that they perpetuate themselves and are relatively stable.

Displacements, shocks, and stimulants

The reader will recall that in our discussion of the graphical illustrations three types of possible quasi-stable equilibrium states were represented. These were: (1) The case where the equilibrium per capita income moved from period to period (see figure 3–8), (2) the case where the per capita income had a tendency to approach the same level period after period but where there was a steady and continuous internally induced growth in resources and population (see figure 3–7), and (3) the case where the Z-function line and X-function line coincide so that there exists a stationary equilibrium position at the outset (see figure 3–2). If, for the moment, we accept the argument that the moving equilibrium case is more likely to involve slowly declining equilibrium incomes rather than growing incomes,[10] and that in the unlikely possi-

[10] There are difficulties with slow equilibrium growth. First, there is no guarantee that it will occur. A slow equilibrium type of decay is also possible. Where the equilibrium growth is caused by exogenous events the economy is at the mercy of these exogenous events. Furthermore, equilibrium growth involves changing institutionalized behavior by very gradual means. It involves substituting slightly different response patterns for old ones. *But there is no reason*

bility of growing equilibrium incomes their rate of growth will be exceedingly slow, we can then conclude that all three types of quasi-stable equilibrium really present for us the same type of problem. To be specific: How stable is this type of equilibrium and how can we escape permanently from the environs of the equilibrium state? Since the generic nature of the problem is the same in all three cases, we may as well use the simplest case as our starting point. Therefore, unless we specify otherwise, we shall proceed on the assumption that the third case is the one that is representative of the general problem. This will require that we tax our memories a little to keep the other possibilities in mind as we go along. On the whole this simplification of the problem makes very little difference to the outcome of the discussion, and we would get substantially the same results by starting with the more complicated models, cases (1) and (2), although accommodating for them would make our discussions more cumbersome.

Having determined the nature of the initial equilibrium position, we now consider the meaning and nature of displacements from this equilibrium position. By "displacement" we refer to any change that comes from outside the system that results in a change from an equilibrium state to a disequilibrium state. Thus, every displacement implies an interference with the system of such a nature that the proportions among the various stocks are altered. However, the initial impact need not come through a direct increase or decrease in any specific stock. It may come through an externally generated change in one of the flows which, in turn, results in an addition or subtraction in one or more of the stocks. Most displacements will probably come about through some intricate mixture of these two means. Common examples of this phenomenon are exogenously determined increases in the capital stock, unusual inventions or other "unexpected" increases in the fund of knowledge, the discovery of new lands or resources, and so on. The critical words in determining what is and what is not a displacement are such words as

---

to expect continued change. There is no reason why at some point the economy would not get bogged down in a stagnant institutional pattern for a long period. This is quite different from the rapid growth case which, if successful, *institutionalizes* change itself. In the rapid growth case there is usually a crucial transition period during which fundamental changes take place. The human population changes not only in its economic structure and role structure, but also in its behavior patterns and expectations. Growth and progress become part of the normal expectations of the populace. They learn to expect and to plan for ever-improving conditions. For example, the process of investment becomes institutionalized so that sustained secular growth is almost guaranteed. In the stagnant equilibrium case, the economy usually has built-in reactions against progress, while in the other, the economy builds in reactions against stagnation.

"exogenous," "unexpected," "unanticipated," "autonomous," etc. An exogenous or autonomous event is an event that could not have been predicted on the basis of our knowledge of the day-to-day operation of the system. Strictly speaking, it is an event whose occurrence cannot be explained on the basis of the initial conditions and behavior equations. If a sequence of events can be explained by knowledge of the operation of the system, such events may be said to be induced rather than autonomous or exogenous. In other words, an exogenous event is an event that causes a sudden change in the value of a variable such that the value of that variable is outside of its expected pattern of behavior.

Distinguishing between displacements as either shocks or stimulants, we shall mean by a shock a per capita income-depressing displacement and by a stimulant a per capita income raising one. Examples of stimulants to growth (some of which we may have mentioned) may be such events as sudden discoveries of land, gifts of capital, the discovery of outlets for excess population, the appearance of especially gifted economic leaders or organizers, etc. Many examples of possible shocks readily come to mind, such as, an unusually heavy flood, an unexpected indemnity payment, etc.

A View of the Economic Development Process

We picture backward economies in terms of a quasi-stable equilibrium system, but we do not picture them as necessarily being in an equilibrium state. It is not important to determine whether they ever are really and completely in an equilibrium state. In most cases the actual per capita income at any point in time is not the underdeveloped equilibrium income, but usually the equilibrium level is being approached. However, from time to time economies are subjected to further stimulants and shocks, and as a consequence the economy rarely, if ever, gets a chance to pursue undisturbed the path toward equilibrium. But because underdeveloped economies do possess at least some degree of quasi-stability (for reasons see later chapters), the stimulants that do occur do not usually lead to sustained growth in per capita incomes but rather to a pattern of change that leads to an eventual return to the low, underdeveloped equilibrium income. This pattern of change, however, will most probably not be permitted to work itself out. It, too, at some points in its progress will be subjected to additional shocks and stimulants. Our theoretical problem is to discover, within this framework, under what conditions, or with stimulants of what magnitude, we can hope to achieve sustained growth in per capita incomes rather than a tendency to return to the low, underdeveloped, equilibrium income level.

Why should the system possess some degree of stability?

This, of course, is one of the crucial theoretical questions. To answer it we invoke our second and third fundamental hypotheses stated at the beginning of this chapter. The second hypothesis suggests that the income-raising forces set in motion, directly or indirectly, income-depressing ones. This means that every stimulant induces or runs up against conditions or activities that repress, at least to some extent, the stimulating effects. Is this a metaphysical idea or can we think of its manifestation in relatively concrete terms? Actually, it is not difficult to think of a number of equilibrating forces and mechanisms that operate in this fashion. For example, population increases accompanied by diminishing returns may wipe out initial advances; or visible increases in consumption by some may lead other groups to try to consume beyond their means and thus eat into existing capital stocks (so-called demonstration effects); or the more intensive use of some kind of resources may lead to the exhaustion of complementary non-replaceable resources; or the initial stimulants bring into play institutional rigidities that serve as bottlenecks to growth or depress the existing expanded rate of productive activities. The literature is full of examples of inhibiting forces that seem to be called into play by attempts toward economic development.[11]

Of course, the mere existence of some income depressing forces in the wake of stimulants is not a sufficient condition to determine the stability (or any degree thereof) of the underdevelopment equilibrium income level. In addition, it is necessary that at some point the depressing forces become more significant than the effects of stimulants. Hence, our third fundamental hypothesis asserts that this is the case for some per capita income levels above the equilibrium level, or at least for the slower rates of growth in per capita incomes. Why this should be so or why it should be reasonable to accept the hypothesis is much more difficult to determine. The hypothesis implies that the system is quasi-stable (with respect to per capita income) for at least small stimulants. The key to the answer to the question of why this should be so probably lies in what we have called the educative process. Sustained growth requires a considerable transformation in the educative process, that is, it requires drastic changes in the mores, habits, and traditions of the populace. But the educative process and the consequent mores and traditions are so fundamental to the life of the society, and so pervasive in the day-to-day

[11] On this point see the United Nations Study, *Processes and Problems of Industrialization in Underdeveloped Countries;* also Buchanan and Ellis, *op. cit.,* as well as the large number of specific country studies made under the direction of the International Bank for Reconstruction and Development.

life of the community, especially within the family group, that it is almost unthinkable that these should respond drastically to small stimulants or shocks. This last is merely meant to be suggestive. We shall elaborate our defense of this hypothesis in later chapters, especially in chapter 8.

Why is the equilibrium state only quasi-stable?

In other words, why do we not accept the fully stable equilibrium as a serious starting point for our conceptual framework? Instead, we visualized a mechanism in which the response to an increase in stocks that implied increased income per head would somehow result, in the long run, in roughly compensating increases in other stocks which, in turn, implied decreasing incomes per head. The main reason for assuming only quasi-stability is that we cannot see any likely mechanism operating that would lead to the reduction of *all* stocks to their former level once they had been increased. Certain stocks and forces appear to be cumulative in nature; for example, certain types of knowledge, skills, discoveries, certain types of capital, etc. Once they come into existence there is nothing that causes them to decrease in magnitude. It is an empirical matter. Some aspects of the process of change are unidirectional. There is no necessary reason why in an underdeveloped economy people should forget skills (or not pass them to succeeding generations), destroy capital or stamp out knowledge, once acquired. These stocks may become more or less widely spread, but their absolute magnitude need not diminish to some initial level. Thus, the three processes may work in such a way as to restore something like the former structure (or balance) between those stocks that determine income per capita but not to reduce the *absolute* magnitudes of all stocks to the initial equilibrium level.

APPENDIX TO CHAPTER 3

On the Definition of a Quasi-Equilibrium System

The purpose of this note is to indicate in a formal and precise way what we mean by a quasi-equilibrium system.

1. By an equilibrium solution of a system we have in mind a vector (or state of the system) the elements of which are values for the variables of the system. A distinguishing property of the equilibrium values, as compared with some other set of values, is that if the equilibrium set

of values exists it will continue to exist as long as the system is not disturbed by external forces. One of the elements in the equilibrium solution we have in mind will be a value for per capita income.

2. For any system the equilibrium solution need not be unique. For each set of parameters there may (or may not) be a different equilibrium vector. Thus, we conceive of a solution set containing all of the equilibrium vectors of the system.

3. We consider two vectors that have identical elements as the same vector. If the solution set contains only one vector, the equilibrium is unique. If the solution set contains more than one vector, there are at least two possibilities. All of the corresponding components of the vectors in the set may be different, or some (but not all) of the corresponding components of at least some of the vectors may be the same.

4. By a quasi-equilibrium system we mean a system whose equilibrium solution set contains only vectors possessing some corresponding elements that are identical for all the vectors and some that are different for all the vectors. Specifically, we have in mind a set of equilibrium vectors containing per capita income elements that are identical.

CHAPTER 4

Characteristics of Backward Economies

Introduction

In this chapter we shall list the characteristics that densely populated underdeveloped areas are often said to have in common. We shall then determine how many of these characteristics can be explained on the basis of simple relationships that connect per capita consumption with the level of per capita income, per capita savings and investment with the level of per capita income, per capita output (or income) with the availability of resources per head, etc. We will find that we cannot explain all the characteristics on this basis, and for that reason we shall leave the explanation of some of the characteristics, indeed some of the crucial ones, to later chapters when we shall try to look at them in the light of the dynamics of the economic and social processes involved. "Explanations" will be brief and suggestive rather than exhaustive, since our aim is to isolate, so that we may concentrate on them later, those factors or aspects of the state of backwardness whose reason for existence is not immediately apparent by the application of relatively simple statical relationships.

It is of interest to note that different observers and scholars, in reporting the characteristics of these backward economies, have frequently come up with very similar lists despite the facts that there are often vast differences in the cultural and political conditions of various backward countries, that the quality of the statistics of different countries varies considerably, and that the politically determined boundaries of countries are, on methodological grounds, relatively poor units for purposes of comparison. Although it is true that all the observations and reports are not independent of each other, there is probably a sufficient degree of independent reporting of a statistical and observational nature to warrant some faith in the near universality of most of the reported characteristics. Indeed, we find, in perusing reports on individual backward economies, that we seem to be reading practically the same thing time and again as we go from the report of one country to another.

The Major Characteristics

It would be too time consuming and too tedious to go through various works, author by author, and to abstract and compare all the lists of characteristics that various writers have included in their discussions of backward economies. Rather, we shall present a combined list of characteristics that includes most of the characteristics most often mentioned.[1] Some writers emphasize some characteristics more than others, but common elements are always evident. Of course, whether or not an author includes something as a characteristic will depend, in part, on how he conceives the backward areas problem. Our summaries include (1) economic characteristics, (2) demographic and health characteristics, (3) technological characteristics, and (4) cultural and political characteristics. We shall see that some of these characteristics overlap some of the categories. This is what we would expect since many of them are closely related to each other and therefore a clear-cut grouping is impossible. After considering the items in the

---

[1] See, among others, the following: P. N. Rosenstein-Rodan, "International Development of Economically Backward Areas," *International Affairs,* April 1944, pp. 159–162. International Labor Office, *The Economic Background of Social Policy Including Problems of Industrialization,* I. L. O., New Delhi, 1947. Alfred Sauvy, "Introduction à l'étude des pays sous-développés," *Population,* Vol. 6 (1951), pp. 604 ff. N. Prokopovicz, *L'Industrialisation des pays agricoles et la structure de l'économie mondiale, après la guerre,* Neuchâtel, Edit. de la Baconnière, 1946. A. L. Minkes, "The Economic Development of Eastern Europe—Review of Materials for Study," *International Affairs,* Vol. 27, No. 1 (January 1951), pp. 46 ff. H. Belshaw, "Economic Development as an Operational Problem," *Civilizations,* Vol. 2, No. 2, Geneva League of Nations (1945), (reprinted 1948), pp. 36 ff. *The Determinants and Consequences of Population Trends,* Population Studies No. 17, Department of Social Affairs, United Nations, New York, 1953, pp. 262 ff.

combined list, we shall consider the general question of whether or not the characteristics listed are necessary concomitants of backwardness. The answer to this question should get us closer to an understanding of the essential nature of economic backwardness.

Characteristics of Underdeveloped Areas (Combined List)

1. *Economic*
   - (*a*) General
     - (1) A very high proportion of the population in agriculture, usually some 70 to 90 per cent.
     - (2) "Absolute over-population" in agriculture, that is, it would be possible to reduce the number of workers in agriculture and still obtain the same total output.[2]
     - (3) Evidence of considerable "disguised unemployment" and a lack of employment opportunities outside agriculture.
     - (4) Very little capital per head.
     - (5) Low income per head and, as a consequence, existence near the "subsistence" level.
     - (6) Practically zero savings for the large mass of the people.
     - (7) Whatever savings do exist are usually achieved by a landholding class whose values are not conducive to investment in industry or commerce.
     - (8) The primary industries, that is, agriculture, forestry, and mining, are usually the residual employment categories.
     - (9) The output in agriculture is made up mostly of cereals and primary raw materials, with relatively low output of protein foods. The reason for this is the conversion ratio between cereals and meat products; that is, if one acre of cereals produces a certain number of calories, it would take between five and seven acres to produce the same number of calories if meat products were produced.
     - (10) Major proportion of expenditures on food and necessities.
     - (11) Export of foodstuffs and raw materials.
     - (12) Low volume of trade per capita.
     - (13) Poor credit facilities and poor marketing facilities.
     - (14) Poor housing.
   - (*b*) Basic characteristics in agriculture
     - (1) Although there is low capitalization on the land, there is simultaneously an uneconomic use of whatever capital exists due to the small size of holdings and the existence of exceedingly small plots.
     - (2) The level of agrarian techniques is exceedingly low, and tools and equipment are limited and primitive in nature.
     - (3) Even where there are big landowners as, for instance, in certain parts of India, the openings for modernized agriculture production for sale are limited by difficulties of

[2] See Chapter 6 for more on this point.

transport and the absence of an efficient demand in the local market. It is significant that in many backward countries a modernized type of agriculture is confined to production for sale in foreign markets.

(4) There is an inability of the small landholders and peasants to weather even a short-term crisis, and, as a consequence, attempts are made to get the highest possible yields from the soil, which leads to soil depletion.

(5) There is a widespread prevalence of high indebtedness relative to assets and income.

(6) The methods of production for the domestic market are generally old-fashioned and inefficient, leaving little surplus for marketing. This is usually true irrespective of whether or not the cultivator owns the land, has tenancy rights, or is a sharecropper.

(7) A most pervasive aspect is a feeling of land hunger due to the exceedingly small size of holdings and small diversified plots. The reason for this is that holdings are continually subdivided as the population on the land increases.

2. *Demographic*

(1) High fertility rates, usually above 40 per thousand.
(2) High mortality rates and low expectation of life at birth.
(3) Inadequate nutrition and dietary deficiencies.
(4) Rudimentary hygiene, public health, and sanitation.
(5) Rural overcrowding.

3. *Cultural and Political*

(1) Rudimentary education and usually a high degree of illiteracy among most of the people.
(2) Extensive prevalence of child labor.
(3) General weakness or absence of the middle class.
(4) Inferiority of women's status and position.
(5) Traditionally determined behavior for the bulk of the populace.

4. *Technological and Miscellaneous*

(1) Low yields per acre.
(2) No training facilities or inadequate facilities for the training of technicians, engineers, etc.
(3) Inadequate and crude communication and transportation facilities, especially in the rural areas.
(4) Crude technology.

Characteristics Explainable on the Basis of Economic Statics

If we study our list of characteristics we are struck by the fact that we can explain a number of them on the basis of two simple relationships and some conventional notions about the demand elasticities for different commodity groupings. These relationships are: (1) that per capita consumption increases as per capita income increases, although the proportion consumed may decrease as income increases, and (2) that investment per head increases as per capita income increases. Income and output are assumed to be identical for a closed economy.[3] Of course, these are similar to the usual Keynesian macro-economic relationships put on a per capita level. In addition, we need to keep in mind an elementary notion about expenditure patterns, namely, that the lower the income per head, the greater the proportion spent on so-called primary needs like food and shelter. Many of the items on the list are income determining, whereas others are income determined. Since we use low per capita income as our criterion of backwardness, it is to be expected that many of the characteristics will be those conditions that produce low incomes whereas other characteristics are the consequences of low per capita income. (But we shall find that there are some items that *cannot* be explained in these terms.)

We may start by elaborating our production relations. For present purposes only, we can assume that the ratio of labor force to the total population is a constant. We generally expect per capita income to increase as any resource per head increases, other things being equal. Accordingly, if capital, labor, entrepreneurial ability per head, technical knowledge, and the credit facilities available increase, the income per head will rise. If we limit our investigations to countries that, by definition, have low incomes per head, we must expect to find that the other side of the production equation holds. Hence, we see the observed characteristics of low capital per capita, crowding on the land or little land per capita, and poor credit facilities, etc., as part of the conditions that determine low incomes. Choosing to observe low income countries, we must simultaneously find conditions responsible for low incomes. The existence of low-income determining conditions accounts for, even if it does not fully explain, at least three of the items on our combined list.

Turning to the consumption side, we are able to account for more of the characteristics considered. Generally the consumption of any specific item depends on income and on price. We would expect a per capita consumption function to be of a similar nature, and given the income level we would find the expenditures to be along the lines of the well-known Engel curves.[4] That is to say, given low incomes

[3] We need not assume a closed economy. But in order to abstract, for the present, the international trade complications, we do assume that the value of imports is always equal to the value of exports.

[4] See Herman Wold, *Demand Analysis,* John Wiley and Sons, New York, 1953, pp. 8–9, and pp. 253 ff. Engel's law states that as income increases the proportions of total expenditure spent on urgent needs decrease, whereas those on semi-luxuries and luxuries increase.

we would, naturally, expect a standard of living for the masses of the populace near the "subsistence" level. Similarly, we would expect most of the expenditures to be on necessities or near necessities, and net savings to be either exceedingly small or absent. For the same reason, we would also expect a considerable degree of indebtedness, especially if there are periodic emergencies such as famines and epidemics. Poor housing is part of the same picture and hardly needs an explanatory comment. To the extent that nutrition and personal hygiene determine mortality, we would certainly expect high mortality rates and low expectation of life at birth in low income countries.

The predominance of agriculture as an economic activity can also be explained, in part, by the demand functions and consumption functions. Since, for the average low-income family, food expenditures take up the major portion of such incomes, demand for agricultural commodities must be the predominant demand; and, given low capital per head, we would naturally expect that the major effort of the labor force should go into agriculture. But this is only a partial explanation. If there is an adequately functioning international division of labor, why should all poor countries be those that seem to specialize in agriculture and primary commodities? There is nothing about agriculture as such that necessarily leads to poverty, and yet there are no exceedingly low-income countries that are primarily industrial.

If the major portion of the labor force is in agriculture, and if the predominant expenditure is for food and housing, it is not difficult to explain the low volume of foreign trade per capita that is usually observed in such economies. We can examine this problem either from the demand or supply side and come up with more or less the same result. Given the internal expenditure pattern determined by the existence of low per capita incomes, we can expect very little effective demand for non-agricultural goods from abroad. Indeed, there is often the need of imports of some agricultural commodities. On the supply side, there is usually very little surplus of the primary commodities, and there are relatively few industries to make possible large exports of industrial goods. When exports are prominent they are usually of a single-crop nature such as rubber, cocoa, and sugar cane. Although such single-crop exports are often striking, and, because of their political implications, quite dramatic, when computed on a per capita basis the result is still usually a low volume of exports per capita as compared with many of the highly industrialized countries.

The prevalence of child labor can, *in part,* also be explained on the basis of low incomes on the consumption side of the picture. It is a characteristic that is income determined. In the first place, alternative activities for children, such as formal education, are often out of the question because of their direct costs. On the other hand, the prevalence of very low incomes per family makes it necessary for families to employ their children economically so that the family income can be maximized.

This question can be examined from still another viewpoint. In underdeveloped areas where mortality rates are high, the cost of rearing a child to an age at which he or she becomes self-supporting is, in proportion to income, greater than in countries where mortality rates are low. In other words, mortality declines lower the cost of rearing an adult worker. For example, Mortara[5] calculates that the ratio of cost of rearing non-survivors to the total cost of rearing survivors dropped in Italy to one-fourth from 1881–1882 to 1930–1932, and in Sao Paulo by about one-half from 1920–1921 to 1939–1941. In typical Western European countries, the ratios have been reduced to one-fourth in the last 50 to 100 years. Hence, to whatever extent the burden of dependency is greater in underdeveloped countries, to that extent can it be reduced by employing people at younger ages.

Savings as a function of income, is the other side of the coin of the consumption function. It is most evident that low savings rates account for the low rate of investment usual in low income countries. This statement explains, in part, the low amount of capital per head and helps to explain some of the implications or consequences of low capital per head, for example, poor and inadequate communications, relatively poor systems of transportation, agriculture, and industrial capital goods of a rather crude nature, and poor training facilities for technicians and engineers. If capital is limited and the inadequacy is widespread, in each use the capital employed is likely to be of a limited and technically backward nature. Of course, this last is not a necessary concomitant of low amount of capital per head. It is conceivable that in some industries capital should be ample and of a most up-to-date nature while in others it is primitive and exceedingly scarce. Such imbalance is not entirely unknown in underdeveloped areas—especially where foreign capital concentrates on one or, at most, a relatively few export industries. Otherwise, the ampleness of capital in a few show industries must be at the expense of others.

The remaining characteristics, those that we were not able to explain in terms of our simple production, consumption, and savings functions, involve considerations of a dynamic nature, factors which

---

[5] Giorgio Mortara, "O Costo de Producão do homen adulto e sua variacão em relacão a mortalidade," *Estudos Brasilieros de Demografia,* Monografia No. 2, Vol. 1 (October 1946), pp. 90 ff.

are really unessential concomitants of economic backwardness, or political and cultural considerations some of which may be beyond our purview. But those within our sphere are taken up in the chapters that follow.

CHAPTER 5

Characteristics of Economic Backwardness—Some Dynamic Aspects

Introduction

The list of characteristics considered in the previous chapter gives us, as it were, a profile of a backward economy. We have seen that the existence of some of these elements can be understood on the basis of simple relationships that explain the internal consistency of the picture that we observe. Thus, given one set of conditions, we can be said to understand its simultaneous concomitants if the implications of the given set of conditions agree with our observations. For example, if we are given a low quantity of capital per head and a low quantity of land per worker, we can readily understand the simultaneous existence of low incomes. But we cannot understand why this should necessarily be a condition that persists.

Technically speaking, in saying that we wish to understand the persistence of low incomes and other characteristics of economic backwardness, we are indicating the need to explain the stability of the system. In other words, we must be able to rationalize why the set of conditions that we find in underdeveloped areas should sustain themselves over long periods. Clearly, these are not conditions that governments or people wish to see maintained, and yet the major reason for the great interest in underdeveloped areas, and the one that makes the problem so challenging, is their persistence. The explanation of why these characteristics maintain themselves is a matter for dynamic analysis.

In this and the next chapter we shall review briefly some of the remaining characteristics in the light of the general picture of development presented in chapter 3. To this end, we shall try to extend our analysis of those matters, previously left unexplained, by introducing some dynamic considerations from time to time. However, the reader should note that our objective is *not* to present anything that pretends to be an exhaustive analysis of each of the characteristics considered. It is intended, rather, to show that these characteristics, their relations to each other, and the broad dynamic relationships that can be introduced to support them are consistent with our view of backwardness as a quasi-stable system.

Broadly speaking, we shall focus our attention on three elements of the problem: (1) the often-found persistence of low yields per acre and per man in agriculture, (2) the lack of non-agricultural employment opportunities, and (3) the role of the general demographic characteristics in the dynamics of backwardness. The closely related problem of agricultural underemployment is examined in the chapter that follows.

Low Agricultural Yields

Whereas it is easy enough to understand low yields per man in agriculture, it is somewhat more difficult to explain low yields per acre under cultivation. The very high density of the rural population implies limited land and capital per man, and, its obvious corollary, low income per head. But looking on the other side of the picture we would expect high yields per acre. It is not too difficult to construct, *a priori,* a case where the normal expectation would be high yields per acre. Other things being equal, the yield per acre should depend on the intensity with which the land is worked. Thus, if land and labor were the only two factors, we should expect high yields where there is high density of labor on the land. Even introducing the capital factor into the picture should not change our conclusions very much, for much of the agricultural capital is likely to be labor saving, and labor is already superabundant. Thus, if we start with land of equal quality, we should expect high rather than low yields in the densely populated underdeveloped areas.

In actual fact, yields per acre are not always lower in backward countries than in *some* advanced countries. For example, wheat yields per acre are much higher in Egypt than they are in Canada but lower than in many Western European countries, namely, Denmark, Belgium, Holland, the United Kingdom, and some others.[1] On the whole, the land-rich countries of North and South America and the backward economies of Asia and Africa have low yields per acre when compared with the advanced countries of Western Europe. (See W. S. Woytinsky and E. S. Woytinsky, *op. cit.,* chapters 15 and 16 for a great deal of the detailed statistics on comparative yields per acre.) The land-rich countries of America use a very extensive (rather than intensive) agriculture, and their output per acre cultivated is understandably quite low. But it is very clear that many of the backward countries, often employing over three times as much agricultural labor per acre as advanced Western European countries and often operating under superior climatic conditions, obtain much lower yields per acre. It is this phenomenon toward which our speculations are addressed.

There are at least three possibilities that can be considered to explain low yields under the stated circumstances. (1) Some of the capital found in advanced agricultural countries may not be of a kind for which we can substitute labor; (2) advanced countries may utilize superior agricultural techniques; and (3) on the average, the quality of the cultivated land may be superior in the advanced countries. To some extent, all these factors play some role. Low capital is associated with low incomes. Primitive techniques may be explained by the rudimentary level of education and the simultaneous lack of necessary complementary capital goods. But, in order to explain differences in the inherent qualities of the land, we need a somewhat more elaborate theory than merely ascribing them to low incomes. Certainly, persistently low yields cannot be ascribed to climatic characteristics since these are often more favorable to high yields in the underdeveloped countries than in the developed ones. But the average quality of the land may be inferior for two reasons. First, because incomes are low, the margin of cultivation is carried much further in the direction of poorer land than in countries where incomes are high, and this, of course, brings the average down. But, second, and more to the point, there may be an inherent dynamic process in the utilization of the land that keeps yields low.

Here we return to one of the principles expounded in chapter 3. Every possibility for improvement that arises, and is taken advantage

[1] W. S. Woytinsky and E. S. Woytinsky, *World Population and Production,* pp. 546–547. See especially pp. 530–549 for numerous tables indicating outputs per acre for various crops for the different areas and countries of the world.

of, sets up counterforces that work toward a return of the quality of the land to its former level—or to a low-quality equilibrium level. Thus, we can visualize a situation in which an improvement in the quality of the land generates a more intensive utilization of that land in such a way that the consequent depletion results in a return of the land to its former quality.[2] We have to visualize at the outset an equilibrium level of nutrients in the soil. As the quality of the land is improved, either through man-made efforts or through some accidental means, such as the overflowing of the banks of a river and the deposit of rich sediment on its shores, the initial effect will be considerably improved yields as the same manpower and capital are applied. However, it is not very difficult to imagine one or more chains of events set in motion by the increased yields that lead to some depletion of the soil. First, we would expect both manpower and capital to be shifted from less fertile lands to the new high-yield lands. This shift should have the effects of eventually raising yields on that land from which the manpower was shifted and of diminishing the soil nutrients on the now more intensively utilized land. There are two opposing forces at work: Yields per acre are likely to be raised by adding manpower to the more fertile land, but, at the same time, the rate of soil depletion will be somewhat higher than otherwise. However, if nothing else occurred, the net effect of these events would be an increased yield on the average acre and some possibility for the landholders and peasants to leave some of the land fallow in order to maintain general fertility. But apparently this does not usually take place.

There are several possible explanations why fertility is not maintained. In the first place, putting land in fallow or taking other measures to maintain the quality of the soil decreases current yields.[3] In other words, it is costly as far as current expenditures are concerned. With incomes already at a very low level there is a tendency to live off

---

[2] On this point, compare the illustrations given in F. Osborn, *Our Plundered Planet,* Boston, Little, Brown and Co., 1948, Chapters 6 and 7. See also K. William Kapp, *The Social Costs of Private Enterprise,* Cambridge, Harvard University Press, Chapter 9. There is, of course, a very large body of literature on the subject of erosion and depletion of resources.

[3] For example, crop rotation, in which one of the rotated crops is a leguminous plant or a vegetable, will produce micro-organisms (for example, *Azotobacter*) that help to bind the nitrogen to the soil, but since the calorie yield of legumes is lower than that of grains, the total calorie yield will be initially lower after the introduction of crop rotation. See Sir A. Daniel Hall, *The Improvement of Native Agriculture in Relation to Population and Public Health,* London, Oxford University Press, 1936. See especially Chapter 1, "The Maintenance of Fertility," pp. 1–20.

the greater current bounty rather than to maintain a steady higher level into an uncertain future. That is to say, when incomes are low there is a tendency to live off capital, especially if that capital is readily convertible into income, and not to replace fully for current depletion. But, even if this were not the case, pressures would arise toward greater depletion of the soil, that is, pressures that increase the current desire to take advantage of maximum yields at the expense of future yields. Increased current yields imply improved nutrition, a diminution of periodic starvation, and consequent diminished mortality rates, resulting in increased population and necessary further subdivision of holdings. Although these smaller holdings yield a somewhat higher fertility than previously, there is now little room for quality-maintenance measures that imply a diminution in the current yield. The net result is a gradual return of the soil to its previous equilibrium quality.

We may ask why the soil is not eventually depleted to a zero level. In some cases, of course, this may actually have occurred, and the vast expanses of deserts (about one-third of the world's acreage) that may have been fertile regions in former times attest to this possibility. Also, there may, in some cases, be physical limitations to the amount of soil depletion that can occur, given the traditional, rather primitive methods of cultivation. Yet we need not believe that the technical nature of the soil is the sole factor that prevents further depletion in many areas. It is more likely that the developed, traditional methods of cultivation determine the equilibrium quality of the soil. That is, those peoples that did not develop traditions which lead to some conservation of the nutrient values of the soil were forced to abandon the land as a consequence of erosion. Those that survived must have developed traditional methods and cultural patterns which permitted a subsistent standard of living while at the same time the quality of the soil was maintained at some low equilibrium level.

Of course, the details would differ from country to country, and, in some cases, from time to time. The actual dynamic process that keeps the quality of the land much below the optimum is certainly a more complicated one than the one we have just sketched. But, it is really not too important whether the details, as we have sketched them, are correct or not for any particular instance. What is important for present purposes is that we can explain low yields in terms of responses to growth that are generated from within the economy and consistent with our picture of backwardness as a quasi-equilibrium state. This becomes especially evident if we contrast such responses with the probable responses to rapid change that are likely to occur in advanced economies. Thus, in the backward economies, we are likely to have something like the following: Reactions to an improvement in the quality of the soil will lead to greater intensity of utilization and consumption because of the very strong time preference of the current population, and because population growth increases the time preference of present agricultural goods for future goods. Present needs cannot be sacrificed for future quality. The abundance and cheapness of labor means that, whenever possible, labor will be substituted for capital. Hence, whenever possible, the land will be worked more intensively rather than employing capital to enrich the soil. By contrast, in advanced, and advancing economies, some capital, in the form of machinery, fertilizer, etc., is constantly being substituted for labor. As non-agricultural opportunities spread, the agricultural activities are concentrated on the best land; complementarity between different types of capital may lead to the adoption of techniques in advanced countries that are impossible in the backward economies. We need not go on indefinitely in this vein. Enough has been said for us to see that in the former case there are dynamic forces that tend to depress yields per acre once raised, while in the advanced economies many of these forces may work in the opposite direction, that is, toward a general expansion of yields.

Lack of Non-Agricultural Employment Opportunities

The persistence of a lack of adequate non-agricultural employment opportunities lies at the very root of the economic development problem. We shall investigate the details of many aspects that touch on this problem elsewhere. Here we shall go into the matter only briefly.

The lack of alternative employment opportunities outside of agriculture, the fact that the predominant portion of the labor force is engaged in agriculture, and the existence of agricultural underemployment are different aspects of the same phenomenon. For it is the lack of alternative employment opportunities that makes it impossible to shift any significant portion of the labor force to the non-agricultural sector. In explaining this lack we explain, in part, the persistence of underemployment and the predominance of agriculture.

The need for such non-agricultural employment opportunities is not difficult to establish. The existence of the exceedingly low productivity of agricultural labor immediately suggests the desirability of employment opportunities where labor productivity might be higher. Although there may at times be a lack of special skills in the non-agricultural sector, the empirical evidence does not usually indicate a general labor deficiency in industry or commerce. Thus, the problem does not appear to be due to any special difficulties of transferring labor from agricultural to non-agricultural pursuits, even if such difficulties may exist. Rather, it appears to be due to a lack of enough non-agricultural employment opportunities or (what amounts to the same thing in this case) to the fact that non-agricultural employment opportunities are not created rapidly enough. Although words like "lack" and "adequate" are normative terms, it is clear that an adequate rate of growth in non-agricultural employment opportunities implies a rate sufficient to absorb the expansion of the labor force and to take some labor off the land.

The exact rate of capital formation that does occur is difficult to assess, but it seems reasonable to accept the United Nations estimate that in most underdeveloped countries net capital formation is below 5 per cent of the national income.[4] Although it is undeniable that such rates are low compared with advanced countries, if such rates persisted in the absence of income depressing changes, we might, nevertheless, expect sustained growth in industrial and commercial employment opportunities, if the allocation were proper. It would appear that there are three general questions to keep in mind simultaneously: (*a*) What accounts for an allocation of investment that is not conducive to non-agricultural employment creation? (*b*) Why is the rate of savings as low as it is, and what are the obstacles to increasing savings and net investment? and (*c*) Why is a low but positive rate of capital formation not sufficient to do the job at hand?

We have already touched on some of the reasons for low savings. A number of obvious ones come to mind: When incomes are low it is difficult to abstain from the consumption necessary for savings and internally created capital accumulation. The banking, monetary, and fiscal institutions to induce greater investment may be primitive or inadequate. Where labor is cheap there is always the incentive to substitute labor for capital. A tradition of thrift may be absent, and the entrepreneurial talent to discover opportunities and marshal other people's savings may be much too scarce. Yet, despite these, and many other reasons, it is clear that the amount of net capital formation in the non-agricultural sector does not, in most cases, come anywhere near to exhausting the savings potential that often exists. And this last is probably as significant a factor as the low savings potential itself.

As is usual almost everywhere, the saving that does occur is accomplished by only a very small proportion of the population. To some extent a considerable amount of potential savings are frittered away. In part, such potential savings are often spent on luxurious living, on items

[4] *Measures for the Economic Development of Underdeveloped Countries,* 1951, p. 35.

that are not all current consumption but which are not productive of sustained industrial employment, such as larger homes, private parks, imports from abroad, etc. Also, in view of the traditional value attached to the owning of land, a great deal of private saving is spent on augmenting land holdings by the wealthy, and sometimes by the less wealthy. This may raise land values but need not result in real net capital creation. Those who sell land may have a very high propensity to consume. This aspect of the savings problem has been well documented, but its extent and importance differ considerably between countries.

What about the net investment that does take place? Some of it will go into agriculture, since agriculture, as a way of life, is highly valued traditionally. Its familiarity and predominance as an endeavor add to its attractiveness as an outlet for investment.

Because of the relative familiarity that the people of backward economies have with agriculture, as against industry, its risks are, more or less, known rather than highly uncertain. And, of course, there is always a greater inducement to invest in undertakings in which the risks are familiar and perhaps roughly calculable rather than those in which they are strange and perhaps unfathomable.

A second significant outlet for investments is the short term commercial venture, often related to the import and export of commodities. Rates of profit are usually quite high on such ventures. Although risks exist, they are short term risks. They do not extend over a long, uncertain period of production. Merchants are familiar with trade in already created goods. This is an activity of less complexity and of a different order from the marshaling, organizing and purchasing of factors of production to make new goods or new types of goods. On the whole such activities do not create a great many additional employment opportunities outside of agriculture. But given whatever net investment there is in the non-agricultural sector, one would expect that, if it is a positive amount year after year, eventually it should have a considerable impact in shifting the labor force outside agriculture. This probably would be true if the labor force remained constant. But the reaction to the fruits of investment is for the population, and hence the labor force, to grow at a faster rate than otherwise. The net result is that the rate of investment has to be of considerable size before it can overcome the force of population growth to shift the distribution of manpower between the agricultural and the non-agricultural segments. A simple numerical example, admittedly based on extreme assumptions, may help to illustrate this aspect of the problem.

Suppose that landowners do not invest in the non-agricultural sector of the economy so that all non-agricultural capital formation arises out of savings in the non-agricultural sector. The other relevant information is as follows:

	Agricultural Sector	Non-Agricultural Sector	Total
Labor force	75	25	100
Income per worker per year	$100	$100	...
National income per year	7,500	2,500	10,000
Rate of savings	20%	20%	...
Capital to income per worker ratio	...	5:1	...

A capital to income per worker ratio of 5 to 1 is, of course, not unusual but a 20 per cent net savings rate is unquestionably exceptionally high. But let us see what happens. In the non-agricultural sector the amount saved will be $500 or 5 per cent of the national income. This, in turn, will create non-agricultural employment for one worker—in this case 1 per cent of the labor force. If the labor force expands by 1 per cent or more there will be no opportunity to reduce the amount of surplus agricultural labor. Even if the savers in the agricultural sector invest one-third of their savings in the non-agricultural sector, this amount would absorb only a 2 per cent expansion of the labor force. Given usual rates of capital formation of less than 5 per cent of national income rather than 20 per cent, as we assumed, we can readily see where the inadequacy arises. We could probably develop many more complex and realistic looking models and still come out with a similar source of inadequacy. Also, we should note that a 1 per cent rate of labor force increase is a relatively low rate in any country that is developing sufficiently to save 20 per cent of its income; a 2 per cent rate of population growth would probably be more realistic. In this case, a rate of net savings of less than 20 per cent, even with the one-third contribution from the agricultural sector, would not permit the maintenance of the old distribution between agriculture and industry. That is, the extent of "disguised unemployment" in agriculture would increase and the proportion of the labor force in agriculture would grow accordingly.

For purposes of simplification some of the assumptions in our example were extreme. We might expect some of the net savings in agriculture to create employment, especially where the savings are used to expand the amount of arable land. Also, in some cases, more of the agricultural net savings may become non-agricultural capital formation. Nevertheless, the example does serve to indicate the essential nature of the problem. If at the outset we have a certain amount of surplus agricultural labor, a certain minimum net investment in the industrial sector has to take place before the surplus can be reduced. And it is not difficult to visualize circumstances in which this minimum is above the rate of capital accumulation actually taking place. Similarly, any lessening of the proportion of the labor force in agriculture requires a certain minimum net investment below which the proportion in agriculture will increase. The central point to be made is that the existence of a relatively low level of investment will insure the persistence of these two characteristics of economic backwardness—surplus manpower and the predominance of agriculture.

The Role of the Demographic Characteristics in the Dynamics of Backwardness

There is, perhaps, a tendency on the part of so-called Malthusian writers to regard the population factor as *the* critical obstacle to economic development. Others have taken an equally extreme position in denying that population growth is a factor of importance. It would seem that neither position is warranted on methodological grounds, as well as on others. As long as population growth is not the *only* obstacle to development, and surely it is not, there is little meaning in regarding it as the crucial obstacle if we look at the whole business in terms of a closely knit set of relationships. If *A*, *B*, and *C* are obstacles that are related in such a way that there is no way of overcoming them one by one, since all of them change as any one of them is tampered with, there is no way of determining that one is much more important than the others. Hence, if we regard population changes as endogenously determined, at least to some extent, then the demographic factor must be considered in relation to other factors, and there is little meaning in saying it is *the* crucial factor. On the other hand, there is a great deal of evidence to suggest, and we shall present some of this evidence later, that this factor is not a variable that can be ignored entirely in considering the development problem.

The demographic characteristics of economic backwardness present a dual problem. In part, they help to explain other aspects of the situation, and from this point of view their particular roles must be delineated. In part, their existence and persistence have to be explained.

It is convenient, as an explanatory device, to start with a closed economy so that the migration element can be ignored. In our analysis two central facts are assumed: (1) that economic growth is always associated with population growth and (2) that population growth always implies growth of the labor force. A third related assumption, whether made explicit or implied, involves diminishing returns. That is, we assume that for the relevant *range,* additions to the labor force are subject to diminishing returns. Where this is not true, population growth is a boon rather than an obstacle to progress. But in the densely populated areas (and this appears to be the general case), capital and arable land are the relatively scarce factors. Indeed, they are usually very scarce. Furthermore, the lack of industrial capital is often the bottleneck factor that prohibits the complete utilization of the available manpower. As long as industrial capital remains relatively scarce, and as long as the vast majority of the labor force is engaged in agriculture, it would appear to be reasonably safe to postulate that under these circumstances, and at least for the early stages of development, the system is operating under diminishing returns with respect to labor.

In densely populated economies population growth is an obstacle to development because it "dilutes" the amount of capital with which the representative worker may operate. Other things being equal, it is a factor responsible for the reduction of per capita incomes. Of course, there may be simultaneous income-raising forces at work. But, in any event, the important point to note is that it can be one of the factors that help to give the state of backwardness a certain amount of stability. Exactly how much stability depends on the significance of all the income depressing factors, among them, population growth, as against the others. Briefly, the mechanism is as follows: Any event that increases incomes will, at first, also increase the rate of population growth. This, in turn, implies an increase in the labor force, and both capital and land per worker are accordingly reduced. Furthermore, this tends to reduce income per capita, which depresses the "induced" rate of population growth, if not the actual rate. The end result may be the sort of fluctuations around an equilibrium subsistence income considered previously.

The actual rate of population growth may not be the same as the "induced rate," by which we mean that rate induced or made possible by a higher rather than a lower level of income. The forces that determine the rate of population growth are very complex. (See chapter 10.) Not all of them can be explained in terms of an economic-physiological connection. In recent years the application of some of the discoveries in the chemical, medical science, and public health fields has often led to spectacular reductions in mortality in countries where high mortality rates were chronic. Since no such spectacular scientific discoveries have occurred with respect to fertility decline, the net result has been larger increases in the rate of population growth. Thus it seems that we have to think of the matter in terms of two types of forces that are constantly being generated. On the one hand, we have *induced* changes in population explainable by changes in per capita income, and, on the other hand, we have exogenous secular forces usually in the form of chemical, bacteriological, and medical discoveries that enable central authorities to reduce mortality rates at very low cost but without the simultaneous increase in per capita income. Once such discoveries are made, they are available forever, as it were. There is no mechanism to unmake them.

Does the rate of population growth always increase as average income grows? This assertion is universally true only for the early stages of development and is not necessarily true for advanced countries. It depends on the related generalization that the high fertility rates found in backward economies have a high degree of stability and will persist unless subjected to very considerable shocks. This being the case, the mortality rate will then be the crucial variable that determines the rate of population growth. As indicated, we should visualize the mortality rate as the result of two types of effects. One we might call the autonomous effect—the effect on mortality that takes place apart from and regardless of changes in income and consumption. Such factors as the medical and public health discoveries previously alluded to are of this nature. The other is the income effect for which we visualize a direct connection between the level of consumption and the related levels of nutrition, sanitation, health, and mortality. Clearly, as mortality rates drop with income increases, population will grow.

But why should high fertility rates persist and have such a high degree of stability in backward economies? Here we have to look to the cultural factors that usually accompany economic backwardness—to the pervasiveness of high fertility rates in environments (1) where behavior is of a highly traditional nature, (2) where there is little experimenting with mores and taboos, (3) where traditionally marriage takes place at an early age, (4) where fertility in women is highly regarded, (5) where birth control is unknown, and (6) where women's position is inferior to men's, etc. But why should this combination of traditions and cultural factors arise and persist? This last question gets us far afield from conventional economic analysis. The detailed explanation of such phenomena is the task of the cultural anthropologist. But, broadly speaking, it can readily be seen that the development of this sort of cultural climate was a necessary evolutionary condition for survival. Given a history of recurrent famines and epidemics and the consequent high mortality rates, only those communities that developed a cultural climate fostering high fertility rates were able to survive.

CHAPTER 6

The Theory of Underemployment in Densely Populated Backward Areas

The Problem

In this chapter we shall examine the problem of actual or "disguised" underemployment as it manifests itself in the agricultural sector. Especially we shall look for a theoretical explanation of the simultaneous existence of surplus labor in agriculture and of labor receiving a positive wage even in those cases where its marginal productivity is zero.

The nature of the problem can, perhaps, best be seen if we review the related questions that are involved. (1) If there is surplus labor in agriculture in the sense that a smaller labor force can cultivate the same amount of arable land, does this mean that the *marginal* productivity of labor is really zero? (2) It is observed that agricultural laborers do, in fact, receive positive wages, but if their marginal productivity is really zero and there is underemployment, should we not expect that competition among laborers or sharecroppers for available jobs or available land would force their incomes down toward a zero level? If, in fact, wages are not zero, does it make sense to infer that the marginal product is zero?

Is the assertion of an absolute labor surplus true? There are two general bases for the belief in the existence of agricultural underemployment in backward economies:[1] (1) casual observation and (2) statistical comparisons of output between what are sometimes assumed to be roughly comparable areas. Although it is impossible to check the casual observer, it is a fact that this type of observation is made time and time again by different people. What can be observed, and what is indisputable, is the existence of exceedingly small holdings and the belief that in other areas a man can cultivate much larger holdings. The statistical observations are of a similar nature. First, an attempt is made to reduce all land to something like units of land of equal or equivalent quality. Then a comparison is made of the number of workers per similar acre of land. Such calculations must, of necessity, be of a rough and ready kind both because of the poorness of the initial statistics and because of the practical difficulties of converting land in various areas possessing quite different characteristics into some sort of comparable units. Nevertheless, despite the rough and ready nature of the methods, the results are not without persuasive power. For it often appears that in some areas the land is cultivated by less than 50 per cent of the labor force used in less developed areas, and yet higher yields are achieved.[2] It is usually difficult to take into account the differences in capital available in different areas. But can this alone account for the vast differences that are observed?

Especially persuasive is the observation that one very often finds in the same area, with precisely the same climatic and soil conditions, both large holdings and small holdings, and yet the large holdings do not use proportionately more manpower although they do have at least as high a yield per acre. Of course, here too, it may be very difficult to account for the differences in capital that may exist.

One possible explanation, for at least part of the picture, is that we have to distinguish between two types of disguised unemployment. The first type is one in which it would be possible to delete a portion of the labor force, reorganize the labor force in some manner or other, make no additions whatsoever to any of the other factors of production, and obtain no smaller yield with the smaller labor force than with the larger

---

[1] See Wilbert Moore, *Economic Demography of Eastern and Southern Europe,* League of Nations, 1945, Chapters 3 and 4; Also Ragnar Nurkse, *Problems of Capital Formation in Underdeveloped Countries,* New York, Oxford University Press, 1953; Doreen Warriner, *Economics of Peasant Farming,* London, Oxford University Press, 1939; W. Arthur Lewis, "Reflections on South East Asia," *District Bank Review* (December 1952), p. 11.

[2] See, for example, the tables in Moore, *op. cit.,* Chapter 3.

one. In this case, the marginal productivity of labor on the land may be said to be zero. Additional manpower would not increase output at all.

A second type of disguised unemployment is involved in the case where a subtraction of a portion of the labor force will yield a smaller output no matter what sort of reorganization of the smaller labor force takes place. Similarly, an addition to the labor force would result in a higher total yield. The sense in which we can have disguised unemployment in this case is that with additional resources or means of creating additional employment opportunities *of the right kind, more effort* could be obtained from the existing labor force. This type of unemployment is due to the seasonal nature of the production process in agriculture, coupled with the fact that there is a lack of alternative employment outlets.

In the second case, the agricultural labor force may be said to suffer from disguised unemployment in the same sense that taxi-drivers may be said to suffer from disguised unemployment. During the daily peak periods, all taxis find riders and if there were additional taxis, they would find additional riders. But during other times of the day a great many of the taxis are idle. The hours of idleness may outweigh the hours during which they are delivering passengers. In this sense, they may be said to be partially unemployed or to suffer from disguised unemployment. Also, any reduction in the labor force of taxi-drivers would raise the average number of riders per taxi.

This second type of disguised unemployment is much easier to understand since it fits in with usual economic ideas. In this case, the marginal productivity of labor is positive and the wage rate is positive. It is directly related to the seasonal type of production process that is fairly well understood. The entire agricultural labor force can be used effectively during the sowing and harvesting seasons but not during the in-between periods. While the marginal productivity of labor is probably exceedingly low in this case, its marginal return may still be sufficient to maintain it at a subsistence level. It is also probable, in view of the fact that the marginal productivity of labor is so low, that the ability to substitute capital for labor is very high. Hence, the introduction of a small amount of capital would permit the elimination of a large portion of the labor force and yet permit the maintenance of the same level of output. Perhaps this second type of disguised unemployment accounts for some of the presumed underemployment that is allegedly observed.

But the first type of disguised unemployment is much more difficult to explain and its existence cannot be dismissed. We shall therefore consider this type of underemployment in the rest of this chapter.

Tenure Systems and Disguised Underemployment

In the case where all of the land is owned by those who work it, there is no problem explaining the existence of surplus labor and the simultaneous fact that those who work the land do have a positive income. But we shall see that when this is not the case, the problem is rather complex.

First then, let us consider the case where the entire country is made up of small holders. Everyone owns his own land. There are, therefore, no employers and no laborers in this hypothetical community. The return to every small holder is a combination of rent and wages. It makes no difference how we divide the small holders income between rent and wages. If we attribute it all to rent, we can square both the theory and the presumed facts. The marginal productivity is zero and, therefore, the imputed wage is zero. Every small holder will work his little piece of land to the point where there is some return just above zero. This will require less labor than he has available. No small holder will want to hire any labor since he has more time than he can use on his piece of land; there is, therefore, no demand or price for labor, and we may indeed say that here we have disguised unemployment and a surplus of labor.

Once we leave our hypothetical world of small holders, it becomes more difficult to work out a neat explanation. Suppose that the agricultural community is made up of landlords who do not work the land and of tenants or sharecroppers who do. In this case, the rent goes to the landlord. The sharecropper gets no return other than what he can get from his labor, which, in turn, depends on the competitively determined share of the crop. Now, suppose each sharecropper has a small plot for which the rent, say, is 50 per cent. In keeping with our problem let us say that it takes him only half his time to work the given plot. The rest of his labor time is to him a free good. It is, therefore, in the interest of each sharecropper to seek an additional piece of land even if he has to pay a higher rent for it. Thus, the competition for additional land must reduce tenant shares. How far can such a reduction go? On the one hand, no matter how low the share becomes, there is always an incentive for an individual shareholder to get more land. However, shares cannot go down to zero since shareholders have to subsist. On the other hand, the tenants' share cannot stay above zero because competition for land must force it down to zero.

Finally, consider the case in which the agricultural labor force is made up of landless laborers rather than tenants or small holders. The analysis, in this case, is very similar to our analysis of tenants or sharecroppers, except that the unemployment would be visible rather than disguised. If we assume perfect markets, we would expect, as usual, that the force of competition would depress wages down toward zero. That is to say, if there is a labor surplus, some members of the work force must be unemployed, and those that are unemployed would be willing to work at less than the going wage. This last would certainly depress the wage level. But can this process of the unemployed forcing wages lower and lower go on indefinitely? Obviously, the possibility of a zero wage cannot be seriously entertained. Therefore, we must either look for some mechanism that permits a determination of a wage that allows at least a subsistence income, or we must come to the conclusion that an absolute surplus of labor, in the sense of a zero marginal product attributed to labor, is an impossibility. Is there a way out of our dilemma?

The Wage-Productivity Relationship

The clue that can lead us out of some of our dilemmas is the often-neglected relationship between the wage level or income level and productivity. Simply put, the extent to which labor is maintained will determine to some degree the amount of effort (or units of work) that will be forthcoming. The amount of work that the representative laborer can be expected to perform depends on his energy level, his health, his vitality, etc., which in turn depend on his consumption level (which depends on income level) and, most directly, on the nutritive value of his food intake.

In brief, we are considering the consequences of the interesting possibility that the energy level of a tenant or worker rises as his income rises and *vice versa*. Thus, a smaller plot implies a smaller income, which in turn implies that the tenant or worker has a smaller energy level to expend on cultivating the land. This forces him to work fewer hours or to do less work in a given number of hours. At some point there is an equilibrium between his energy level, his income, and the number of hours he is able to devote to working his land. We should note that this picture is consistent with the notion that the same work force could cultivate more land if more were available and more income were created accordingly. It is also consistent with the notion that a smaller work force could cultivate the same amount of land if its share remained roughly the same, and hence, income per worker would grow in proportion to effort spent. That the relation in question exists for some income levels may appear to be intuitively obvious, but the extent of the relationship may perhaps best be illustrated if we consider briefly some of the relevant facts stressed by those in the fields of nutrition and public health. Of course, we cannot review this body of literature in a critical and exhaustive fashion, but it is nevertheless worthwhile to point to some of the highlights in order to show that there is a substantial empirical underpinning to the basic relation that we shall employ in our analysis.

To avoid repetition, the arguments that follow will usually be in terms of laborers and wages, but very similar arguments could be made in terms of tenants and crop-shares, among others.

The wage-productivity relationship can best be examined if it is broken up into two parts: (1) the relation between income (= wages) and nutrition and (2) the relation between nutrition and productivity. A 1936 study by Lord Boyd Orr shows clearly that in England the value of the nutritive components of diet (that is, calories, proteins, fats, calcium, iron, etc.) are monotonic increasing functions of income.[3] Similar studies reported by the League of Nations' Committee on Nutrition gave similar results for a number of other countries.[4] It is also evident from the Food and Agriculture Organization estimates of calorie consumption in various countries that low calorie consumption, generally speaking, goes with the low income per capita countries and high calorie consumption with high per capita income countries.[5] Also, it is clear from a number of the detailed studies of workers in various underdeveloped countries that for the groups studied, the calorie intake per man per day is, in these cases, considerably below that designated by nutrition authorities as adequate for the maintenance of health, of normal body weight, and for the carrying out of a full day's work at "normal" speed.[6] In general it is believed that in the underdeveloped areas calorie intake per day is around 2100, that in a group of middle per capita income countries the calorie intake is between 2200 to 2800, and that

---

[3] *Food, Health, and Income,* A Survey of Adequacy of Diet in Relation to Income, London, Macmillan and Company, Ltd., 1936, pp. 34–35.

[4] *Nutrition,* Final Report of the Mixed Committee of the League of Nations on the Relation of Nutrition to Health, Agriculture and Economic Policy, Geneva, 1937, pp. 247 ff. See also International Labor Office, *Workers' Nutrition and Social Policy,* Geneva, 1936, Chapter 3, "Facts on Workers' Diets," especially p. 68.

[5] Food and Agriculture Organization, *The State of Food and Agriculture (1948),* Washington, D. C. See also, F.A.O., Committee on Calories Requirements (1950), *Calorie Requirements. Report of the Committee . . . ,* Washington, D. C.

[6] On this see, among others, V. Ramalingaswami and V. N. Patwardhan, "Diet and Health of South Indian Plantation Labor," *Indian Journal of Medical Research,* Vol. 37 (1949), pp. 51–60. On the plantations studied, over 3000 calories per day were required to carry out the work well but over 50 per cent of the workers consumed less than 2000 calories per day. See also E. R. DeMello, C. J. Modi, et al., "A Nutritional Survey Among Factory Workers in Bombay," *Indian Journal of Medical Science,* Vol. 4 (1950), pp. 337–360.

only in the advanced countries is it above 3000 calories per day.[7] In this connection we should relate these figures with the usually designated calorie requirements of between 2800 to 4500 calories per day for many types of work.

On the relation between calorie intake and productivity there are two types of evidence to be considered. The first derives from numerous physiological experiments the results of which enable one to calculate the calories needed for various types of activities.[8] Of course, the amount of calories required depends on the size of the man and on the nature and strenuousness of his activities. A 5-foot, 6-inch man weighing 130 pounds requires about 1400 calories for his resting metabolism alone, while a 6-foot man of normal weight will usually require over 1700 calories for this purpose. For every activity additional calories are needed. Thus, for simply sitting an additional intake of 15 to 20 calories per hour will be needed, but for moderate work the additional calories required will probably be between 80 to 240 per hour. For example, walking requires 130 to 240 additional calories per hour while activities that involve climbing may require from 400 to 900 calories per hour.[9]

The significance of these figures can be seen if we consider a few calculations. Let us assume 1500 calories for resting metabolism, and a day that is made up of eight sleeping and sixteen waking hours. Counting 1500 calories for resting metabolism, adding approximately 100 calories per hour for moderate work for a period of four hours, and adding to this about 20 calories per hour for the remaining twelve hours of relaxation, we get a total of 2140 calories needed to support a 4-hour work day. Now we observe that an addition of 320 calories, or a total of 2460 calories, will support an 8-hour work day of the same degree of strenuousness as before. What this implies is that if at the outset an employer pays a wage that is sufficient only to enable his workers to obtain a diet of no more than 2140 calories, the employer can approximately double his *effective* work force by paying a wage that would enable the workers to purchase a diet yielding 2460 calories. Of course, in actual practice the workers will, in both cases, be working what appears to be a full day, but in the former case (under the 2140 calorie regime) they will work much more slowly, with less energy and

---

[7] F.A.O., *op. cit.*

[8] See Henry C. Sherman, *Chemistry of Food and Nutrition,* New York, Macmillan, 1941, Chapters 8–11. Also, Magnus Pyke, *Industrial Nutrition,* London, MacDonald and Evans, 1950, Chapter 2.

[9] *Ibid.* There are many standard works in this field that yield similar calculations.

enthusiasm, in a more lethargic fashion, and probably with a greater degree of absenteeism.[10]

The direct connection between calorie intake and productivity is shown very clearly in a number of studies by Kraut and Muller made in Germany between 1942 and 1945.[11] Twenty men building earth embankments shifted 1.5 tons of earth per hour per man when they consumed 2400 calories, but when the calorie intake was raised to 2900 the output rose to 2.2 tons per man (and at the same time body weight increased by about 9 pounds per man). Allowing 1600 to 1800 calories for metabolism and relaxation, we see that (approximately) a 60 per cent increase in "working" calories leads to an almost 50 per cent increase in output. But of greater interest for our purposes is that a 21 per cent increase in total calorie intake results in an almost 50 per cent rise in output. In another study of 31 miners an increase of 1200 to 1600 work calories led to an increase in output from 7 to 9.6 tons per day. The experience of miners in the Ruhr district also reported by Kraut and Muller confirmed these general results. On the average, the mining of a ton of coal required about 1200 calories, and when, during the war period, the calorie intake of the miners was reduced, output fell proportionately, and when at a later stage the diet was increased, production rose proportionately. Even more spectacular results are reported in a study of construction workers in Central America where it was found that the efficiency of workers increased threefold when they were provided with an adequate calorie allowance. Since the original calorie intake of the workers is not reported, it is not possible to compare the relative change in calorie intake with the relative increase in output, but the report is, nevertheless, suggestive of the sort of results that can be obtained by increasing the calorie intake of workers.[12]

It would be easy to continue to pile up additional experimental and empirical evidence relating not only calorie intake to output, but also relating other nutritive elements to output either directly or indirectly

[10] See R. K. Mukerjee, "Food and Food Requirements of the Indian Labourers," *Indian Journal of Economics,* Vol. XII, 1932, p. 263. The inverse relation between quality of diet and absenteeism seems to be fairly well established. On this point see also C. E. A. Winslow, *The Cost of Sickness and the Price of Health,* World Health Organization, Geneva, 1951, pp. 35 ff.

[11] "Calorie Intake and Industrial Output," *Science,* Vol. 104 (1946), pp. 495–497. In this connection see also the more recent studies by G. Lehman, E. A. Muller, and H. Spitzer, "Der Caloriebedarf bei gewerblicher Arbeit," *Arbeitsphysiologie,* Vol. 14 (1949–1950), pp. 166 ff. Here they determine the extent of the deterioration in work output resulting from different levels of calorie feeding, and develop prediction tables for various workers for various occupations.

[12] Winslow, *op. cit.,* p. 33.

through their effect on debilitating diseases, absenteeism, lethargy, etc. But enough has been said to suggest our main point. There is an obvious and clear cut relationship between income and output, and furthermore, it is clear that up to some point, the effective work units are increased as wages are increased.

It follows from the above discussion that we must distinguish between the supply of labor-time (that is, man-hours or man-years) and the supply of work (or effort), and between the average and marginal

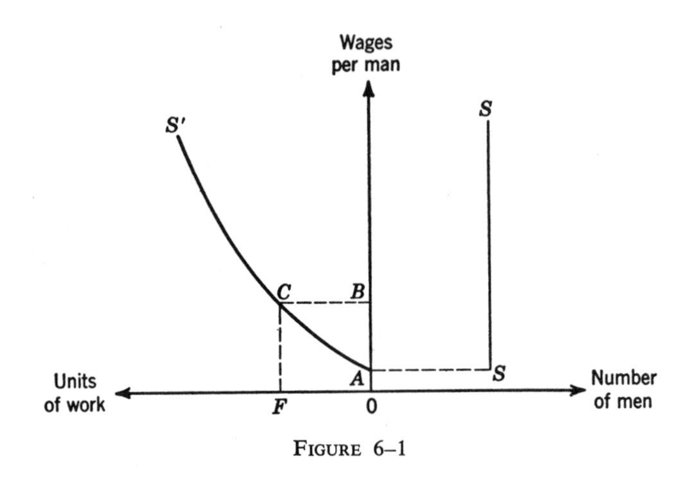

FIGURE 6–1

product per man and the average and marginal product per unit of work. We must keep these distinctions in mind throughout the rest of this discussion. The significance and implications of these distinctions can probably best be seen with the aid of figures 6–1, 6–2, and 6–3 that follow.

In figure 6–1 we illustrate the distinction between the supply of labor-time and the supply of units of work. In the short period the supply of labor-time may be said to be approximately fixed, and hence the supply curve of labor-time is the vertical line *SS*, as shown in the right quadrant of the figure. Below some minimum wage the work force would starve and there would be no work forthcoming. Therefore, the supply of labor-time starts only above that minimum wage *OA* necessary to sustain life in the labor force. However, the number of units of work supplied will increase gradually as wage rates and consumption rises. Hence, the curve *AS′* in the left quadrant of figure 6–1 slopes upward gradually to the left. Each point on the curve indicates the number of units of work that would be forthcoming in response to a given wage rate. Of course, above a certain wage the supply of work curve becomes absolutely vertical. In other words, beyond some point, increases in consumption are unlikely to add appreciably to the health, vigor, and vitality of the average worker so that the work performed per unit of time is no greater than at a lower wage.

Now, what this means is that the average productivity (and the marginal productivity) of a group of men will depend on their wage. Up to some point, the higher the wage the higher the per capita productivity for the group, because the higher the wage the greater the units of work per man. The nature of this relationship is illustrated by the

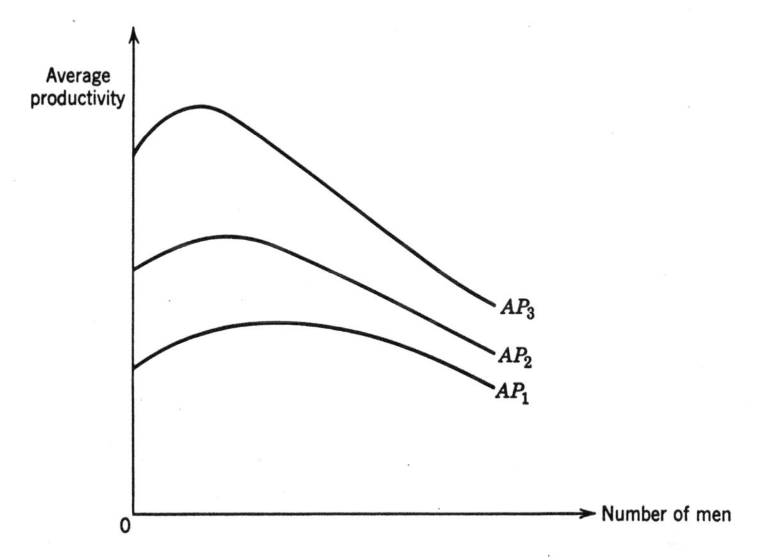

FIGURE 6–2

family of average productivity curves in figure 6–2. Each curve in figure 6–2 illustrates what happens to average productivity as the number of men in the work force increases. As usual we assume that beyond some point, diminishing returns are in effect, and, therefore, beyond some point the average productivity curves are negatively inclined. AP_1 is the average productivity curve for a low wage (say w_1), AP_2 is the average productivity curve for a somewhat higher wage (say w_2), and AP_3 is the average productivity curve for a still higher wage. The curves are always above each other because for any given number of men the higher the wage, up to some point, the higher the output.

As usual for each average productivity curve there is a related (and derived) marginal productivity curve. Of course, just as there is a separate average productivity curve for each wage there is also a separate marginal productivity curve for each wage. And it is the relation between the different marginal productivity curves for different wage rates that is of special interest for our purposes.

As already indicated, we expect the average productivity curves for different wage rates to be one above the other, but it is important to observe that this need not always be the case for the related marginal productivity curves. Indeed the interesting case for our purposes, and the one that we shall concentrate on, is the case where the marginal productivity curves for different wage rates cross each other. This is the case that we illustrate in figure 6–3.

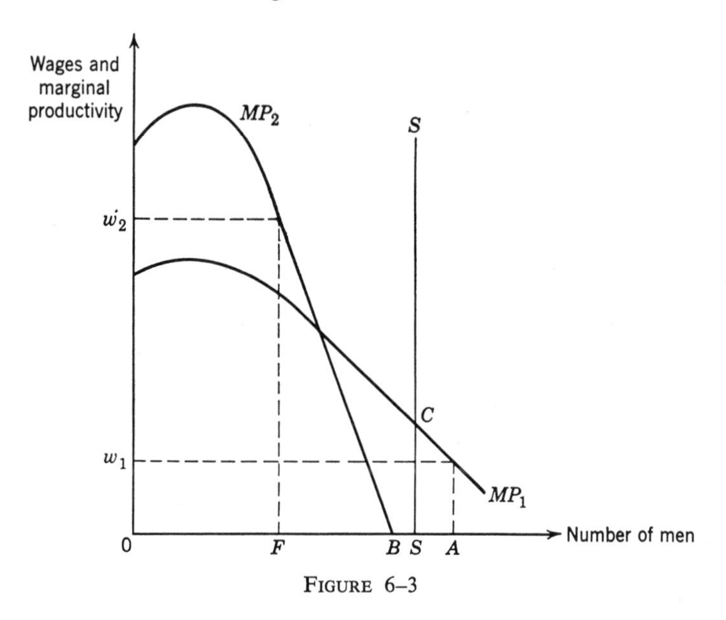

FIGURE 6–3

The curves marked MP_1 and MP_2 in figure 6–3 are the marginal productivity curves under consideration. The *MP* curve for a higher wage rate is likely to start at a higher level than one for a lower wage, but beyond the point where diminishing returns are in effect, the marginal curves for the higher wage rates may fall much more rapidly than the marginal curves for the lower rate.

Consider the two curves MP_1 and MP_2 in figure 6–3. The marginal productivity per man curve (MP_1) for the low wage rate w_1 falls much more slowly than does the marginal productivity curve (MP_2) for the high wage rate w_2. At some point the marginal productivity curve for the high wage rate will fall below the one for the low rate. To see the reason for this we have to observe that there are two forces in operation that work in opposite directions. (1) On one hand the higher the wage the more units of work that are put forth per man per unit of time. (2) But on the other hand, as more units of work are put forth, the marginal product per *unit of work* declines. Beyond some point the marginal product per unit of work may decline quite rapidly. The rate of decline may be so rapid that for the higher curve (representing more work units per man) the rate of decline in the marginal product per man (as men are added) is greater than it is for the lower curve (MP_1). It is, therefore, possible for the higher wage curve (MP_2) to cross the lower wage curve (MP_1) and then fall below it. In other words, beyond some point, we expect the declining marginal productivity per unit of work to become more important than the fact that each man accomplishes more units of work.

Let us look again at the possibility depicted in figure 6–3 and see what it implies in terms of the problem under consideration. We note first that the curve MP_1 is drawn in such a way that at its related wage there is actually a scarcity of labor. As drawn, the supply of labor is equal to OS but the demand is OA, assuming that demand is determined at the point at which the marginal product equals the wage. The reason for this possibility is not difficult to conceive. At this low wage (w_1) the labor force is in such a low state of health, vigor, and vitality, that it produces relatively few units of work and, as a consequence, the marginal product per final unit of work as well as the marginal product per man is considerably above the wage rate. Or, what is the same thing, the number of work units produced are so few at this low wage that the existing resources could be combined advantageously with more units of work. At the low wage w_1 more men can be hired before the marginal product is equal to the wage per man. As the curve is drawn the reverse is true with respect to the curve marked MP_2 and the related wage w_2. At the wage w_2 the supply of labor on SS is greater than the demand of OF, assuming that the demand is determined at the point where the marginal product is equal to the wage.

What all this implies is that at very low wages there may be a labor deficit because the units of work produced per man are so few. But at higher wages the units of work per man increase so rapidly that a labor surplus is created. For the underdeveloped areas this may mean that the allegedly observed manpower surpluses in agriculture do not really exist when wages are very low, but that they do indeed become a fact when wages rise sufficiently.

In addition it is worth observing (in figure 6–3) that at the low wage (w_1) the marginal product of the fully employed labor force is in fact above zero ($= SC$), but at the higher wage the marginal product per man may fall to zero (as at point B) or even below zero.

Institutional Rigidities, Wage Rates, and Marginal Productivity Theory

An interesting consequence of the wage-productivity relation discussed in the last section is that we can show that there are circumstances under which it is to the benefit of landowners to pay a wage above the competitive level. Specifically, we shall see that in circumstances where competition among the visibly unemployed depresses wage rates toward the zero level, it may be to the benefit of landlords as a group to operate under institutional arrangements (or traditions) that would not permit wages to fall to their competitive levels, but, rather, to operate under conditions which permit wage rates above competitive levels.

We shall not examine in detail the specific type of institutional arrangements that would enable landlords to employ the entire labor force at a wage in excess of their marginal product, but it is not difficult to think of some possibilities. The appropriate institutional arrangements will usually arise from the historical situation under which the backward economy operates. A system of serfdom, where landlords have to utilize all the serfs born on and tied to the land, is essentially of this nature. Another system of this nature is that which, by virtue of its mores, permits people born into certain castes to perform only a limited range of tasks. Other institutional arrangements of this type are found in various backward economies. The point of the discussion that follows is that such institutions need not be irrational, and indeed, we shall see that such institutional arrangements may lead to a greater total product than otherwise.

To see that the results mentioned above are actually possible we need to continue our analysis from the point where we left it in the previous section. Starting with the marginal productivity curves in figure 6–3, we shall build up through diagrammatical illustrations (figures 6–4, 6–5, and 6–6) a comparison of the possible outcomes to landlords as a group under two alternative situations: (1) the situation wherein landlords can ignore the effects of visible unemployment and (2) the situation wherein visible unemployment does have a depressing effect on the wage rate, and in which the effect on the wage rate also affects landlords' incomes.

In figure 6–4 we draw a family of marginal productivity curves similar to those in figure 6–3. Each curve is related to a specific wage rate. As before, the curve MP_1 indicates the alternative marginal productivities per man for alternatively greater numbers of men if the wage rate is w_1. MP_2 is the marginal productivity curve if the wage rate is w_2, and so on. Let us suppose that landlords as a group can hire any number of men they wish without regard to the possible results of a labor deficit or of a labor surplus, and also without regard to the possible consequences of such a deficit or surplus. How many men would they hire? In other words, we examine the demand side first without regard to supply conditions. (Later, of course, we shall take into account the supply aspect.) For each wage rate and its related marginal productivity curve there is

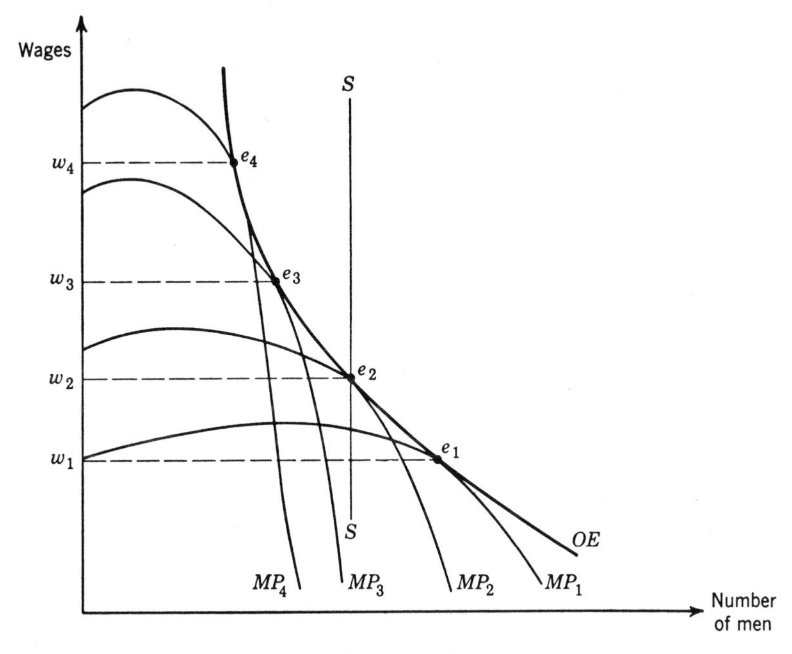

FIGURE 6–4

an optimum number of men whom landlords as a group would hire if they were to maximize their group income. The optimum number of men to be hired is determined, as usual, at the point where the wage is equal to the marginal product of the labor force. In figure 6–4, for the curve MP_1, this optimum point is e_1, where the marginal product is equal to w_1. Similarly, we obtain e_2, e_3, for the curves MP_2, MP_3, and so on. Thus for every wage we obtain the optimum number of men to be hired. The locus of such optimum employment points is indicated by the curve *OE* in figure 6–4. This curve is, *in a sense,* a demand curve for labor. At each wage it tells us the number of workers that landlords as a group would hire if they had a choice of hiring the number that would maximize their group income without regard to the consequences of any labor deficit or surplus that may be involved.

In figure 6–5 we combine the curve *OE* and the related inelastic supply curve for labor *SS*. We observe that at the higher wage rates the optimum number of men employed is less than the supply, whereas at the very low wage rates the reverse is true. A question that comes to mind is whether the *OE* curve need cross the *SS* curve at any point. Generally speaking, it is probable that there would always be some wage rate so low that the optimum employment would be greater than the supply.

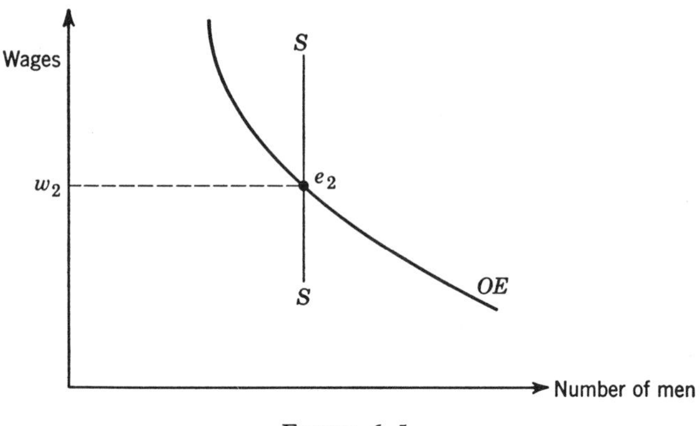

FIGURE 6–5

But we need not worry about this general point at present. For present purposes it is sufficient if we concentrate on the possibilities depicted in our graphs.

The next step in our argument is to relate the points on the optimum employment curve with the net revenues obtained by landlords at various wage rates. Associated with every wage rate and every optimum number of men employed there is a given net revenue to landlords as a group. This relationship is illustrated by the curve *OR* in figure 6–6. (For each *MP* curve the net revenue is equal to the area under the marginal productivity curve that is above the "wage line.") For every wage rate and related point on the *OE* curve there is a related net revenue shown on the left quadrant of figure 6–6. The locus of these points may be called the *optimum employment revenue curve OR*.

Next, suppose that the *entire* labor force is employed. Then, in a similar fashion, we can obtain the *full employment* revenue curve *FR*. That is, for every wage, assuming that the full labor force *SS* is employed, there is a related net revenue that will accrue to the landlords. At some wage rates the employment of the full labor force will involve employing a greater number of workers than landlords wish to employ and, at other wage rates, a smaller number than that which would maximize their group incomes.

Some remarks about the shape of the curves *OR* and *OF* and their relationship to each other are of special interest. Consider first the general shape of the optimum employment revenue curve *OR*. (As usual we assume diminishing returns per unit of work.) For exceedingly low wage rates per man, the amount of effort per man is also exceedingly low, hence the marginal product per man is very low. In this case a great many units are each doing very little work. The per capita costs

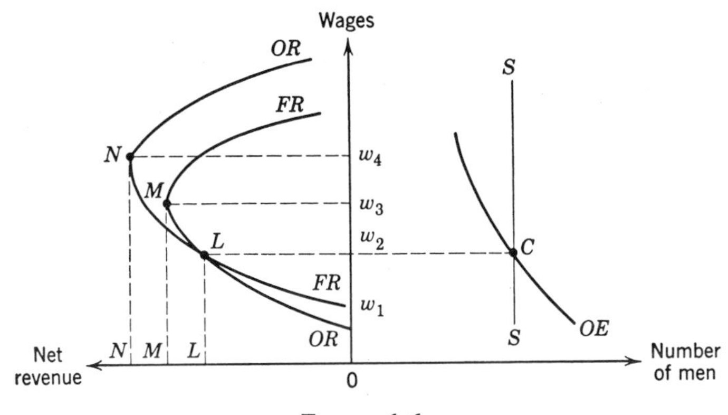

FIGURE 6–6

of coordinating the work force, and other overhead costs, are likely to be high in relation to output. It seems reasonable to believe that there is some very low wage rate at which the net revenue due to landlords would be just slightly above zero. As wages increase, as effort per man grows, and as the optimum number of men decline, overhead costs per *unit of work* decline accordingly, and, as a consequence, we would expect net revenue to rise. At least two general factors are responsible for increases in net revenue as wages rise: (1) As wages rise, work per man may increase more than the proportionate increase in wages. (2) With the greater amount of units of work produced by the work force, it may be possible to combine resources and labor so that we come closer to the optimum combination of factors and, as a result, increase the output per unit of work. Up to some wage rate, net revenue is likely to increase as wages increase. However, beyond a certain wage, we would certainly expect a reversal of this tendency, for beyond some point, an increase in wages will bring with it no increase whatsoever in units of work supplied per man, and, therefore, at some wage, as wages rise, the units of work done per man will increase less proportionately than wages. Hence, beyond some point the higher the wage rate, the less the net revenue. Of course, at some very high wage rate the net revenue will drop to zero since there is obviously a wage that is greater than the maximum productivity per man possible. For these reasons we depict the *OR* curve, as illustrated in figure 6–6, in the shape of a "U" on its side.

The main thing to observe about the full employment revenue curve is that at each wage rate, except one, the full employment revenue is always less than the optimum employment revenue. Of course, at the wage where the optimum employment curve *OE* crosses the labor supply curve *SS*, the optimum employment revenue and the full employment revenue are identical. In figure 6–6 this is shown at the point *L* where the *FR* curve touches the *OR* curve.

It should be clear that the full employment revenue curve need not be at a maximum above the wage w_2 where the labor supply and the optimum employment are equal. Although it is true that at wages above w_2 the full employment revenue must always be less than the optimum employment revenue (since there must be a reduction from the optimum employment revenue occasioned by the necessity of employing excess manpower whose wages are below their marginal product), it may nevertheless be that the full employment revenue is higher than what it was at a lower wage. The reason for this possibility is similar to those reasons given in explaining the increase in optimum revenue as wages rise. Namely, above the wage w_2, the work units per man increase by a greater proportion than the increase in wages, and this effect may, up to some point, be more significant than the depressing effect of the greater wages bill on net revenue.

Three points in our illustration (*N*, *M*, and *L*, on the curves *OR* and *FR*) are especially worthy of attention. If landlords could pay any wage they pleased and could hire any number of workers, they would pay a wage of w_4 and achieve the maximum net revenue possible, *ON*. But at this wage there would be an excess supply of labor. If there were some means of eliminating the excess labor in a costless fashion, this would be the optimum solution from the landlords' point of view.

But if there is nowhere for "surplus" labor to go, and competition among the unemployed and the employed depresses wages, the wage rate will decline below the level, w_4. The wage decline will continue as long as an excess supply exists, and wages will eventually drop to w_2, the wage at which the optimum employment curve crosses the labor supply curve. *But at this point net revenue drops to level OL.* It is clear that in our graphical illustration employers can improve their position, by employing the entire labor force (simultaneously raising wages to w_3), and consequently can enjoy a net revenue of *OM*, which of course is greater than *OL*. This is the best solution under the circumstances, because as long as they leave some of the excess labor unemployed, there is the danger of wage rates being driven down to a level at which revenue is less than OM. Hence, landlords, as a group, are in an improved position if institutional arrangements permit them to employ the entire labor force, pay a wage of w_3, and yet not utilize the entire labor force. Possibilities and institutional arrangements of this sort *can* account for the phenomenon of disguised unemployment.[13]

Let us examine some of the characteristics of the solution in our diagrammatical illustration. First, we note that this solution (a wage of w_3 and a net revenue of OM) can account for the existence of surplus labor and of disguised unemployment. At this wage the labor force could cultivate more land with the same auxiliary resources if there were more land available. Second, and this is a crucial aspect of the foregoing argument, we see that under the postulated conditions the wage can be above the marginal product of labor. Indeed, it is to the benefit of both landlords and labor that this be the case.

The essential aspect of the argument is that the position of landlords can be improved by employing excess labor, where the units of work produced are related to the wage, rather than by employing the "optimum" amount of labor which permits the unemployed surplus to drive wages down to a level where the amount of work produced is reduced to such an extent that the landlords' net revenue is lower than otherwise.

Let us now consider the extreme case where M and L coincide, that is, where the maximum full employment revenue is at the wage at which the optimum employment curve and the supply of labor curve cross. In this case, the landlords' optimum solution is to pay a wage, w_2, and to hire the entire labor supply. Labor's marginal product will be equal to the wage. It may appear that under such circumstances the situation depicted is not quite consistent with the notion of an excess labor supply and disguised unemployment. Determining such consistency depends on how we interpret the notion of excess labor. It is true that in this case (where M and L coincide) at the optimum wage w_2 there is no surplus of labor, and the marginal product is above zero. But if our criterion is that excess labor exists where the existing labor supply can cultivate more land, this criterion can be met even in this extreme case. For under these circumstances the existing labor force could cultivate more land if they received some portion of the produce of the additional land cultivated. Given a greater output, we would expect some increase in

[13] Indeed, we have illustrated the possibility that such institutional arrangements may lead to a greater total product than otherwise. Thus, we come to the rather curious conclusion that, far from being a vice, institutional arrangements that permit a degree of disguised unemployment may actually enable the economy to be more productive than otherwise.

wages, which in turn would lead to more units of work per man, thus enabling the fixed labor force to cultivate more land. However, it is of interest to note that should the country undergo industrialization and try to shift some of the labor force off the land without increasing wages per man, we would have a shortage of labor. This last may perhaps shed some light on situations like those experienced by some of the countries in the Soviet orbit, where a shortage of labor appeared in the agricultural sector after attempts at forced industrialization were put into effect, whereas prior to this, it was believed that there was a considerable amount of disguised unemployment.

CHAPTER 7

Specialization, Income Level, and Occupational Structure

The Problem

One of the most persistently noted characteristics of low per capita income economies is the very high proportion of the economically active population engaged in primary industry (agriculture, mining, fishing, etc.), the very low proportion engaged in manufacturing, and the usually low proportion in commerce, transportation, and services. In this chapter we examine some aspects of this characteristic of economic backwardness.

In connection with the characteristic just mentioned, a number of writers have commented on the remarkable statistical relation between the occupational distribution of a population and economic growth. Colin Clark attributes the discovery of this relationship to Sir William Petty and refers to the relationship as Petty's law.[1] In recent years this relationship has, of course, been rediscovered and popularized by both Colin Clark and A. G. B. Fisher.[2] Classifying occupations as primary,

[1] Colin Clark, *The Conditions of Economic Progress,* London, Macmillan and Company, Ltd., 1951, pp. 395–396. See especially Chapters IX and V.

[2] A. G. B. Fisher, "The Economic Implications of Material Progress," *International Labor Review,* July 1935, pp. 5–18. See also, J. H. Boeke, *Economics and Economic Policy of Dual Societies,* as exemplified by Indonesia, Haarlem, H. D. T. Willink, 1953, pp. x and 324.

secondary, and tertiary industries Clark and Fisher claim that the following relationship between the proportions of the population in these occupational categories and economic progress holds at least approximately. As progress is made, the proportion in primary industries declines steadily, the proportion in secondary industries grows, reaches a certain plateau, and then either stops or declines somewhat, while the proportion in tertiary industries seems to grow steadily. By primary industries we refer, for the most part, to agriculture, mining, and fishing; secondary industries refer to manufacturing and construction; tertiary industries refer to services.

The support for this thesis is of two kinds: (1) statistical evidence and (2) statements that appear to be of a theoretical nature. First, it is observed that poor countries have a very high proportion of the labor force in primary industries and very low proportions in secondary and tertiary industries. As the investigation shifts from poorer to richer countries, the occupational structure shifts more or less in accordance with the postulated relationship. Investigations of occupational statistics of the labor force in time seem to yield similar results.[3]

The theoretical argument is based mostly on the way consumption patterns shift as incomes grow and on the belief that primary industries are subject to diminishing returns whereas secondary and tertiary industries are probably subject to either increasing or constant returns.

In recent years some controversy has arisen with respect to the tertiary industries part of what we may call the Clark-Fisher thesis. Bauer and Yamey[4] especially have argued that a high proportion of the economically active population of some backward economies do engage in the provision of direct services. They especially argue against the Colin Clark explanation of his occupational distribution theory that low-income purchasers will prefer material goods to non-material things. However, no statistical evidence is presented by Bauer and Yamey, and a good deal of the argument depends on personal observations in West Africa. The discussion started by Bauer and Yamey and taken up by others does suggest quite clearly that the tertiary industries part of the Clark-Fisher

[3] See Clark, *op. cit.*

[4] P. T. Bauer and B. S. Yamey, "Economic Progress and Occupational Distribution," *The Economic Journal,* December 1951, pp. 741–755; S. G. Triantis, "Economic Progress, Occupational Redistribution and International Terms of Trade," *The Economic Journal,* September 1953, pp. 627–637; and S. Rottenberg, "Note on 'Economic Progress and Occupational Distribution' ", *The Review of Economic Studies,* May 1953, pp. 168–170. Note especially the excellent reply by Triantis to the arguments put forward by Bauer and Yamey. See also the illuminating article by Richard H. Holton, "Marketing Structure and Economic Development," *Quarterly Journal of Economics,* April 1953, pp. 344–361.

thesis may be its weakest link. It is probably true that the extent of tertiary employment does depend on more than simply the stage of economic development. Other factors do enter the picture, especially the nature of the resources and institutions of the economies. For example, a poor country that attracts many tourists may have a higher proportion in tertiary industries than a richer one that attracts very few. However, it is important to note that there is nothing in the discussions considered that would cast serious doubt on the validity of the primary and secondary industries part of the Clark-Fisher thesis. For our purposes we need not concern ourselves excessively with the unique tertiary industries that may exist in some underdeveloped economies. Statistically it would appear that the important problems have to do with the vast proportion of the population engaged in agriculture. As a consequence, we shall emphasize in our examination of this phenomenon the parts of the Clark-Fisher thesis which deal with the primary and secondary industries.

The question of interest, and one that may be of importance with respect to development policy, is whether the occupational change pattern in the Clark-Fisher thesis is a necessary one. For example, must labor be shifted off the land for economic development to occur? In this chapter we shall argue that for the most part the Clark-Fisher thesis is correct, but we shall examine the question from a somewhat different viewpoint than that used by other investigators, that is, neither from the side of consumption, nor exactly from the side of diminishing and increasing returns, but rather from the point of view of the relation between specialization, production methods, and growth. In brief, we shall first indicate the relationship between per capita income growth and the degree of specialization and then proceed to show the connection between specialization and occupational distribution. Specifically we shall show that even apart from the consumption side of the argument, that is, even if the proportion of the different commodities remains the same throughout, as a country progresses from low to high per capita incomes there will still be a shift away from the primary industries and into the secondary and tertiary industries.

Production Theory and Specialization

The usual exposition of the theory of production is reasoned from inputs to outputs or from factors to commodities without explicitly considering intermediate elements such as the activities, operations, and functions that the factors perform. Although it is true that writers on production theory have been aware that there is more to the process than merely combining inputs and obtaining outputs, and they often allude to some intervening elements, it nevertheless remains the case that the formal theory is usually presented in terms of inputs and outputs. Whether or not it is desirable to complicate the theory with intervening elements depends, of course, on the problems we have in mind. For many problems the input-output approach is sufficient. But to understand the relationship between changes in the degree of specialization and occupational distribution, it is hardly adequate.

The phenomenon of specialization cannot be understood simply in terms of inputs and outputs or in terms of factors of production and commodities. These categories almost limit the discussion of specialization in terms of the *variety* of the commodities produced but not in terms of the *way* a specific commodity is produced. Thus, in the usual discussion, in international trade the virtues of specialization are in terms of the benefits to be achieved by concentrating on *few* commodities. But for a closed economy the significant manifestation of different degrees of specialization is in different ways of producing the same commodity or the same bundle of commodities. In terms of the conventional theory, all that can be said is that the different degrees of specialization involve different combinations of the factors. Clearly this last can shed very little light on the nature and advantages of specialization. What we have to know is what it is that the factors *do* that is different where a higher rather than a lower degree of specialization is involved. Thus our first step will be to visualize the production process in terms of what the factors of production *do* rather than the mere fact of their existence.[5]

We now turn to such a model. The definitions of the basic categories are as follows:

1. A *commodity* is the entity that is the object of the production process, and has a specific set of attributes or specifications.
2. A *factor* is an entity, units of which can be purchased on the market, that has the capacity to carry out one or more activities.
3. An *activity* is our primitive concept. It refers to those necessary acts carried out by a factor, or functions of a factor, necessary in the productive process. We define a set of related activities as an *operation.*
4. A *process* is a specific set of operations necessary to produce the commodity in question. There may be a number of possible alternative processes.
5. By a *firm* we refer to the entity that purchases factors, creates commodities, and sells commodities.

---

[5] The problem was handled in a somewhat similar fashion by George Stigler in his excellent article "The Division of Labor is Limited by the Extent of the Market," *Journal of Political Economy,* June 1951, especially pp. 187–189. Stigler's analysis is in terms of "the functions of the firm" rather than "activities."

This is our vision of the productive process: The firm purchases the necessary factors. The firm's purpose for doing so is to create some quantity of a commodity which can be defined in terms of a set of attributes. The attributes are created by a set of operations. The operations are made up of activities. In our rather broad notion of an activity, it is any contribution to the creation of the commodity. The contribution may be passive so that an entity that permits itself to be manipulated is engaging in an activity. For example, we conceive of some specific raw material, say a piece of wood, being capable of performing the activity of becoming the necessary physical matter out of which the commodity, say a bench, is made.

In the course of economic growth the nature, definition, and variety of commodities produced by firms change. As firms specialize, they may buy raw materials in a more finished state than formerly, or they may sell commodities in a less finished state or sell a lesser variety of them than before. But for purposes of our analysis we have to keep something constant. Assume that the commodity that we have in mind and its specifications remain constant, and that this is true whether the commodity is made by one firm or by a number of firms in sequence in which each firm produces only a portion of that commodity. In other words, we define the commodity from the point of view of the final consumer and not from the point of view of the firm.

By increased *specialization* we shall mean an increased concentration of the factor of production on fewer *kinds* of activities. For the most part we shall think in terms of labor specialization, and hence, by an increased degree of specialization, we shall have in mind each individual performing fewer types of activities in a given time period. In the extreme in specialization, an individual is involved in one activity, continuously repeated, all the time.

But is there meaning to the notion of a narrowing of the range of activities if the nature of the activities changes? Although it is true that the activities need not be invariant with different degrees of specialization, the specifications of the commodity are invariant. Here we have a useful constant. What we shall mean, therefore, when we speak of a narrowing of the range of activities is that the activities performed by an individual establish a smaller number of characteristics of the commodity or meet fewer specifications than previously. If the activities do not remain invariant, this implies that to establish a smaller number of characteristics of the commodity, fewer of the invariant activities could have been used, although it is more economical to change the nature of the activities in the new circumstances. Hence, there is meaning to the notion of a narrower range of activities even when the nature of the activities does change.

If the range of activities narrows, the number of times an activity can be performed increases at least proportionately or more than proportionately to the extent that the activities have been narrowed. Thus, if ten operations each took one hour to perform during a ten-hour working day, we would expect that one of the operations could be performed *at least* ten different times during the same working day. Indeed, we would expect that usually that same operation could be performed *more than* ten times during a working day. This assertion is one basis for the belief that specialization increases productivity. The reason for this is that there is no loss of time in starting, stopping, and switching from operation to operation. Furthermore, repetition of the activity increases the degree of skill and dexterity in performing the operation so that it can be performed more rapidly and more accurately. While narrowing the range of activities increases the efficiency with which any activity is carried out, it simultaneously creates the necessity for certain new activities and decreases the necessity for others. The new activities needed are the coordination and synchronization of the activities of the larger number of individuals involved in the creation of the product. At the same time the need for activities required in shifting from one operation to another is reduced.

A significant consequence of specialization is that in narrowing the range of operations performed per individual, new ways of performing operations become possible that previously were impossible. The most obvious manifestation of this phenomenon is in the case of specialized machinery the use of which is prohibited when a larger range of activities per man is carried out because of the high cost of idle machine time. The necessary economies can be obtained only if such machines are employed a certain minimum amount of time. Therefore, narrowing the range of activities per factor unit permits the longer runs per man that enable the more specialized machinery to be used economically.

Per Capita Output and the Degree of Specialization

We now turn to an examination of the relationship between specialization and per capita output. At low output levels the following conditions are likely to exist: (1) The variety of activities engaged in per man will be very large. Not only will single individuals and production units produce much more of a single commodity but they are also likely to produce a number of commodities. (2) The performance of many operations is of a seasonal nature and therefore it is usually very difficult to spread the necessary work very evenly over the year. (3) There will be considerable time lost in shifting from one activity to the next. (4) The skill displayed in performing any given activity or operation is likely to be very low, on the average. (5) The nature of the activities is such that very little capital per unit of product is required.

To facilitate analysis we postulate that for every level of per capita income there is a degree of specialization that is optimum and that this optimum is in effect. For the moment let us also postulate that population size is constant. Since we assume that the proportion of different goods remains constant, an increase in income (or output) manifests itself in an increase in output of all commodities in the same proportion. The increased output of every commodity permits the concentration of each worker on fewer activities. If workers are employed the same period of time as before, the economy as a whole can then produce more units of each commodity with the same labor force. It can do so because labor efficiency increases via specialization in the following ways: time lost in shifting from activity to activity is eliminated, activities are somewhat better synchronized than before, repetition leads to increased skill in performance, and, last, efficiency is increased, because increased specialization permits a better distribution of men among the activities in which they are most skilled.[6]

But the crucial question is this: Why was not the increased degree of specialization possible at the lower level of output? Increased specialization, given the smaller bundle of goods, would have meant less time needed per man to produce that bundle of goods, and hence the gain could have been taken in greater leisure per man. Surely, this represents a better solution than the one that involves less specialization. Why is this not done? Briefly, the answer that suggests itself is that specialization is costly, and its cost is both of a fixed and a current nature. But it is the fixed part of the cost that is significant, because this implies that increased specialization requires additional capital.

In discussing the costs of specialization two types of costs must be distinguished. One is the cost of shifting from one stage of specialization to the next; the other is the differential cost of different degrees of specialization. The first type of cost is dynamic in nature. Some part of the costs of labor mobility and urbanization, as they are usually considered in discussions of economic development, involves the first type of cost. It really has to do with the cost of shifting from one resource and manpower base to another. But it has nothing to do with the question of why there is not a greater amount of specialization for a *given* resource and manpower base; this is a question of statics. Our argument will be that (1) for any given resource base there is only a limited degree of

---

[6] This last reason is, of course, the classic argument for both international and domestic trade.

specialization that is economic, and (2) the larger the resource base, other things being equal, the larger the degree of specialization that is economic, and, conversely, a greater *optimum* degree of specialization can be achieved only with a larger amount of capital resources.

Of course, at any one time there are many factors that determine the degree of specialization, for example, the state of technological knowledge, the technical nature of the capital stock, etc. Also, at any moment the economy need not be operating at its optimum degree of specialization, under which circumstances it is possible to increase the degree of specialization and output without any increase in capital stock. But clearly there must be limits to such possibilities. At some point the gains from increasing the degree of specialization will be equal to the costs of doing so, and it is at this point that we have the optimum degree of specialization. The reason that beyond some point it does not pay to carry specialization any further is that with a given capital stock, not only are there limits to the amount of specialized capital that can be provided, but, more important, there are also significant limits to which it is advantageous to divert capital from less specialized uses to more specialized uses. There is some degree of indivisibility in almost all types of machinery and related capital equipment and in a great many types of capital goods. For any piece of specialized equipment necessary to carry out an activity in a specialized manner, there is a minimum amount of that activity that makes it just worth while to use the specialized equipment, and less than which it will not pay to do so. But again, beyond some point, in order to have enough of the activity going on, a larger capital stock will be required. This last is clearly the case when the activity in question involves the use of one or more raw materials and when more capital is required in order to produce a greater quantity of raw materials. That is to say, more capital is needed not only to support the additional activities required by a greater degree of specialization, but also in order to make possible the greater output that will necessitate larger amounts of the given activities so that it may be advantageous to specialize these activities.

Let us now consider some of these ideas in greater detail. Specialization involves the concentration by firms or other entities on a lesser number of activities and operations and, hence, the separation of the location of activities. This means that the commodity has to travel more between laborers, which, in turn, implies the need for more transportation facilities as well as increased facilities for the coordination of activities among individuals. That is, the separation of productive activities gives rise to necessary commercial activities in order to recombine the productive efforts of different individuals in order to obtain final commodities. Narrowing the range of activities implies an increased dependence on the market for both the purchase of commodities and the sales of factors. In part this will mean that a greater risk is involved than under a regime of self-sufficiency. Also some of the other costs of increased dependence on the market must be considered.

An increased degree of specialization and the implied concentration and separation of activities and operations necessitate a greater entrepreneurial effort, and, therefore, a payment for such effort. Increased specialization can come about only when someone finds it profitable to organize and coordinate such activities. Indeed, doing so requires a very high level of entrepreneurship. In practice it would mean organizing new firms that purchase the narrower range of commodities or the less finished commodities of the existing firms and reselling them to other firms at a cost below the one that would have to be incurred by the buying firms if they were to bring the product to this stage of completion. It would involve the organization of production units engaged in a narrower range of activities that displace, because of their increased efficiency, those production units engaged in a wider range of activities. But it may be argued that some of these costs are the costs of achieving a greater degree of specialization and not of maintaining it.

It is true that our present concern is mainly with the costs of maintaining a greater degree of specialization, but even the maintenance of greater specialization requires a greater degree of entrepreneurial ability, for the entrepreneurial function is required even in the stationary state. The entrepreneurial function involves not only the decision to undertake new activities but also the types of decisions that involve the maintenance of existing activities, the ultimate decisions necessary for the continuance of the going concern. Narrowing of the range of activities of individuals implies a simultaneous increase in the number of coordinating units. But these coordinating units, even as going concerns, require entrepreneurial talents for their maintenance, as well as the additional complementary capital to maintain these additional coordinating units.

Yet another limiting factor to having a greater degree of specialization with the same aggregate demand lies in the nature of the capital that may be required. Clearly the capital needed is not neutral in determining the degree of specialization. Certainly the *type* of capital needed for greater specialization will be different from the type of capital needed for less. But will the *amount* be any different? If we grant, to take an extreme case, that when a person concentrates on a single activity he needs quite a different type of equipment than if he spreads his energies over a very large number of activities, would it take more resources for the economy to produce specialized equipment for everybody than it would to have provided everybody with a more general type of equipment? To examine this question, compare figures 7–1 and 7–2.

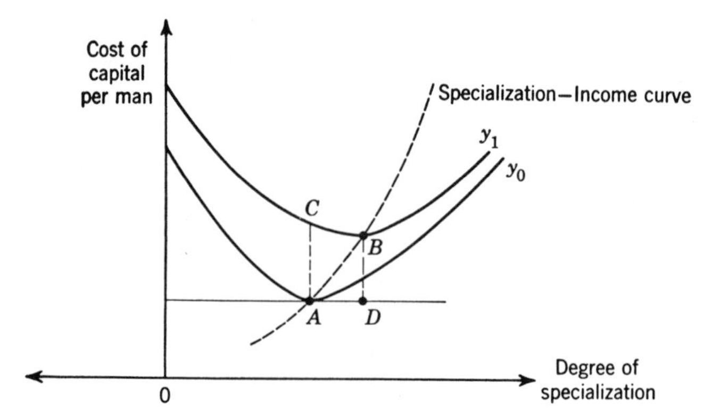

FIGURE 7–1

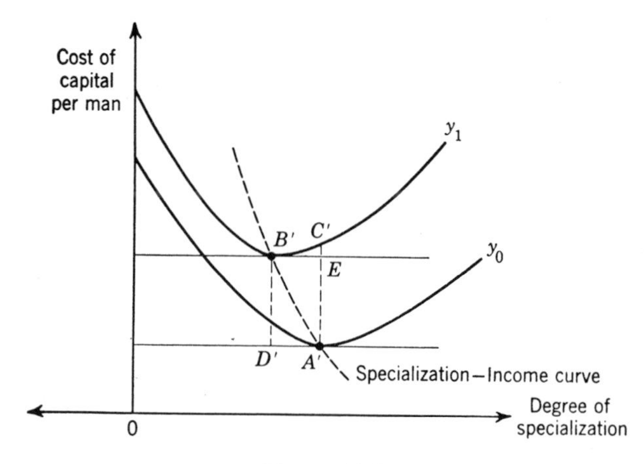

FIGURE 7–2

In figures 7–1 and 7–2 the ordinate measures the cost of capital per man to produce a given output.[7] The curve y_0 indicates the cost of capital per man for various degrees of specialization in order to produce an output, y_0. Similarly, y_1 is a curve that shows the costs of capital per man for alternate degrees of specialization required to produce a larger output, y_1. All points on y_0 are lower than the corresponding

---

[7] We assume that the labor force remains constant in all cases.

points (for the same degree of specialization) on y_1. This last reflects the notion that for a given degree of specialization we can always produce the smaller output with less capital or, at worst, with the same amount of capital.

That the capital specialization curves are likely to have a U-shape appears to be a reasonable proposition if we reflect on some of the major factors that are likely to be involved. Consider what happens in the extreme case of complete self-sufficiency for each consumption unit compared with some degree of specialization. Capital for transportation increases with increased specialization. But machinery or implement needs will at first decrease with increased division of labor since under self-sufficiency some implements to aid in the production of *every* kind of commodity are needed. Since some implements or machinery are indivisible the need for them is likely to be larger under self-sufficiency than when there is some division of labor. Capital needed to carry out commercial transactions, record keeping, etc., is also likely to increase as the division of labor increases, whereas the need for minimum inventories will at first decrease as the division of labor increases. As we can see, there are forces that suggest that at first there are decreasing capital needs and afterwards increasing capital needs, hence the U-shaped curves. In figure 7–1 the point marked A is the optimum degree of specialization to produce output y_0, and similarly B is the optimum degree of specialization to produce output y_1.

The curves illustrate the notion that beyond some point the greater the division of labor, the more the capital cost. As already indicated, this may occur for at least two reasons: First, because of the greater cost of more specialized types of capital and, second, because the greater the division of labor, the more the capital need for coordinating and trading activities necessitated by the greater division of labor. But in addition we have to consider that there may be some waste involved in not using multipurpose capital for less than all the purposes to which such capital can be put.

The line AB, which we designate as the specialization-income curve, is the locus of optimum degree of specialization points. Adam Smith's famous dictum, that the division of labor is limited by the extent of the market, involves the direction of the specialization-income curve (AB). Does a greater demand (and output) always imply a greater *optimum* division of labor? It is certainly easy to visualize situations where this is indeed the case (see figure 7–1). Greater output permits longer runs per unit of man and, hence, enables the use of specialized machinery that is not economic at the smaller output y_0. This is in conformity with Adam Smith's dictum.

But is the case depicted in figure 7–2 a possibility? This figure illustrates the reverse of Adam Smith's dictum. A greater output is related to a lesser optimum degree of specialization. Although this goes counter to usual expectations and beliefs, we do have to admit it as a possibility. What it implies is that a greater output permits the utilization of a type of capital that goes with a lower degree of specialization. The new capital is such that the division of labor is decreased. Therefore, a laborer carries out a greater range of activities than previously. The gains from specialization must here be *more* than counterbalanced (1) by the gains from using multipurpose machinery and implements more effectively and (2) by the gains that can be attributed to the decrease in the commercial, transportation, and trading activities that are the concomitants of less specialization. Since we assumed manpower to be constant, each worker can now produce more despite the fact that he is doing a greater variety of things. This last can only be possible if there exists multipurpose capital subject to indivisibilities so that a proportionately smaller amount of such multipurpose capital could not have produced y_0. Broadly speaking, it seems to imply that multipurpose capital is more subject to indivisibilities than special-purpose capital.

But as an empirical matter, the situation is likely to be quite the reverse. It is the *highly efficient* special-purpose equipment that, for the most part, is subject to indivisibilities at points where the cost per unit of capital is quite high. It is the degree of indivisibility per unit of efficiency that matters. It appears reasonable to suppose, on the basis of observation and on *a priori* grounds, that highly efficient, rapidly operating, and fully automatic machines can be constructed, although subject to a high degree of indivisibility, if they are of a special-purpose rather than of a multipurpose nature. It is important to note that a machine that may appear to be a multipurpose one in the technical sense may yet be a special-purpose machine in its economic uses. That is, it may be capable of doing many things but it may be more efficient per unit of output if it is used for only one task. From this point of view it appears likely that an increasing specialization-income relationship (as in figure 7–1) is empirically the correct one.

In sum, we have seen that the gains from specialization arise from (1) overcoming indivisibilities, (2) distributing activities where they are most efficiently performed, (3) the better synchronization of activities, (4) the elimination of certain activities, and (5) increasing skill per activity. None of these gains are reduced and some may be increased for greater outputs. The first two factors are likely to be improved for increased output whereas the last two will, at worst, not be affected. On the other hand, the counterbalancing losses from increased specialization arise out of (1) new activities necessitated by specialization, (2) the possible greater risk and cost of risk bearing under greater specialization, (3) the need of additional capital either to carry out the new activities or to acquire more costly specialized capital needed to carry out more specialized activities, and (4) the possible cost of learning new skills to carry out more specialized activities. Most important, some of the counterbalancing costs of increasing the degree of specialization are likely to involve factors of production that are indivisible, that is, they involve additional fixed capital. Up to a point costs per unit can be reduced by increasing output, the degree of specialization, and the capital stock simultaneously. Hence, our conclusion that for a given composition of commodities, the degree of specialization is likely to increase with output.

Specialization and Occupational Distribution

We now return to our main theme—the relationship between specialization and occupational distribution. Before we can proceed with the main question we must consider, at least briefly, the problem of defining the basic occupational groupings.

Colin Clark, in the first edition of *The Conditions of Economic Progress* (pp. 337–338), defines primary, secondary, and tertiary industries as follows:

1. *Primary* ". . . is defined to include agriculture, livestock farming of all kinds, hunting and trapping, fisheries and forestry . . ."
2. *Secondary* ". . . is defined to cover manufacturing production, building and public works construction, mining and electric power production. Mining and electric power production are in certain countries included with primary production, on the grounds that they represent the exploitation of natural resources. This is true; but in many respects the operation of these industries resembles that of manufacturing industry, and certainly bears little resemblance to agriculture. The building and construction industry presents certain difficulty. There might be some case for including it with the service industries, especially that large part of its output which consists of repair and maintenance work conducted on a small scale."
3. *Tertiary,* or ". . . services includes commerce and distribution, transport, public administration, domestic, personal and professional services. . . . All paid domestic work is included and all unpaid domestic work is not included."

Other writers use roughly similar definitions although there are differences at times with respect to some specific industry.

The really important point to note for our purposes is that such categories as primary, secondary, and tertiary industries do not usually depend on what workers actually *do*. That is, the categories do not depend directly and exclusively on the actual activities performed. Similar activities may be performed in all. For example, records may be kept in each of the three categories, and yet a farmer who keeps his own books part time is a farmer (primary) and not a bookkeeper (tertiary).

The distinction between tertiary industry and the others is somewhat easier to discern and so it may be well to start here. Those involved in tertiary occupations do not produce a *physical* commodity of any sort. They do not provide form utilities. The product involved does not contain physical materials of any sort, although physical goods may be utilized in providing this service. But we cannot turn around and say that all factors or laborers that do not create form utilities are engaged in tertiary industry. Once again, the timekeeper in an automobile factory will usually be classified as being engaged in secondary industry. From all of this it is clear that whatever the criterion of classification employed, the activities and operations performed are not the only considerations in the determination of the occupational category.

Of course, for different countries the rules for statistical collection will differ somewhat. But, in the main, it is likely that the allocation of individuals among primary, secondary, and tertiary production depends on the nature of the production processes of the major commodities sold by the institutionalized production unit to which the individuals belong.[8] (1) If a man belongs to a productive unit that sells, for the most part, a commodity whose production process involves considerable utilization of natural forces, such as those provided by land and sea, the man is engaged in *primary production*. (2) If the productive unit is engaged in selling a commodity whose creation involves manipulating materials or non-human factors, without substantial aid of the forces provided by nature, anyone attached to such a unit is in *secondary production*. (3) If the commodity sold by the production unit is a service, that is, something that does not contain any physical material elements in it, anyone attached to this production unit is in *tertiary industry*.

A number of things may be noticed with respect to such classifications. It is the activity of *the production unit* rather than the activity of the individual that counts. Thus, as the production units change in response to economic growth, the occupational distribution also changes. Yet this approach to classifying people into one of three occupational

---

[8] See Bauer and Yamey, *op. cit.*, p. 753.

categories is not really arbitrary but follows notions that are suggested by the names of the categories. For the categories, primary, secondary, tertiary, suggest a hierarchical scale in the resultant types of commodities. Primary suggests commodities closest to nature, closest to our needs, and without whose existence nothing else would be possible. Secondary suggests a stage removed from the primary commodities. It involves the manipulation of the primary materials into a somewhat different form so that they may be more useful, although the primary commodities may be useful without additional manipulation. And tertiary suggests still another stage of removal from primary materials, namely, the creation of services in which tangible materials are not part of the final product.

Of course, the problems with which we are dealing are in part of a semantic nature. The statistical result does depend, in part, on how we define our occupational categories. But only in part. To some extent, the type of occupational shift (with respect to income growth) that we suggest would take place even if the classification method depended entirely on the actual activities that people carried out regardless of the nature of the production unit to which a person belonged. Our point is that increased specialization must lead to a new distribution of activities even if the composition of the commodity bundle remains the same. But, in fact, a farmer is probably always classified as being entirely in agriculture even if a portion of his time is spent on record keeping. Therefore, let us return to our previous classification scheme and continue with our analysis. Thus, if it is the nature of the commodity sold that determines the occupational grouping, it must be what the production unit does rather than what the individual does that is the controlling factor.

We saw that increased income implies an increased division of labor, which, in turn, implies a decrease in the variety of activities performed by the individuals in the community. Now what happens to the occupational distribution as this process occurs?

First consider the primary industries. The range of activities in agriculture narrows. But if the range of activities *per person* is reduced, *where* are the operations necessary to create those goods previously produced entirely in the agricultural sector carried out? Some of the operations will, of course, still be carried out by production units engaged in agriculture although these production units are more specialized than previously. Some operations will be carried out by new production units no longer primarily engaged in agriculture. This is almost necessarily the case. To the extent that some of these activities involve the creation of form utilities, a sufficient increase in the division of labor would lead to the location of such activities in new production units, that is, to strictly manufacturing units. Thus, greater specialization, with a given labor force, must lead to a shift from agriculture to manufacturing. Similarly, to the extent that the narrowing of activities leads to the separation of clerical, marketing, and other activities from agriculture, it leads to an increase in tertiary production units.

In a similar manner, increases in specialization in secondary industry lead to the creation of new production units that can be classified as tertiary. Narrowing the range of activities per man must mean that some men cease to spend any of their time transforming raw materials. If such activities are coordinated in independent production units, they become tertiary industry. We note that there is no shift from manufacturing to primary industries since, to begin with, primary types of activities are not performed to any extent by secondary industry.

Tertiary industries cannot lose to the other classifications because of further specialization but only as a consequence of a greater integration of activities. But the need for "tertiary activities" is increased by greater specialization in view of the greater need for transportation and commercial activities. Simultaneously, a greater need for secondary industry is also established. Therefore, we see that solely on the basis of the specialization-income relationship are we able to get some confirmation of the Clark-Fisher thesis.[9]

Of course, the actual process is more complicated than indicated. In our approach toward greater realism, some additional factors might be mentioned that also tend to reinforce the thesis. First, as capital accumulation takes place, the nature of the capital has important effects on the distribution of labor. Agricultural capital is most likely to be of the labor-displacing variety. In other words, it leads to a substitution of mechanical power for manpower more than it increases yields and

[9] A summary of the formal argument runs as follows: We designate three types of industries, A (primary), B (secondary), and C (tertiary), and three sets of activities $(a_1 \ldots a_k)$, $(b_1 \ldots b_m)$, and $(c_1 \ldots c_n)$. For each person to produce some of every good under self-sufficiency requires that he carry out all activities $a_1 \ldots a_k$, $b_1 \ldots b_m$, $c_1 \ldots c_n$. If any person performs activity a_i (for all i) then regardless of other activities that he may carry out simultaneously he is classified as belonging to industry A. If he performs *no* activity, a_i, but an activity, b_j (for all j) then the industry he belongs to is classified as B. As people narrow their range of activities some will cease to carry out any a_i activity, and they will, therefore, enter industry B or C. But those whose concentration leads to the elimination of activity b_j (for all j) enter industry C. No concentration of activities by those in B can lead to the establishment of any A industry since there are no a's in B. Similarly, no concentration in C can result in the establishment of a B industry. In addition, concentration requires an increase in activities of the c variety. Hence, our general thesis.

the consequent demand for more manpower. We should also take into account the income elasticity of demand for tertiary products. The initial labor-displacing machinery leads to greater incomes which, in turn, may lead to a proportionately greater demand, at the margin, for the products of tertiary rather than secondary industry. On this score, too, the Clark-Fisher thesis is reinforced.

CHAPTER 8

The Critical Minimum Effort Thesis

Introduction

One of the main arguments of this book is that in order to achieve sustained secular growth, in the general case, it is necessary that the initial stimulant or stimulants to development be of a certain critical minimum size. In this chapter we shall analyze this thesis, delineate its nature, and examine its persuasiveness.

First, what is the thesis? The thesis is sufficiently broad and general so that a sentence definition is hardly likely to be immediately meaningful; it can be only a beginning. For so complex a phenomenon as economic development a central explanatory principle is likely to be somewhat elusive at the outset. We may look at the matter in this way. Economic backwardness is characterized by a set of related factors that have a certain degree of stability. The *degree* of stability is characterized by the fact that some of the crucial variables have equilibrium values that possess at least stability in the small though not necessarily perfect stability.

The actual values are different from the equilibrium values because the economy is always being subjected to stimulants or shocks. These stimulants, which have to be defined, tend to raise per capita incomes above the equilibrium level. But in backward economies long-run economic development does not occur because the magnitude of the stimulants is too small. That is to say, the efforts to escape from economic backwardness, be they spontaneous or forced, are below the critical minimum required for persistent growth.

It is clear that a number of the terms we have used in our brief explanation beg for clarification and elaboration. What do we mean by the magnitude of a stimulant? How is the critical minimum effort notion related to the idea that backward economies are bedeviled by a series of vicious circles? We turn to these and related matters.

The Vicious Circle Idea and Its Relationship to the Critical Minimum Effort Thesis

We have already noted that it is quite common to find references to vicious circles in the literature.[1] Such phrases as "A country is poor because it has little capital, and it cannot raise capital because it is poor" are suggestive of the kind of ideas we have in mind. The vicious circle idea is usually mentioned *en passant*. It is rarely worked out carefully in technical economic terms. It is, therefore, very difficult to know what more exact meaning we should attach to it. Should it be taken merely as an elliptical allusion to the fact that the problem of economic backwardness is a very difficult one, or does it imply nothing more than the notion that there is an internal consistency in the factors and relationships that determine poverty, or is it meant to be an explanation of the persistence of poverty? One can never be sure.

A possible interpretation is that the vicious circle idea implies nothing more than the fact that the determinants of economic backwardness are mutually consistent. But since we must believe that economic relationships in general are mutually consistent, this is more or less what we would expect. In many cases the vicious circle idea alludes to the twin notions of the persistence of backwardness and the difficulty of seeing a way out. If the circle is truly vicious, there would appear to be no way out. If poor countries cannot augment their stocks of capital because of their poverty, and if their inability to raise capital is the

---

[1] H. W. Singer, "Economic Progress in Underdeveloped Countries," *Social Research,* Vol. XVI, No. 1 (1949), pp. 1–11. August Maffry, "Problems of Economic Development," *The American Journal of Economics and Sociology,* Vol. 11, No. 3 (April 1952), pp. 327–342. S. Enke and V. Salera, *International Economics,* New York, Prentice-Hall, 1951, Ch. 28, p. 530. N. S. Buchanan, "Deliberate Industrialization for Higher Incomes," *Economic Journal,* Vol. 56, No. 4 (December 1946), pp. 545–548. International Labor Office, *The Economic Background of Social Policy Including Problems of Industrialization,* New Delhi, 1947, pp. 148–152.

cause of their poverty, we would expect their poverty to persist into perpetuity. But this, of course, does not explain how countries that were once poor are no longer poor, or are not as poor as they were.

Thus, we see that, at best, the frequent vicious circle allusion tries to say something about the stability of the state of economic backwardness. The idea of ascribing to the state of economic backwardness stability in the small is a much more exact way of viewing the matter. What this says is that the state of backwardness, as viewed from a day-to-day basis, represents fluctuations of the variables around a low income per capita equilibrium. The values of the variables are consistent with each other for any economic state, but the low income equilibrium state which has *some* stability serves as a magnet, so to speak, so that the values of the variables tend to go toward it. Periodic stimulants and shocks result in a dance of the values of the actual variables around the equilibrium state. In this way the persistence of general economic backwardness is explained, although the explanation allows for small variations from time to time.

If we continue to think in terms of vicious circles, and it is sometimes a convenient shorthand mode of thinking about the problem, at some point we have to explain how the vicious circle can be broken. It is here that the critical minimum effort idea appears.

Can the Vicious Circle Be Broken?

In previous chapters we have argued that the characteristics of economic backwardness have some degree of stability. Why are they not perfectly stable? What sort of relationships must we assume in order to believe that the vicious circle can be broken? Or, what is the same thing, under what types of circumstances does the critical minimum effort thesis hold? A number of possibilities exist.

The simplest example of the thesis is a system in which for small values of the stimulant the income-raising factors are zero, but for higher values they are positive. But for so complex a phenomenon this simple case is not very interesting.

We can obtain the result we want if we assume that for small values of the stimulant the generated income-depressing factors are, in the long run, more significant than the induced income-raising forces, but that for high values of the stimulant the reverse is true. This implies the corollary explanation that where economic backwardness persists the stimulants have been small in the past, whereas in advanced countries there was some point or period during which the magnitude of the stimulant(s) was great. How this works out in detail will depend on what the specific stimulants are, how the stimulants are related to *specific* income-raising factors, and how both, in turn, are related to income-depressing factors. An example may help to clarify matters. Suppose that the stimulant is an agricultural discovery of some sort that results in an increase in output per acre. Now, assume that for small increases in output the peasants' marginal propensity to consume is so high that the entire increase is taken up in greater consumption. There is, therefore, little left for capital accumulation. But if the stimulant is very large, the upward adjustment of the consumption level may permit investment and capital accumulation. This is a simple case in which there are no income-depressing factors but in which a minimum increase in output is needed to get capital accumulation started. But it is not difficult to introduce reasonable income-depressing factors into our example. Let us suppose that the effect of the stimulant is for the peasants to expect an annual increase in their consumption level. If the stimulant is small, the amount of reinvestment in the land is insufficient to bring forth steady increases in yields and yet maintain the fertility of the soil. The likely alternative is for the peasant to work the soil more intensively which, in turn, results in erosion and the consequent reduction in yields. If we add autonomous and/or induced population growth to our system, and consider the usual consequences of such growth on the consumption and output levels in the densely populated and backward agricultural setting, the role of the income-depressing factors becomes all the more evident. But if the magnitude of the stimulant is "large," the outcome could quite readily be the reverse. The initial much larger increase in yield can now be sufficiently large to allow for (*a*) the initial increase in the peasants' consumption level, (*b*) the investment required for subsequent increases in the peasants' consumption level, (*c*) the increased yields necessary to take care of the autonomous and/or induced population growth, and (*d*) a sufficient increase in yield to permit some of the land to lie fallow to prevent soil depletion or to permit crop rotation.

An alternative possibility already mentioned is that the consequences of the income-depressing forces have an upper limit but the simultaneously generated income-raising factors have either no upper limit or a higher upper limit. Thus, the income-depressing factors may be operating autonomously or be generated by the stimulant, and up to some maximum effect they may be more significant than the income-raising factors. As a consequence, if the income-raising factors are stimulated beyond the maximum of the income-depressing factors, the critical minimum has been reached and the economy would, in this case, be on the road to development. The population growth effect fits this case. It may happen, although it need not, that any small increase in capital will stimulate a more than equivalent increase in population. Thus, a 1 per cent increase in capital will generate (via raising incomes and depressing mortality rates) a more than 1 per cent increase in population and a proportional decline in average income. Of course, the line of causation will be more complicated and not so direct but we need not go into these matters now. There is a biologically determined maximum rate of population growth between 3 and 4 per cent. Thus, persistent capital accumulation above a certain minimum rate would permit development. And if the sustained rate of capital accumulation is positively related to the size of the stimulant, the minimum effort thesis applies.

Many other variations are possible, but all of them need not be spelled out now. From what has been said, it should be clear that the minimum effort idea is both consistent with the vicious circle notion and at the same time offers a way out. In other words, the only reason the vicious circles appear vicious is because it is so very difficult to find and marshal stimulants to development that are of sufficient magnitude.

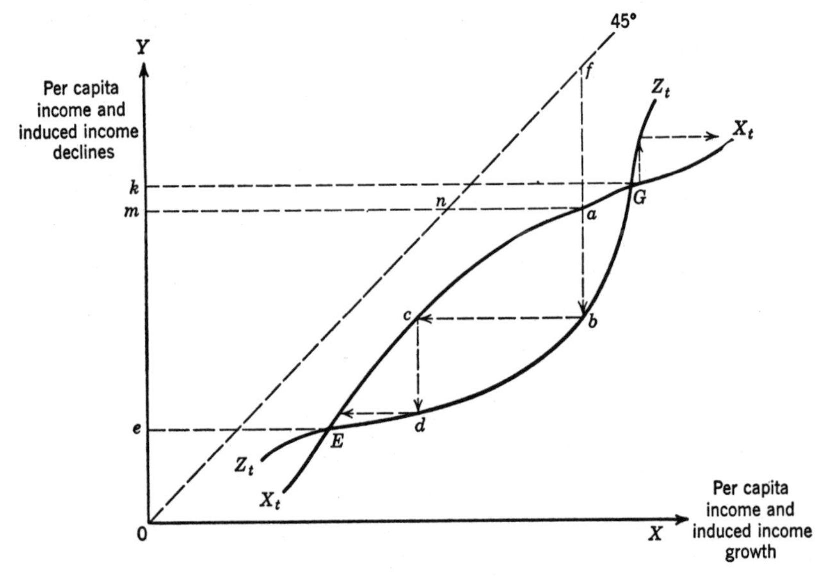

FIGURE 8–1*a*. Critical minimum effort case.

Is the Minimum Effort Thesis Logically Necessary?

Graphically, the critical minimum effort thesis, and some of the alternative hypotheses, can be illustrated by the diagrams below.

In figures 8–1*a*, 8–1*b*, and 8–1*c* we show the outcome of the struggle between two opposing sets of forces: the per capita income-raising forces and the per capita income-depressing forces. In our illustration the income-raising forces are generated by the previous level of per capita income, and the strength of the income-depressing forces is determined by the level to which per capita income would have been raised had the income-raising forces been the only forces in operation. The ordinate Y represents the level of income per head. X represents the effects of all the per capita income-*raising* forces in the system, and Z represents the effects of all the per capita income-*depressing* forces. Note especially that we measure the induced increases and decreases in per capita income from the 45-degree line in the figures. The curve X_t indicates the extent to which income would be increased in the current period, given the related per capita income level of the previous period shown on the ordinate, *if the income-raising forces were the only ones in operation.* Let us look at figure 8–1*a.* If the income level of the initial period is *Om,* the income-raising forces generated will in the next period raise the income level by *na.* But at the same time the effects of the income-depressing forces will reduce income below the point to which they would have been raised by the income-raising forces. We measure Z, the effects of the income-depressing forces, vertically down from the 45-degree line. Again note that the curve Z_t indicates the extent to which income is depressed for each alternative level to which income would have been raised if the income-raising forces had been the only ones permitted to operate. Thus, figure 8–1*a* shows that if income had been raised to the point on the abscissa opposite *f,* the income-depressing forces would have reduced income by *fb.* The rest of the curve Z_t is to be interpreted in a similar fashion. Keeping in mind the meaning of the two curves, we can see, if we follow the events step by step, that an initial income level *Om* will generate the path *abcd,* and so on, until the path eventually settles at the point *E.* Similarly, we can show that if we begin with a level of per capita income above *Ok,* we generate an explosive income growth path. In all the figures, the path of per capita income, period by period, from various initial points, is shown by the arrows between the curves.

Figure 8–1*a* illustrates the critical minimum effort thesis. If the initial stimulant or stimulants raise per capita income above *Oe* but not above *Ok,* the path of change, as shown by the arrows, will eventually lead to a return to the equilibrium position *E.* But if the stimulant is sufficiently large so that income does rise above *Ok,* the path of change is one of endless expansion—a clear illustration of the critical minimum effort thesis.

Figure 8–1*b* illustrates the case in which the situation is hopeless, in which the income-depressing forces are always, in the long run, more significant than the income-raising ones. Here, no matter to what extent the stimulant or stimulants raise per capita income, the path of change that follows is always toward the low-income equilibrium E.

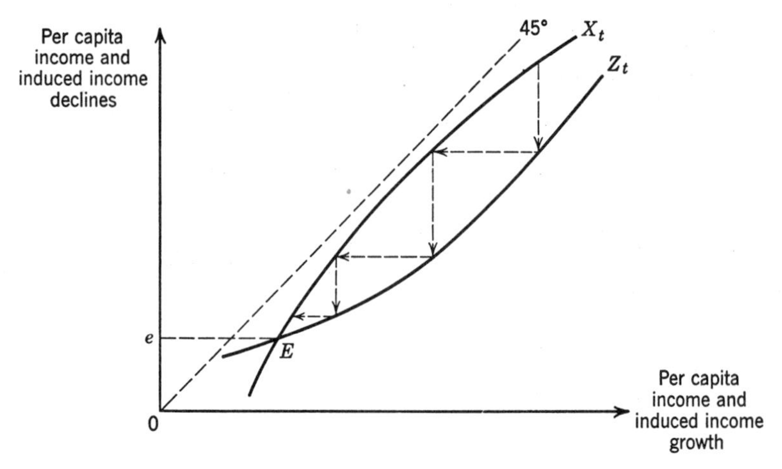

FIGURE 8–1b. Completely stable case.

Figure 8–1c illustrates the case of slow progressive growth. It represents the optimist's idea of the development problem, whereas figure 8–1b represents the pessimist's vision. Here, given any initial position, slow growth from that position is induced from within the system. For some countries the X_t and Z_t curves may be closer together, for others further apart, thus illustrating the conditions for lesser and greater sustained rates of growth. At the lower end these curves may or may not cross. If they do, a low income equilibrium exists that is unstable, since any stimulant, no matter how small, leads to growth in this case.

The diagrams suggest that the persuasiveness of the minimum effort thesis does not depend on logical necessity. We have seen that it is possible to concoct economic-growth models that do not have this property. We can, perhaps, best analyze the problem in the following manner. Divide the vast variety of growth models that can be constructed into two types—those that imply the minimum effort thesis and those that do not. We then examine the properties of some of these models, see how they fit the properties of the problem with which we are concerned, and judge which type of model best fits our problem.

1. Low-income equilibrium models. First consider those models whose variables have a set of equilibrium values consistent with low income per capita. This implies, at the very least, that the equilibrium income level will remain at that level once it occurs. Let us suppose that this equilibrium is stable in the large (as illustrated in figure 8–1*b*) so that the minimum effort thesis cannot be invoked. This would explain those cases in which economic underdevelopment persists, but it would fail to account for the fact that some economies that were once backward are no longer so.

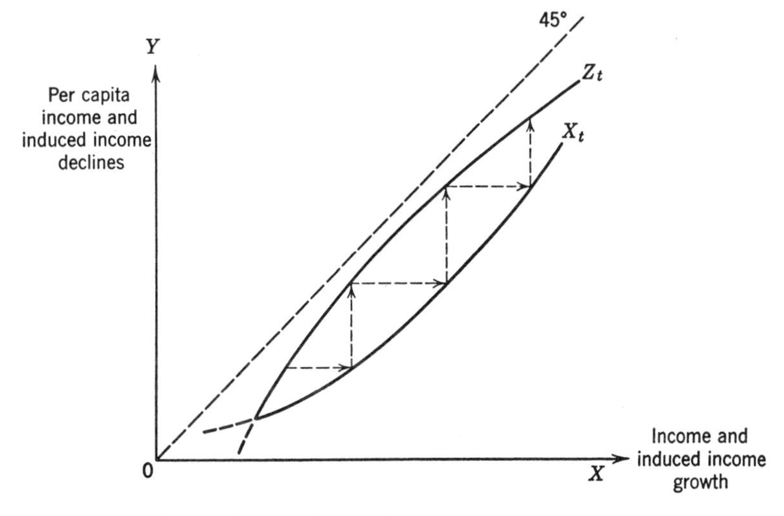

FIGURE 8–1*c*. Disequilibrium slow growth case.

Let us turn to the other polar case of a completely unstable equilibrium (as in figure 8–1*c*). This would imply that any stimulant, no matter how small, would lead to escape from low-income equilibrium. But if this is so, what explains the persistence in many areas of economic backwardness? There are two possible answers to this question. Backwardness appears to persist because economies are subjected to both stimulants and shocks. The incidence of these stimulants and shocks is more or less randomly distributed, and most economies are subjected, more or less, to as many stimulants as shocks. Hence backwardness usually persists, explaining why most of the world remains underdeveloped. The developed countries have simply been luckier in the distribution of stimulants and shocks that they have had to bear. But there are several aspects to such an explanation that are not especially satisfying. First, apart from its being fatalistic, it explains development on the basis of luck which, itself, remains unexplained. Thus, in the end nothing is really explained. Second, it does not explain why the backward countries should be concentrated geographically if the stimulants and shocks are randomly distributed. We would expect an advanced country in the midst of underdeveloped countries and vice versa. Thus, the presumption that low-income equilibrium has some degree of stability would appear to be more satisfying.

Let us consider yet another argument against the critical minimum effort thesis. We can argue that for the backward economies their low-income equilibrium is stable in the large, but that for the advanced economies it was always unstable. This argument implies that the situation in backward economies is quite hopeless, that the gap between the backward and advanced economies must forever grow. This viewpoint may be consistent with some of the facts of history, but it implies that there is something unique about present backward economies that is of a lasting nature. But, we know, generally speaking, that the broad characteristics of backward economies today are not different from what they were in advanced economies in a former period. In some countries these characteristics existed (for example, in Sweden) not much more than three-quarters of a century back, in others several centuries at most. This statement may not be a foolproof reply to the notion that backward economies are stable in the large, but it does carry with it some degree of persuasiveness.

Another possibility is that the equilibrium is either neutral or unstable (figure 8–1*c*). In view of the fact that economies are subject to shocks and stimulants, economies, as such, are never in equilibrium. The spread of knowledge, inventions, innovations, and technology, and the accumulation of capital have their effects everywhere, but in some places much more than in others. As a consequence, no economy is stagnant but some economies are advancing so much more rapidly than others that the slower ones appear backward by comparison. However, they would not appear so on the basis of any absolute measure. Of the possibilities we have thus far examined this is probably the most appealing doctrine. It is certainly an optimistic doctrine for it implies that the consequence of any stimulant is improvement, no matter how small. Even very small rates of growth, if they persisted over a number of centuries, would result in considerable improvement, but this does not seem to be the impression we get from reading the history of many backward economies. Indeed, some calculations seem to show[2] that for some countries there were periods centuries-long during which real incomes or the expectation of life at birth had not risen. Furthermore, we shall see that we can

[2] For example, two Indian economists, P. A. Wadia and K. T. Merchant, point to the fact that the frequency of famines has actually increased considerably in the period 1876–1900 as compared with the previous century. Also cultivated land per man has declined considerably. See Wadia and Merchant, *Our Economic Problem,* Bombay, New Book Company, 1954, pp. 105 ff.

point to a number of income-depressing factors that are generated by stimulants to development, and that it is likely that such factors can be, and probably are, more significant for small stimulants than the income-raising factors.

2. *Non-equilibrium models.* It is not necessary that the variables of a model have a set of equilibrium values. The economy may be in constant flux without tending at any time toward any specific state. In such an instance, it may be argued that the factors that promote growth, such as technology, innovations, the spread of knowledge, and capital accumulation, exist everywhere but in greatly varying degree. And the difference between advanced and backward economies is explained simply by the roles that these growth stimulants play, greater in one country than in another. But this view of the matter is almost identical with the view we have to adopt in the unstable equilibrium case, and similarly it does not fit very well with the persistence of low per capita incomes for centuries in many areas. We need not consider again the arguments that we have just examined in our discussion of the unstable equilibrium case.

Another approach is to argue that the economic condition of a people is explained by institutional or extra-economic factors. Such arguments at one time enjoyed a considerable vogue among some American economists. Along such lines we may argue that it is political disorganization or mismanagement or exploitation of some sort that causes the persistence of low incomes. Or a similar argument is that it is in the interest of some group or power to keep per capita income and output low in order to keep "the people" enslaved. The burden of such arguments usually appears to be the visualization of a devil of some sort whose removal would permit the natural progress inherent in the economy. But such a view of the matter, if it is to be persuasive, must show a connection between these extra-economic forces and the economic variables that determine per capita output. Once this is admitted we are led back to a consideration of the relationships between the economic variables, which, in turn, leads us to the familiar questions of equilibrium, stability, and the possibilities for change that we have already considered. All of this is not to deny that such phenomena as colonial exploitation, governmental mismanagement, etc., can and often do play important limiting roles. It may, indeed, be necessary for the economy to struggle against and rid itself of such limiting forces if development is to occur. In addition to the limited stability of low-income equilibrium that is to be overcome, it may be necessary for the economy to rid itself of the superimposed limiting factors that have political or other non-economic origins.

In sum, we can say that the critical minimum effort thesis is not a logical corollary of *all* conceivable growth models. The persuasiveness of the thesis must lie on somewhat more tenuous ground than that of absolute logical necessity. Its persuasiveness lies in the fact that it appears to be more reasonable than its alternatives on three general grounds. First, since human beings are basically similar, we should expect that the same theory should explain the existence of both the advanced and the underdeveloped countries. Second, the persistence of low-income economies in the face of the existence of stimulants to growth suggests that such economies have some degree of stability. Third, we can point to at least some of the income-depressing forces that are generated by stimulants which, when taken together, can explain a degree of stability for low-income countries. (See especially the chapter that follows on this last point.)

Dimensions and Meaning of the Critical Minimum Effort

Thus far, we have discussed the idea of a critical minimum effort only in very general terms, and this was unavoidable. If this thesis is to be a significant part of a theory that involves a great many variables, it is bound to contain generality and abstractness. But the use of the word minimum obviously implies a quantity of some sort, and hence a discussion of the dimensions of the minimum effort and the definition of some of the terms involved are required.

Our central variable is income per head, and, therefore, we will define what we mean by the minimum effort, as well as some of the other notions employed, in terms of or in close connection with income per head.

To simplify matters, let us assume at the outset that the state of low income equilibrium exists. We have defined a stimulant to growth as any event that changes the value of a variable away from its equilibrium value so that the consequence of this event is an *initial* increase in per capita income. Similarly, we have defined as a shock any event external to the system the consequence of which is to reduce per capita income initially. An obvious possibility for defining the critical minimum effort is in terms of the magnitude of the stimulant that it takes to achieve sustained development. Thus, if the stimulant is investment obtained externally, we could name some amount of externally created investment as the critical minimum effort. But a moment's reflection would indicate that this would hardly do since there is a variety of stimulants, and the money value of the critical minimum effort for different stimulants may be quite different. We would hardly expect that $1000 that can be spent in a number of directions would raise per capita incomes by the same amount in each and every direction. At this point we may introduce some efficiency principle that results in a single number. That is, we may argue that for purposes of calculating the minimum effort, that distribution among stimulants which minimizes the cost should be chosen. But here there is an additional obstacle. Not all stimulants can be translated into a money value or cost. Investment, of course, does have a money value, but unusually good climate or a discovery of some sort need not be translatable into such terms.

Another alternative is to measure the minimum effort in terms of its effect on raising income. In other words, we may come up with a number that indicates the amount by which per capita income has to be raised by some stimulant in order to achieve sustained development. This would solve the problem for those stimulants to which it is difficult to attach a money cost.

Under both alternatives there is the problem that the stimulant has a time dimension. Not everything can be done at once. A certain expenditure stretched over ten years may be more effective than the same expenditure spent all at once or all in one year. This implies that the critical minimum effort viewed as a *minimum minimorum* of all possible efforts that would lead to sustained real income growth involves an optimum time pattern of expenditure or effort.

What is the upshot of this discussion and elucidation of difficulties? First, it is probably impossible to define the critical minimum effort in such a way that we always, under all conceivable circumstances, mean exactly the same thing by it and at the same time state it in terms of a number along a single dimension. Even if this were possible, it is not at all clear that such a definition would be desirable. But, whatever we may mean by it, it is clear that the critical minimum effort is something that either directly or indirectly (for example, in terms of its ability to raise per capita incomes) has a magnitude of some sort, part of which can usually be stated in terms of money value. Its exact meaning will have to depend upon the context in which it is being used. Usually, if the relevant stimulants can be stated in terms of a money value, it will be the money value of the stimulant, although we may have to add some statement to indicate the nature of the time dimension that we have in mind. In any event, any statement that attempts to indicate a specific critical minimum effort under specific circumstances will imply a number (for example, the discounted value of a certain investment stream) or a set of numbers, each number having a time point or period attached to it such that we could conceive of a smaller number that would *not* lead to sustained development.

Types of Determinants of the Critical Minimum Effort

To understand more fully the nature and need for a critical minimum effort we have to examine some of the reasons and mechanisms that suggest the necessity for such a minimum.

The factors that determine the need for a minimum effort are of four kinds. In brief, there is a need for a minimum effort in order: (1) to overcome internal diseconomies of scale due to indivisibilities in the factors of production, (2) to overcome external diseconomies due to external interdependencies and to achieve what has sometimes been called "balanced" growth, (3) to overcome income-depressing obstacles that may be generated by the stimulants to growth, and (4) to generate sufficient momentum in the system so that the factors that stimulate growth continue to play their part.

1. Internal diseconomies. This factor bears a close resemblance to the usual type of infant industry argument, but we shall see that, taken together with some of the other factors, it is not quite the same thing. The essential aspect of the argument is that firms have to be above a certain minimum size in order to be reasonably efficient; hence the investment has to be of a certain minimum size. For any large country it would appear that this factor alone could not be a very serious obstacle. For size of plants is a kind of absolute matter and is not relative to the size of a country or its national income. Thus, even if the proportion of national income that goes into investment is very small and the country is large enough, the absolute amount of investment, if it can be marshaled, can be sufficiently large to enable the start and operation of some firms of optimum size. All that this limitation implies is that investment must be concentrated among a few industries rather than spread widely. Hence, for large countries this factor would not seem to be a serious detriment. However, we shall see that when we combine this factor with the next one the matter can become quite serious.

2. External economies, interdependencies, and balanced growth. Although there is some controversy as to the exact meaning of external economies,[3] the general nature of these phenomena is fairly well known. External economies usually refer to the fact that

[3] For an excellent discussion of the meaning and nature of external economies in both equilibrium theory and in the theory of economic development, see Tibor Scitovsky, "Two Concepts of External Economies," *The Journal of Political Economy,* Vol. 62, No. 2, April 1954, pp. 143–152. See also H. W. Arndt, "External Economies in Economic Growth," *Economic Record,* November 1955, pp. 192–214.

as an industry expands, costs for all firms within the industry are reduced, although no firm within the industry is any more efficient than it was previously. This may be due to the existence of internal economies in industry *A* generated by the expansion of industry *B*, or due to the fact that the expansion of industry *B* permits certain functions to be carried out more efficiently by firms in industry *B*. But the major source of economies of this sort will be due to the interdependence of different industries. Industry *A*, to produce what it must produce, will have to purchase materials and services from a host of other industries, and the same will be true for industries *B*, *C*, *D*, etc. Therefore, for one to exist, all have to exist if we assume a closed economy. But, if to be efficient they each have to be of a certain minimum size, it can readily be seen that to create them, the minimum investment has to be considerable.

Ideas of this sort have led to the notion and advocacy of what has been called "balanced growth."[4] If there were no serious technological indivisibilities to overcome, balanced growth could be achieved with any level of investment; but if the indivisibilities are considerable, balanced growth is bound to take a considerable amount of investment initially. But the incentive effect may be just as significant a reason for the need of a critical minimum effort. Only if costs can be kept sufficiently low so that profits are attractive will there develop an appetite for continued investment. There is a greater chance of achieving low costs if both internal and external economies can be exploited. Hence the need for the large initial effort. Otherwise, the competition of low cost labor and the restraining effect of frustrated anticipations due to lower profits than anticipated may dampen or eliminate the reinvestment momentum so necessary to sustained growth.[5]

For the most part, we have looked at the matter of internal and external economies in the static sense, in the sense that at any point in time a larger scale is more economic than a smaller one. But in both cases there is also a time-delay aspect that may be equally significant. This has to do with the fact of the delayed profitability of many new projects.

The reasons for the delayed profitability of projects are numerous, and the major factors are reasonably well understood. It obviously takes time to build facilities and get operations under way. Thus, for

---

[4] See Ragnar Nurkse, *Problems of Capital Formation in Underdeveloped Countries*, New York, Oxford University Press, 1953, pp. 11 ff. Also M. Fleming, "External Economies and the Doctrine of Balanced Growth," *The Economic Journal*, Vol. 66, June 1955, pp. 241–247.

[5] See the next three chapters for more on this point.

many projects, especially those of a more elaborate kind (for example, the creation of a railroad system), there is a long gestation period. During this period the amount of real income creation may be close to zero, and there is certainly no possibility of plowing back funds out of profits for investment. Also, the mere existence of complementarities and interdependence between industries creates a situation in which there is likely to be delayed profitability, or what is the same thing, delayed income-creation sufficient to cover all costs. Not all industries of precisely the right size can be established at once so that all production complementarities between industries can be met exactly. Thus, industry *A* may be profitable as soon as industry *B* is established and reaches a certain size, and the same may be true of *B vis-à-vis A*, or some other industry, but because of different gestation periods, lack of capital, or some other reason, they cannot all be profitable at the same time. The outcome must be delayed profitability for at least some.

Furthermore, both technological and organizational efficiency and progress depend, and feed, on industrial and technical experience. Early managerial and work experience is bound to be inefficient compared to later developments and progress. Also certain promotional, organizational, and even social overhead costs may be very high initially, although they can be eliminated or reduced as experience is gained.

The consequences of the delayed profitability of certain investments are clear. Some enterprises have to be subsidized by current income. This clearly reinforces the necessity of a critical minimum effort initially, since that portion of the current savings used for the subsidization of "immature" industries is lost to current capital accumulation. In sum, the initial stimulant has to be sufficiently large to cover temporary losses and generated income-depressing forces and, also, to provide a surplus for growth.

3. Overcoming induced and autonomous depressants. We have already considered, to some extent, this facet of the minimum effort thesis in connection with other matters.

Two intertwined forces are involved. At any time the economy may be subjected to autonomously generated income-depressing factors and at the same time be subjected to depressants induced by some aspects of the process of growth. Here, again, population growth can serve as an example. Public health measures such as the spraying of houses and swamps with DDT may cause a decline in mortality rates and an increase in population. As a consequence, a certain minimum investment is necessary in order to create the subsistence essential to the additional population. At the same time, stimulants to per capita income growth will force mortality rates still lower, increase the rate of population growth, and necessitate still larger increases in capital before additions to per capita income can be achieved. But, as argued previously, there is a maximum to the rate of population growth, and hence there is a finite critical minimum effort above which sustained income growth can be attained.

Another example, previously mentioned in passing, is the following one. For development to take place, food must be provided for the growing portion of the labor force that is taken off the land. If yields in agriculture increase but little above what they were before the labor shift, the additional food grown may never get to the non-agricultural sector due to the rising consumption standard of the peasant, that is, "peasant hoarding." Hence, the rate of investment must be sufficiently great not only to enlarge the non-agricultural sector, but also to increase simultaneously the yield in agriculture in order to meet the increased demand of the agricultural sector and to provide a surplus for the growing non-agricultural sector.[6]

More examples will be considered later in connection with other phases of the problem.

4. Non-economic aspects and the growth momentum. The more elusive determinants are those that may depend on the rate of growth itself. Here we have in mind factors that are, at least partially, of a non-economic nature and are quite difficult to pin down, but which may be very important nonetheless. We have in mind the culturally and institutionally determined attitudes that are conducive to performing the functions necessary for economic growth. From the evidence available it would appear that the attitudes that exist and persist in backward economies are attitudes that inhibit growth.[7]

A partial list of the attitudes that it would be desirable to develop in order to promote economic growth are: (1) Western "market" incentives, that is, a strong profit incentive, an eagerness to maximize money incomes, etc., (2) a willingness to accept entrepreneurial risks, (3) an eagerness to be trained for industrial and "dirty" jobs rather than white collar jobs or those that have cultural prestige value, and (4) an eagerness to engage in and promote scientific and technical progress rather than devotion to an honorifically valued "cultural"

---

[6] See N. Kaldor, "Characteristics of Economic Development," in *International Congress of Studies of the Problem of Underdeveloped Areas,* Milan, October 1954.

[7] See United Nations, *Processes and Problems of Industrialization in Underdeveloped Areas,* pp. 18 ff. See also Buchanan and Ellis, *Approaches to Economic Development,* New York, The Twentieth Century Fund, 1955, pp. 74 ff.

education. In sum, it is necessary to create an outlook in which success is gauged by market performance and in which rational, rather than conventional or traditional, considerations are the determinants of action.

This cultural and institutional barrier is difficult to pierce. The shift from centuries' enforced, traditional patterns of behavior, which may have had significant survival value in the past, is not easy to achieve. Behavior patterns which have had such a high degree of stability in the past are unlikely to be dislodged by mild stimulants. The precise mechanism for achieving such changes does not appear to be known. However, when such attitudinal changes have occurred, they were often the concomitants of a significant rate of economic change. It would appear a reasonable hypothesis that such changes require a certain minimum rate of economic expansion for them to become effective. The rate of economic growth must be sufficiently large in order that it may appear to people that there are new values and new experiences that are a challenge to existing values, and that if the trend can be projected, these new values and modes of behavior will become the predominant ones. In other words, the rate of change has to be sufficiently large and sufficiently pervasive so that a significantly large number of people may begin to feel that this change in values will persist and endure, and that the adoption of these values will be rewarded and respected.[8] There is a two-way causal connection. If people feel that the new values will persist, they will contribute to their persistence. Change breeds more change once a certain minimum momentum has been achieved. Hence, a sufficiently large minimum effort is necessary at the outset if the necessary minimum momentum is to be achieved.

[8] As Professor A. Gershenkron has put the matter: "Precisely because some value systems do not change readily, because economic development must break through the barriers of routine, prejudice, and stagnation, among which adverse attitudes towards entrepreneurship are but one important element, industrialization does not take place until the gains which industrialization promises have become, with the passage of time, overwhelmingly large, and the prerequisites are created for a typical spurt-like upsurge." *Economic Progress,* Papers and Proceedings of a Round Table held by the International Economic Association, Louvain, 1955, p. 319.

CHAPTER 9

Growth Incentives, Agents, and Activities, and the Minimum Effort Thesis

In the earlier chapters we focused mostly on the characteristics of economic backwardness, on the question of what it is that keeps a country from developing. We consider the obverse side of the same problem when we ask what the underlying factors are that act to promote growth. Predominant among such factors are the motivations of the populace and the incentives to which they respond. But motivations and incentives are meaningless apart from the main actors that are spurred by and respond to them in the drama of development—the entrepreneur, the inventor, the discoverer, the innovator, those who marshal, accumulate, and utilize wealth, and those who accumulate skills, disseminate knowledge, and so on. The cast and their activities are seemingly endless, but we can look at the major types under their broad generic titles and relate them to the plot that we have in mind. We shall be especially concerned with the development of entrepreneurship, knowledge, and skills.

Attitudes, Motivations, and "Zero-sum" Incentives

Economic growth does not occur automatically. It is not simply a matter of setting it in motion. It occurs only because of the constant striving of the human agencies that are involved. It occurs because of a special type of human response to motivations and incentives that are created, at least to a considerable extent, by the economic and social environment. The question of incentives is most often mentioned in relation to the problem of the development of an entrepreneurial class in backward economies. But the significance of incentives and the nature and importance of the reaction to them is much more pervasive. There are considerable differences in attitudes toward work, accumulation, taking risks, etc., between the mass of the people in developed areas and the bulk of the population in underdeveloped areas. These attitudes are culturally determined; they depend entirely on environmental conditioning. There is also little doubt that such attitudes can be changed. But the rates at which such attitudes can be changed and the impact of such changes are unquestionably significant. Thus, we find Kaldor[1] saying:

> In my view the greatly accelerated economic development of the last 200 years—the rise of modern capitalism—can only be explained in terms of changing human attitudes to risk-taking and profit-making. It was the result of the displacement of production units governed by a traditionalist outlook—the peasant and the artisan—by business enterprises led by men who found risk-taking and money-making their chief interest in life; by men who were out to make a fortune rather than just a living. The emergence of the "business enterprise" characteristic of modern capitalism was thus the cause rather than the result of changes in the modes of production; and it was the product of social forces that cannot in turn be accounted for by economic or technical factors.

On the other side of the picture we find an I.L.O. report lamenting that:

> Among the principal factors which have favoured or retarded the growth of modern industry in Asia, the most important so far is doubtless the general lack of enterprise. Men of enterprise, ready and able to respond to market opportunities, have been scarce in all Asiatic countries. Not only capital, but also the initiative in developing modern industry has come mainly from abroad.[2]

---

[1] N. Kaldor, "Characteristics of Economic Development," *International Congress of Studies of the Problem of Underdeveloped Areas,* Milan, October, 1954.

[2] International Labor Organization, *The Economic Background of Social Policy Including Problems of Industrialization,* New Delhi, International Labor Office, 1947, p. 97.

Quotations of this sort could be multiplied without too much difficulty. There appears to be a fairly general and also well-founded belief that one of the requisites of economic growth is a transformation of attitudes of a sufficient number of people from a traditional outlook and motivations toward honorific activities to drives toward profit making, monetary gains, and risk taking.

Unquestionably the proper psychological attitudes and motivations must somehow become imbedded in the consciousness of a sufficiently large number of people for development to take place. It is a necessary if not a sufficient condition. Furthermore, in addition to proper motivations, we must have the proper externally determined incentives, that is, there must be either profit-making or income-earning opportunities available. But are these sufficient?

The fact that profit-making opportunities and profit-seeking individuals exist does *not* imply that their combination will yield economic growth. The reason for this is that there are two types of profit-making or income-earning opportunities, and the entrepreneur or wage earner is quite indifferent in his choice between them. *What may be a source of income creation for the individual need not be a means of income creation as seen by the community at large.* To put the matter in the language of Von Neumann's and Morgenstern's *Theory of Games:* There are zero-sum games and non-zero-sum games. In either type of game, solutions will permit gains or profits to some players. A player is interested only in the possible winnings. He does not particularly care whether he plays in a zero-sum or positive-sum game. Indeed, individual abilities, proclivities, and environment may be such that they incline him toward the zero-sum game although in either case he is equally keen on the prize.

Translating this notion into the economic environment makes it clear that enterprising individuals can make money either by "exploiting" their fellowmen or by the creation and marshaling of resources in more productive combinations. The opportunities for "exploitation," the "zero-sum enterprise," may in many instances be more congenial and accessible than the second alternative and may even be socially more acceptable. In the zero-sum enterprise there is only a distributive effect. Profit or income is shifted from some individuals in the economy to the fortunate entrepreneurs, or from some entrepreneurs to others. In productive creation of resources there need not be, although there may be, a distributive effect. There is a net gain in national income, and it may be shared by everyone. Or, in any event, no one need lose. Quite clearly it is the second type of activity that is conducive to economic growth, and not the "zero-sum game." But what assurance can we have that the economic opportunities created will be of the positive-national-income-gain type?

This aspect of the problem is often considered, in somewhat different terminology, in connection with the problem of inflation. Thus Bernstein and Patel[3] point out that continuous inflation usually induces the wrong kind of investment. They distinguish between investment in *holding* wealth and investment in *using* it. Using wealth increases the demand for labor as well as the supply of consumption goods. However, during inflation quick profits and increases in capital values induce *holding* wealth in the form of certain types of construction, inventories, etc. Furthermore, Bernstein and Patel argue that when large credits are extended by banks it cannot be assumed that the volume of investment is increased accordingly. Investment financed through bank credit is offset by a decrease in investment financed from savings of the non-profit receiving group; when prices rise, the real income of some groups fall, and these attempt to maintain consumption by reducing current savings.[4]

But the problem is much more pervasive and general than these views would indicate. It is not limited to attempts to *use* inflation as a means of obtaining necessary investment funds. Considering the matter on a broader level, we shall refer to the incentives to *hold* wealth and to engage in other profitable activities that do not increase national output as the *zero-sum incentives*. Similarly, we shall refer to incentives to engage in activities that lead to increases in aggregate output as *positive-sum incentives*. It is the positive-sum incentives that have to be engendered by the economic environment for economic growth and development to take place. But what is needed is much more than just the initial creation of positive-sum incentives.

To see a little more deeply into the nature of the problem, let us look at some probable relationships between incentives and growth. First, it is likely that backward economies are such that at the outset the positive-sum incentives have a tendency to degenerate and disappear, other things being equal. Second, positive-sum incentives often lead to activities that stimulate zero-sum incentives. Thus, a very special set of conditions must be created to obtain an environment in which we can count on the *persistence* of positive-sum incentives.

We now consider these assertions in some detail. In a backward economy where there is little experience with industry, it is common

[3] F. M. Bernstein and I. G. Patel, "Inflation in Relation to Economic Development," *International Monetary Fund,* Staff Papers, Vol. II, No. 3 (November 1952), pp. 383 ff.

[4] *Ibid.,* p. 376.

that a great deal of prestige is attached to the ownership (and, therefore, *holding*) of land. The environment is one in which behavior is traditional and social approval is significant. The new is more likely to be disapproved of than the known and the certain. Although there is unquestionably some risk involved in the ownership of land it is a known risk, not in the sense that it can be calculated specifically but in the sense that it is the type of risk with which enterprisers are very familiar. Similarly, although to a somewhat lesser extent, the risk involved in the purchase and sale of goods and in the building-up of inventories is a familiar risk.

Additional factors help to fill out the picture. One is liquidity, and the other is the possibility of monopoly gains. Both land and inventories of familiar commodities are likely to be the sort of goods that is either readily salable or on which it is quite easy to raise money. There is no long and uncertain gestation period. Fellner[5] makes the point that the uncertainty in industry is a particular type of uncertainty that differs from the risk involved in ordinary commercial transactions. Not only is the return, as such, uncertain, but it takes a considerable period of time before the extent of the uncertainty can be gauged. In other words, until the plant is built, goods produced, some market and production experience obtained, and some knowledge as to how consumers are likely to react to the commodity obtained, no estimate of the risk can be made. This matter may be put another way: in the commercial[6] and usual zero-sum sort of enterprises, there is only a trading risk that is involved; in the industrial enterprises there is a combined *exploration* and trading risk involved.

In view of what has been said, what does it take to maintain positive-sum incentives? This is, obviously, a difficult question to answer. But, speculating upon the matter, we, it would seem, have to compare the deterrent effects of the various types of uncertainty with the anticipated gains from the positive-sum activities. Since economic growth *usually* involves providing the labor force not only with more but also with different types of capital goods, it therefore involves engaging in new types of enterprise and new types of work. The nature of the gains is largely unknown since it is difficult to assess and compound the

[5] William Fellner, "Individual Investment Projects in Growing Economies," an unpublished paper submitted to the Center of International Studies, S.S.R.C. Conference on Economic Growth, October 15, 16, 17, 1954, pp. 8 ff.

[6] This is not to suggest, by any means, that all commercial ventures are of the zero-sum type. Far from it. But neither is there any reason to believe that, in the absence of the never-realized conditions of perfect competition, the profits of commercial ventures reflect equivalent increases in national output.

exploration risks, production risks, and trading risks that may be involved. Thus the magnitudes of the expected gains must be high enough to overcome the feelings of risk and still appear superior to the familiar alternative opportunities in zero-sum activities. This last condition is most likely to hold in an atmosphere in which there is a general availability of complementary industries, of continued sources of raw material supply, and of a skilled labor force. It probably also involves the creation of an atmosphere of growth in order to induce the production of goods for an expanding market.

It is also likely that the positive-sum incentives, *in the absence of an atmosphere of considerable growth,* have within them the seeds of their own degeneracy, as well as seeds that tend to generate zero-sum incentives. A few examples of each type should illuminate the argument. If the enterprise is not successful it establishes bad precedents and increases the aversion to this type of risk. If it is successful, then for any specific enterprise, there is likely to be a saturation of the market at some point unless a high rate of general economic growth is maintained. If it is successful it will stimulate followers into the industry,[7] which, in turn, increases output and reduces profit margins and, therefore, the incentive to growth. On the other hand, the initial stimulus to engage in this positive-sum activity may have been achieved by the entrepreneurs having obtained monopoly rights and privileges of some sort. But for such a monopoly position to be exploited, a restriction of output and the diminution of incentives of this type are involved. Not only on the entrepreneurial side but also on the labor side of the picture are degenerative practices likely to come into being. The usual activities of this sort come under the heading of featherbedding, that is, the development of regulations favoring the maintenance of current methods of production rather than the development of new and superior ones. Once the new becomes familiar, the familiar becomes traditional. Broadly speaking, tradition, aversion to risk, and the desire to do things the way they have always been done are likely to have their degenerative effects on the positive-sum incentives.

Of probably even greater importance are the zero-sum incentives stimulated by the temporary success of the positive-sum incentives. Here, again, the examples are of a familiar nature. The credit expansion generated by the initial growth may have an inflationary effect, which, in turn, is conducive to the appearance of zero-sum incentives.

The very success of the positive-sum incentives, by their nature,

[7] On this point Schumpeter's famous analysis of this aspect of the development process immediately comes to mind. See Joseph A. Schumpeter, *The Theory of Economic Development,* Cambridge, Harvard University Press, 1951, Chapter VI.

sets in motion motivations, activities, and practices conducive to zero-sum activities. As the positive-sum incentives become effective and are exploited, this exploitation manifests itself in increased price competition, which stimulates activities of a monopolistic or price-fixing nature. Similarly, some of the manifestations of economic growth appear to threaten workers with technological unemployment, which in turn stimulates the adoption of policies that inhibit further technological change. In summary, the success of the positive-sum investments that engender economic changes enables the skilled and fortunate enterpriser and laborer to attain a position of profit which is threatened by equally skilled followers, and as a result creating the stimulus to turn positions of temporary profits into positions of permanent privilege.

Much of what we have said may appear to go counter to received theory. According to the usual textbook theory, all trading activities result in mutual gain and, hence, in gains to the national product. If this is the case, how, then, can we have our so-called zero-sum activities? First, we are concerned with the disposition of scarce entrepreneurial energies and entrepreneurial resources. Second, some activities, or the results of activities, may be of such a nature that there are great disparities between the valuation of individual and social gains from them. The social gains may be zero while the individual gains are positive.

The main point is that neither the existence of a stock of entrepreneurial ability and energy, as it were, nor the existence of opportunities to engage in activities that lead to growth is in itself sufficient to promote growth. How entrepreneurs utilize their capacities will surely depend on the incentives to which they respond. Note that the potential or actual entrepreneurs may spend their time and energy in any of the following ways that may directly or indirectly increase the personal wealth and income of some of them but which involve activities that add little or nothing to the productive capacity of the economy. (1) They may spend their time in *non-trading* activities in order to secure for their interests a greater monopolistic position, increased political power, more prestige, etc. Such activities can conceivably lead to greater financial gains for some of them than the alternative of engaging in investment activities that lead to increases in national product.[8] (2) They may engage in *trading* activities that may secure for some of them a greater monopolistic position or simply what they believe to be better ways in which to hold their wealth so that such activities will not increase aggregate resources in any way. (3) They may use their talents and

[8] See Jean Marchal, "The Construction of a New Theory of Profit," *American Economic Review*, Vol. XLI, No. 4, September 1951, pp. 549–565.

marshal wealth in order to engage in speculative trading which, in turn, need not increase aggregate resources or aggregate income. Such activities, even when they do not use up savings, do waste rare entrepreneurial resources. (4) Finally they may engage in activities that do use up net savings, but the investments involved are in enterprises of such a nature that their "social value" is either zero, or their social value is very much lower than their private value.

Let us suppose that we have an economy in which there is no growth. Does this imply the absence of entrepreneurial activities? Certainly not. But the entrepreneurial activities that take place under these circumstances will probably be largely of the zero-sum kind. Each enterprising individual can still engage in business activities the purpose of which is to gain for that individual a financial advantage at the expense of another. There can be little doubt about the existence of such activities in the real world. Furthermore, where the country has a long history of comparative stagnation such activities will be the predominant ones with which the entrepreneurial class has any experience; hence, the often-found lack of familiarity with the positive-sum activities and the traditional resistance to them.

Although there may be some scope for positive-sum activities even in the absence of net growth, in order to counterbalance activities that are destructive of the existing stock of capital, we would certainly expect the sphere of such positive-sum activities to be a highly restrictive one. Only under conditions of growth can there be much scope for positive-sum activities. Furthermore, considering the relative unfamiliarity with industrial investment, the different nature of the risk that is involved, the longer period of gestation, etc., we would expect that only with a fairly rapid rate of expansion, under which even the inexperienced and awkward entrepreneurs can make their anticipated gains, can we have a situation in which the initial positive-sum incentives neither degenerate nor stimulate a predominance of zero-sum incentives.

But it may appear that our use of the notion of zero-sum investment activities is really an illusion—that, from the point of view of the community as a whole, they are not really investment activities at all but merely transfers of liquidity from some holders to others. For, it may be argued, if the rentier chooses to purchase land rather than to build factories, the liquidity position of the seller of the land increases to the same extent, and he, in turn, is in a position to invest. To the extent that there are real savings there must be real investment. Otherwise all that has occurred is a shift in the distribution of assets among the members of the community, and nothing more. Thus, there is no zero-sum investment as seen by the community. But this is not really the case because we are here being misled by Keynesian-type definitions which do not make the appropriate distinctions for development problems.

The point is that not all assets are real income creating. Objects that have economic value as such, and that bear a real cost to the economy, since they require resources that could be used elsewhere, do not necessarily add to productive capacity. For example, precious metals and jewels fall into this category, and investment in such objects is not necessarily income creating. Similarly, investment in old masters, monuments, unnecessarily luxurious buildings or administration facilities *may* fall into this category.[9] A more obvious and universal example is investment in inventories or other objects for speculative or precautionary purposes. A certain minimum inventory may be needed for production, but there is surely a surplus that adds nothing to productive capacity. Examples of this type can be found without much difficulty.

On the whole the analysis suggests, in a somewhat impressionistic way, that the rate of economic expansion must appear to be sufficiently rapid so that the newly created positive-sum investment opportunities are more significant than the continuously generated zero-sum incentives. In order to delve a little more deeply into this hypothesis and related ones, we turn to consider in some detail those agencies that respond to and are responsible for the creation of positive-sum opportunities and activities; mostly we shall concentrate on those activities that come under the rubrics of entrepreneurship, inventions and innovations, and the creation of skills.

---

[9] In essence it depends on how we define "investment" for development purposes and whether or not we accept unrestricted consumer's sovereignty as the sole criterion of valuation. If we assume that the social objective is economic development, it may be reasonable to define investment as the creation of assets that add to the productive capacity of the economy, in the sense that these assets increase the economy's ability to provide goods and services for the community at large. If, in addition, we add the value judgment that commodities whose only functions are that they serve as unusual luxuries for a small, wealthy group do not count as part of the "social income," then the creation of durable consumers' goods that fall into this category would not be considered investment. Thus, the construction of a Taj Mahal, or other private monuments, would not be looked upon as acts of investment. Of course people may quite rightly differ about the propriety of the criterion of welfare employed. Such welfare judgments are arbitrary. But we may easily conceive of welfare functions, whether or not we accept them, that would discriminate against unusual luxuries for a small group at a time when the country as a whole was striving to escape from a low income equilibrium. The social valuation of an act of investment may be different from its private valuation.

Growth Agents and Growth Activities

The predominantly visible aspects of the growth process are those activities that seem to lead most directly to economic growth, primarily the activities that result in new capital goods. The building of factories, the erection of a transportation system, the digging of canals and irrigation ditches, the construction of dams, the creation of systems of communication, etc., are activities of this nature. It seems natural to have such activities in mind when we think of economic development. But there are other activities that often do not come under the heading of investment that may be even more important. We have in mind those activities that lead directly or indirectly to the expansion of what we shall call the growth agents, namely, the expansion of those human faculties, traits, and capacities that increase the potential growth-promoting activities that can be derived from the population.

First, we must distinguish between growth agents and growth activities. By growth agents we mean those individuals who have the capacities to carry out growth-contributing activities. The stock that we are interested in here is not the number of people involved but the quantum of capacities. There probably is not a name for every type of person capable of growth-contributing activities of some sort, but we have in mind such categories as the entrepreneur, the investor, the discoverer, the teacher of new skills, the disseminator of useful ideas, the saver, etc. Some related growth-contributing activities are the ferreting out of new investment opportunities, the invention of new production processes and techniques, the discovery of new resources and commodities, the teaching and learning of skills, the spreading of ideas, and, finally, the important act of saving, that indispensable act, passive though it may often appear to be, of releasing resources from current consumption to make them available for the construction of capital goods.

To obtain an adequate view of the growth process, we cannot assume that the stock of growth agents (the stock of capacities that enable people to engage in growth-promoting activities) is fixed.

In other words, we must consider in our theory not only the direct growth activities, such as savings and investment, but also the less direct activities that lead to an expansion of the growth agents, activities that result in increases in the stock of entrepreneurial abilities, in the propensity to invent and innovate, in the increase in work skills and managerial capacities, etc. The discussion that follows on entrepreneurship, innovations, and skills and their probable relation to incentives and the rate of growth is stimulated by a conviction that when we do obtain a really good understanding of the economic growth process, a key part of that understanding will be a knowledge of the connection between these four factors: the expansion of growth agents, the growth activities, the resulting rate of growth, and the incentives generated by the growth process.

Entrepreneurship

Growth can be generated when the economy is subjected to a stimulant of some sort. The stimulant will generate a set of consequences which can be looked upon as a change in the matrix of economic values, such as incomes, demands, prices, etc. The consequences of the stimulant generate entrepreneurial activities; therefore, we have to examine what is meant by entrepreneurship and the nature of entrepreneurial activities.

1. Requisites of an entrepreneur. Entrepreneurship is a quality that inheres in some members of the population. Certain members of the population will possess characteristics that will enable them to carry out "entrepreneurial activities." We can list the characteristics or capacities that an entrepreneur must possess. The entrepreneur must:

(*a*) have the ability to discover investment opportunities, and/or the ability to seek information the analysis of which can lead to the discovery of investment opportunities;

(*b*) have access to resources and the capacity to marshal whatever resources are necessary for the venture so that the requisite factors of production can be obtained;

(*c*) and/or have the ability to "promote" the venture, that is, sell the venture to others who may be interested in investing;

(*d*) have the ability to organize the enterprise, that is, purchase the factors and get operations started, as well as retain or transfer into competent hands the ultimate responsibility for the continued coordination of the operations. Anyone possessing these qualities can be said to be an entrepreneur.[10] Anyone having only some of these

[10] Our definition of entrepreneurship may appear to be a little broader than that employed by Schumpeter. Schumpeter limits entrepreneurship to the act of combining resources in *new* combinations. He argues that, "As a rule the new combinations must draw the necessary means of production from some old combinations . . . . we shall assume that they *always* do so, in order to put in bold relief what we hold to be the essential contour line. The carrying out of new combinations means, therefore, simply the different employment of the economic system's existing supplies of productive means . . . ." (*The Theory of Economic Development,* p. 68.) Thus Schumpeter seems to assume that the resources remain fixed. This is an assumption that we find untenable for our purposes. Although we agree that a considerable amount of the type of entrepreneurial activity that goes with growth will be of the "new combinations" kind, there is no need to restrict entrepreneurial activities to this variety if we permit the simultaneous expansion of the factors of production.

qualities may, of course, combine with others to carry out entrepreneurial acts.[11]

2. *Meaning of the growth of entrepreneurship.* If we speak of a lack of entrepreneurship, it must be a capacity that has a size of some sort. We must be able to visualize some way of measuring it, at least in principle, otherwise we cannot tell whether it has grown or diminished.

A first thought might be to measure the amount of entrepreneurship by the number of people possessing the requisite qualities. But a moment's reflection would indicate that this would be misleading. A large number of people who can each marshal a few dollars is surely no more significant than a single person who has access to more than all of them combined. Any measure must attach to each a weight that reflects the capacity of that individual entrepreneur.

A more reasonable measure would appear to be the amount of money (or value of resources) that can be marshaled for entrepreneurial activities. We could sum the real values of the amount of money that each entrepreneur could obtain and have a notion of the magnitude of entrepreneurship. But this amount would depend on the existence of incentives or entrepreneurial opportunities. In the absence of investment opportunities there would be no funds forthcoming regardless of the entrepreneurial capacities of the people. Therefore, the measure would have to be in terms of the number of dollars that the entrepreneurial group could gather on the assumption of a given set of available investment opportunities. This is similar to the notion of the demand for a commodity on the basis of a stipulated or given income. Actual estimates of this kind would, of course, be exceedingly difficult or nearly impossible to make, but, conceptually, it is a measurable notion. At the very least it is not meaningless to speak of a larger, as against a smaller, amount of entrepreneurship.

3. *The growth of the entrepreneurial group.* We can visualize entrepreneurship growing via (*a*) the expansion of the number of people

---

[11] Although entrepreneurship is an activity that we usually visualize taking place in a capitalistic environment, this need not be the case. Entrepreneurial activities are needed in other than purely or even partially capitalistic economies. In a growing socialist economy some people would have to carry out what are essentially entrepreneurial activities; some people would have to determine the location of investment, that is, discover investment opportunities; some people will have to "sell" new ventures to the appropriate "planning board" or "commissars"; some will have to marshal the resources in order to start the venture; and so on. Of course the system of rewards for entrepreneurial activities might be quite different, but the necessity for the activities, and for people with the capacities to carry out such activities, would remain nevertheless.

possessing the requisites as well as (*b*) an increase in the capacities of those already members of the group.

At any time some will enter the entrepreneurial group through the acquisition of the appropriate capacities and desires, while others will leave the group through death, retirement, and the shift to other activities. The acquisition of the requisites probably depends on a combination of innate ability, training, motivation, and access to opportunities. In the absence of other evidence we may assume the distribution of innate capacities to be more or less constant regardless of income. To the extent that training can help, the amount of entrepreneurial capacities probably depends more on the level of income, given the proper motivation, than any other factor. But access to opportunities are more likely to depend on the rate of economic expansion, that is, on the rate of growth of per capita income.

Access to opportunities depends on the social and economic position of a person as well as on the extent of social and economic mobility. Imagine, for a moment, a complete absence of economic and social mobility. In that case we would expect that the potential entrepreneurs would come from the upper rather than the lower income groups. But fertility rates in upper income groups are so low that upper income groups often do not replace themselves, or their relative rates of growth are considerably lower than those of the lower income groups. This is simply part of the familiar observation that as one goes down the income scale, family size is usually larger. Hence, on the basis of fixed groupings determined by birth, we would expect the proportion of the population having access to opportunities conducive to the development of entrepreneurship to decline in time. If the proportion of people having access to such opportunities is to rise, it must be because of the existence of some social and economic mobility. But the *growth* of social and economic mobility depends not on the income level but on the extent of economic expansion, that is, on the rate of per capita income growth.

The reasonableness of this proposition may be clearer if we look at the matter in the following light: Are the barriers to social and economic climbing most likely to be relaxed under conditions of declining, constant, slowly rising, or rapidly rising per capita income growth? Surely there is a greater chance of barriers being lowered when everything appears to be expanding, when scarcities in certain capacities become apparent, when the threat to established economic positions appears to be diminished due to an apparent ampleness of opportunities rather than when the reverse conditions hold—in other words, when per capita income is growing rather than declining. Conversely, entry will be much more closely guarded if incomes are constant and the fierceness of the struggle for economic position and privilege is undiminished. In sum, the numbers of people with access to opportunities allowing them to acquire the entrepreneurial requisites are surely larger, the greater the rate of per capita income growth.

The drive of some people to acquire the necessary capacities and to engage in entrepreneurial activities will depend on the rewards for such activities, on the interest in such rewards, and on the disappearance of alternative endeavors. The greater the rewards, the greater the number that will enter the entrepreneurial group. Of course, the interest in such financial rewards will depend on the attitudes of the community at the outset. Where the attitudes are still of a traditional nature and the most highly prized rewards are non-economic, a shift in attitudes toward economic aspirations will help to expand the numbers entering this group. Usually the push is more effective than the pull. Thus the drying up of alternative social and economic opportunities either in agriculture, civil service, or in other non-entrepreneurial categories would help. The importance of this last point is made evident by the frequent observation that in backward economies entrepreneurial activities are engaged in temporarily only as a means to amass sufficient wealth so that the person involved can purchase land, and possibly a title or a sinecure, in order to become one of the landed aristocracy. The expansion of social and economic opportunities may be a two-way sword. It will permit and induce some to enter the enterpreneurial class, but at the same time it may enable valuable members of the entrepreneurial group to leave in pursuit of more highly valued non-economic rewards.

An equally significant way in which entrepreneurship can expand is through the increase in the capacities of those already in the entrepreneurial group. In part this is likely to be a self-accelerating process. A sustained experience of reasonably favorable outcomes to entrepreneurial activities will have this effect. Necessary funds certainly become more accessible as a result of entrepreneurial success, not only because the entrepreneur's own funds are likely to become more ample as a consequence of success, but also because both private and institutional savers are more likely to entrust their funds to such entrepreneurs. Also, the ability to ferret out investment opportunities is clearly likely to increase with experience. Similarly, the appropriate motivations are likely to be enhanced by successful experience, although, as already mentioned, too successful an experience may lead to a desire for other than economic rewards. Finally, experience is also a factor that will increase one's ability to promote and organize entrepreneurial ventures.

We have attempted to indicate the ways in which the quality we call entrepreneurship *can* expand. We must now proceed to consider two very closely related questions, namely, how investment opportunities are created, and what determines the rate of entrepreneurial expansion.

4. The creation of investment opportunities. The expansion of entrepreneurship is the demand side of the investment activities picture. On the other side we have the supply of entrepreneurial opportunities.

In conventional economic analysis an investment opportunity exists wherever the internal rate of return implied by the discounted net revenue stream is greater than the interest rate. But why should such situations arise? There are several possibilities, prominent among which are: (*a*) a change in the relative availability of factors, (*b*) shifts in demands for final goods, and (*c*) monetary changes. For example, inventions and discoveries of new production techniques, resources, or products, greatly emphasized by some writers, manifest themselves in either the first or second possibility just mentioned. Anything that contributes to a change in these three factors contributes to the creation or drying-up of investment opportunities. Economic entrepreneurial opportunities are created by changes in the supply of the factors and the consequent changes in factor prices. The new factor prices change the relationship between demand prices and costs, and create situations in which prospective profits change accordingly. These changes occur not only as a result of stimulants but also as a natural consequence of day-to-day economic processes. Among such day-to-day events are the following: (1) Period by period there are new savings which can have the effect of lowering interest rates and creating investment opportunities. (2) Similarly, the period-by-period population growth adds to the supply of labor and, therefore, changes the price of labor. (3) Also the day-to-day accretion of knowledge, as well as discoveries, enables the entrepreneur to experiment with new modes of production.

Even if factor prices remain constant, increases in the demand for products create new investment opportunities. Among the day-to-day processes that change the demand are population growth and income growth due to the investments of the past coming to fruition. If the rate of aggregate income growth is no larger than the rate of population growth, the new investment opportunities created may permit an expansion only up to, or less than, the amount necessary to absorb the growing labor force. Any change in the demand per capita would probably require per capita income growth. Changes in the propensity to consume are more likely, at first, to come about through exogenous means via changes in tastes as a result of contacts with foreign standards of consumption.

Monetary and fiscal changes brought about through the intervention of government can affect a number of factors such as the interest rate, the propensity to save, and available income (that is, income after taxes). A great portion of standard economic literature is concerned with the analysis of just such problems making it unnecessary for us to go into detail here on this matter.

Of course, we need not begin with a state of equilibrium. It would unquestionably be more realistic to assume that a disequilibrium state exists at any time, and that as a consequence there are usually some investment opportunities available, *if they but be discerned.* The usual situation is such that there are always *some* industries in which price is above long-run marginal costs, although it is possible that on balance, in periods of stagnation, there are probably more industries in which retrenchment is taking place. However, it is important to note that one of the reasons for disequilibrium may be a lack of entrepreneurial perceptiveness of opportunities that do exist.

5. The determinants of the growth of entrepreneurship. What combination of factors can explain the rate of growth of entrepreneurship? With respect to this question we formulate a simple hypothesis.

From any time point the growth of entrepreneurship will be conditioned by the attitudes of the people toward entrepreneurial activities at the outset plus the spectrum of existing opportunities. But given these, we might posit the following relationship: The growth of entrepreneurship depends on (*a*) the *size* of the entrepreneurial group, (*b*) the level of per capita income, and (*c*) the rate of growth in per capita income. There may be some lags in the reactions, but on the whole these are the major factors. The size of the entrepreneurial group determines the extent of the contacts and the degree of familiarity that potential entrepreneurs can have with members of the entrepreneurial group. Size may be some indication in determining the importance and prestige of the group in the community at large, and it may determine the extent of the potential "bandwagon effect" as the group grows. To the extent that behavior is imitative, we can say that the more people there are to imitate, the greater the growth. The attraction of potential entrepreneurs toward a group, where the members of the group are successful, will depend, in part, on its size. The lower the level of per capita income, the smaller the supply of entrepreneurship in response to the demand that may exist. At low per capita income levels people cannot afford to take the time to acquire the necessary skills to become potential entrepreneurs. They cannot be relieved from the day-to-day activities necessary in earning a livelihood and, therefore, cannot engage in the exploratory and promotional activities that go with entrepreneurship.

Nor can they spend much time in the acquisition of entrepreneurial skills since in the early stages such activities carry few rewards and involve mostly costs. But since a low level of per capita output implies the utilization of primitive techniques, one would think that there are greater opportunities for entrepreneurship in the form of borrowing and introducing superior techniques. Obviously, at higher levels of per capita output there is less technique to be borrowed. But at low levels the perceptiveness of entrepreneurs to such possibilities may be limited since their perceptiveness is conditioned by their long experience of the traditional and customary.

More significant is the fact that low incomes are accompanied by low wages, and under such circumstances primitive techniques appear to be the more profitable.

A most significant factor in determining growth in entrepreneurship is the *rate* of growth in per capita income. For it is the fact of experiencing income growth that will determine the expectations of entrepreneurs and potential entrepreneurs. Growing per capita income is likely to permit sufficiently larger profit margins so that even inexperienced entrepreneurs are rewarded and early errors covered up. A continuing state of income growth enables the inexperienced to become experienced, the experienced to continue in their field and to grow in perceptiveness and technique, and tends to create a situation in which entrepreneurship becomes profitable and attractive. Furthermore, as entrepreneurship continues to be profitable the entrepreneurial group is likely to grow in power and prestige.

Underlying the theme of the last paragraph is an implicit assumption that is significant. The assumption is that as income per head grows, the payment to other factors does not rise as rapidly as the payment to entrepreneurship, and that the greater the rate of income growth the greater is the extent to which this is likely to be true. What can account for such a lag? In the first place, the entrepreneur, at least in the capitalistic, institutional setting, is the residual claimant to the income of the enterprise. His job, essentially, is to buy future outputs at current rates. Thus labor, funds, capital goods, etc., are purchased for future delivery at current prices. It takes time before contracts can be renegotiated on better terms. As incomes grow, other claimants will get their increased return only gradually and not so rapidly as the growth in income. For example, consider the matter of rent recipients. The entity rented may be for a year, and the landlord cannot renegotiate until that time. Such a state is enforceable under conditions of growth because most incomes appear to be rising. It is likely that there will be some inertia in worrying about *relative rates* of improvement as long as the real conditions of those concerned appear to be getting better.

Another way of looking at the matter is to say that during per capita income expansion, prices in the expanding industries are likely to be above marginal costs. This last is due to the fact that in the real world the act of investment takes considerable time. During the expansion period the expansion of industry cannot occur as rapidly as opportunities appear. There is always a gap between the discernment of the opportunity, the act of investment, and the consequent sale of commodities. As a result, in the absence of forecasting errors, supply does not quite catch up with demand. Price is therefore above marginal cost.

Consider for a moment the limiting case in which aggregate income does not change. Under such circumstances there may be no need for entrepreneurship. All that is required is that the managers repeat their performances period after period. There may, however, be a need for potential entrepreneurs as an equilibrating force. Where managers mismanage, entrepreneurs must be there to seize the entrepreneurial opportunity created. But the size of the entrepreneurial group need not grow in such a state.

The more interesting case is the one in which both labor and capital are expanding at such rates that the consequence is a constant per capita income. Will the simultaneous, proportionate growth of capital, population, labor, and the expansion of output require growth in entrepreneurship? Unlike other factors that may be visualized performing some routinized type of activity or providing some routinized service, entrepreneurship is in part a unique factor, one that carrries out exploratory and promotional capacities. To the extent that any activity becomes routine, it need not be explored and promoted. Since the major function of entrepreneurship, from the standpoint of development, is to discover and organize the needs and means for expansion, an almost constant amount of entrepreneurial capacity *will be sufficient* to provide for a steady rate of expansion. To the extent that the pattern and the rate of expansion are of a similar and routinized type, period after period, to that extent the exploratory and promotional activities will not be needed after a while. Indeed, we may expect some of the entrepreneurial capacities to atrophy in the steady routinized expanding state. Routine eliminates the need for entrepreneurship. Therefore, to stimulate the steady expansion of entrepreneurship sustained per capita income growth is probably required.

6. Growth and contribution of entrepreneurship. How can an entrepreneurial class be fostered and made to grow? Clearly, the economic environment must provide a stimulus to develop in men the characteristics of this group. In order to promote growth, the entrepreneur must often be, to use Schumpeter's definition, an individual who creates new combinations of the factors (or an individual who introduces new commodities which, of course, implies new combinations of the factors). Not all stimulants are favorable to the creation of new combinations of the factors or to the introduction of new commodities. For example, a stimulant like an invention, or the discovery of new resources, will obviously be more favorable to the creation of new combinations than, say, a good harvest. Thus the initial stimulant or stimulants must generate some obvious opportunities for new combinations. Also, new combinations involve new risks, unfamiliar risks, and hence the ensuing growth process must foster attitudes favorable to risk taking. What does this entail? *The initial entrepreneurs must have a more than satisfactory experience.* This means that the economic environment must be such that, on the average, the risks taken pay off better than anticipated. This obviously would serve as a stimulus to the spread of this particular type of risk taking. At the same time an environment is created in which risks can be more readily shared. As the nature of the risks becomes known, familiar institutional arrangements can be fostered that permit the sharing of the risk on a wider basis. Also, the nature of the stimulants and the growth processes that ensue must create an environment in which there are penalties for not taking risks. This will usually come about, directly or indirectly, through the force of competition. The better than favorable experiences can have two effects. First, they create a demand for complementary industries and, hence, opportunities for new but related combinations. This last might be looked upon as the "pull" effect to new combinations. Second, they displace existing combinations, or existing processes and modes for producing commodities. And this may be looked upon as the "push" into new combinations and risk taking. A penalty is created via the competitive advantage of the lower cost of production of the risk takers so that risk taking becomes a necessary way of economic life for the capital-owning portion of the community. Except for the highly adventurous, the "push" is usually a more compelling stimulus to action than the "pull." Thus, unless there is a penalty for not taking risks, the majority of investors will prefer the peaceful existence of the non-risk taker.

The lack of prestige attached to entrepreneurial and trading activities often found in backward economies is unquestionably an obstacle to growth. Thus the rate of growth of the new entrepreneurial class must be sufficiently rapid and its success, power, and importance sufficiently evident, so that entrepreneurship, in some form or other, becomes an "honorific" mode of life in men's minds. It appears that economic growth must displace not only existing combinations of the factors but also existing values. Since it is unlikely that such long-established values can be transformed by almost imperceptible gradual changes, this last may also imply a rather rapid tempo of change.

To further clarify these ideas and to illustrate them graphically, we have to concentrate on the relationship between the features that are conducive to the development of an entrepreneurial class and the rate of growth of real income per head. To generate attitudes favorable to growth, and to obtain a better-than-anticipated experience with respect to the results of risk taking, it is necessary that the actual rate of growth be better than that implied by anticipations. This implies, roughly speaking, that the direct and indirect *contribution* of additional entrepreneurial activities to growth must be at least as large as the anticipated rate of growth that called forth the additional entrepreneurial efforts.

The contribution of entrepreneurship depends on the stock of entrepreneurship and the available entrepreneurial opportunities. The interaction of the two determines the amount of entrepreneurial activity that takes place. Every successful *positive-sum* entrepreneurial act yields real income which is to be divided among the factors of production. We now compare the income attributed to the entrepreneurial activity with what those factors, including entrepreneurship, would have earned had no entrepreneurial act taken place. The difference yields the contribution to national income for the period of that particular entrepreneurial act. By aggregating the contributions of all the entrepreneurial acts, we obtain the contribution of entrepreneurship to national income. Dividing this last sum by the population, we obtain the contribution of entrepreneurship to per capita income.

But it may be argued that entrepreneurs do not base their decisions on anticipated per capita income growth. Indeed, for the pursuit of their activities they need have no notion as to what it is at any time. For any entrepreneurial opportunity they need be concerned only with the anticipated reward for engaging in the activities implied by the opportunity. Thus, for every entrepreneurial opportunity we visualize the entrepreneur with a specific profit expectation, or some notion of a profit range that would lead him to act as if he had the equivalent specific expectation. It is the size of the anticipated profit that determines whether or not he will engage in the entrepreneurial activity involved. But how is this related to our notion that the amount of entrepreneurial activity and the expansion of entrepreneurship somehow depends on the "anticipated growth in per capita income"?

Consider this: (*a*) Every profit anticipation that induces a given entrepreneurial act (one that does not displace an existing entrepreneurial activity) implies a vision on the part of the entrepreneur of an entrepreneurial opportunity. (*b*) For such an opportunity to be created, the expansion of the economy is necessary, to some extent. (*c*) For the sum total of such opportunities to be created, the expansion of the economy (and the population) is necessary, to a certain extent, which in turn implies a certain per capita income growth for that period. Thus every set of visualized investment opportunities implies a certain necessary income growth for them to materialize, that is, it implies what we have called a certain "anticipated per capita income." Since we can visualize alternative sets of possible investment opportunities, we also visualize the alternative rates of per capita income growth necessary to bring them about.

The actual contribution of entrepreneurship may or *may not* create the entrepreneurial opportunities on which the entrepreneurial activities are based. There is no reason why the sum of the entrepreneurial activities should of necessity lead to an economic state that creates the opportunities visualized in the anticipations. The created opportunities may be more than anticipated and of a more favorable nature, or less than anticipated. The reason is that each entrepreneur cannot foresee, in assessing an opportunity, the simultaneous activities of all other entrepreneurs, the consequences of such simultaneous activities, or the expansion of the other factors of production. Each assessment of an opportunity, and the anticipation that arises therefrom, implies a guess about the availability of other factors, and the creation of demand for the commodity through simultaneous income-creating activities in other parts of the economy. The lower the aggregate anticipations, the less likely it is that the complementary activities will take place which were implied in these anticipations. For fairly high anticipations the net aggregate advantages of all the complementary activities that take place will probably be greater than anticipated. But for exceedingly high anticipations, unforeseen "bottlenecks" are likely to arise. Competition for the scarce factors of production may eventually lead to costs higher than planned, and as a consequence high anticipations may be disappointed. These broad ideas are illustrated in the diagrams that follow.

In figure 9–1 the ordinate represents the rate of growth of anticipated income per head for the period. The abscissa represents the rate of expansion of the stock of entrepreneurship in terms of its capacity to yield increases in income per head, that is, in terms of the contribution of the addition to the stock of entrepreneurial capacities. The curve marked *G*, the entrepreneurial expansion curve, represents the alternate increases in entrepreneurship above the initial level measured in terms of the rate of growth in per capita income resulting from the expansion of entrepreneurial capacities.

The growth agent expansion curve is in three parts. *LM* is the section where the contribution to income resulting from the expansion of entrepreneurship is smaller than the anticipations upon which their expansion depends. *MN* is the section in which the contribution of entrepreneurship is greater than the anticipated rate of growth in incomes. *NP* represents the section where the relationship is again reversed. The reasonableness of this last section of the curve is evident if we consider that there must be some maximum contribution that the expansion of

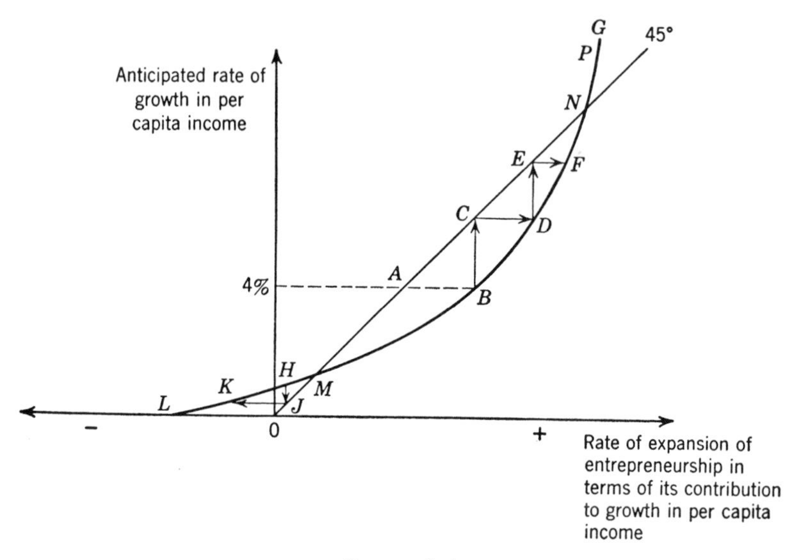

FIGURE 9–1

the entrepreneurial capacities could make. To take an extreme case, if in response to exceptional anticipations *everyone* attempted to become an entrepreneur, the net result would be chaos rather than growth.

The really interesting sections are *LM* and *MN*. Why should the contribution of entrepreneurship sometimes be smaller than anticipated, while at other times it is larger than anticipated? Consider first section *MN*. Suppose that a 4 per cent anticipated growth rate falls within *MN*. This is a reasonably substantial rate of growth. Why such a high anticipated growth rate may stimulate a sufficient amount of entrepreneurial and other activities so that the result is better than anticipated has already been discussed under such headings as the advantages of complements in production, the advantages of external economies, the greater chance that the other growth factors will expand simultaneously, the greater ease with which the demographic hurdle can be overcome at that rate of growth. To return to our diagram, suppose we begin with an expectation of a 4 per cent rate of income growth (the point *A*); this will result in an expansion of the growth agents, which in turn will yield a rate of income growth of *B* (as measured from the ordinate). At *B* the appropriate growth anticipation rises to *C*, which, in turn, yields an expansion of the entrepreneurial contribution to *D*, and so on. Eventually the equilibrium growth rate of *N* should be reached, if the entrepreneurial expansion curve remains constant (see figure 9–2).

Let us now suppose that the anticipated rate of growth is very small, say ½ of 1 per cent, and assume that this falls on the segment *LM*. Why should the contributions to growth by the expanding growth factors be smaller than anticipated? To a considerable extent it is so for precisely the opposite reasons that we used above to explain the segment *MN,* such as the competition of zero-sum activities, the lack of adequate expansion or creation of complementary industries, the lack of external economies, the lack of growth of complementary factors of production, and so on. Furthermore, during each period, ventures begun in former periods come to fruition. Their gestation periods are over and some of their harvests are to be reaped. Some ventures will have been well thought out, well planned, and well managed, while others will not be —reflecting the wide range of abilities among entrepreneurs and managers. A rapid rate of growth will permit a higher proportion of these ventures to survive than a slow rate. Returning to our figure 9–1, we can trace the declining growth path *HJK,* etc., if the initial anticipated growth rate is too low.

Figure 9–2 reflects the probability that the higher the level of income, the greater are the potentialities for growth and the more readily can the expansion of the growth agents achieve anticipated results. Thus, as income grows, the growth agent expansion curve shifts to the right, reflecting the greater capacity to expand. The curves marked G_1 to G_3 are the entrepreneurial expansion curves, each based on a higher income as we proceed from G_1 to G_3. Beginning with the anticipated growth rate of *A,* we obtain the accelerating growth pattern *ABCDEF,* where in each step we shift to a lower growth agent expansion curve. (A similar decelerating growth or accelerating decline pattern can be depicted by appropriate changes in the order of the curves and by beginning at a sufficiently low rate of anticipated income growth.)

Two points need be made about such processes. First, they are not reversible. We cannot show both the accelerating and decelerating processes on the same map of growth agent expansion curves. The reason is that the reactions to favorable experiences are not the same as the reactions to unfavorable experiences. A favorable experience with respect to anticipations will itself affect the positions of the curves. Second, the entrepreneurial expansion curves may not shift to the right indefinitely as higher income levels are reached. This relationship is likely to be reversed when incomes become very high, for under those circumstances the possibilities of expansion, for example, through the borrowing of technology, disappear. Other growth possibilities of a similar nature may also disappear at very high incomes. But we must leave this tantalizing aspect of our problem for other occasions.

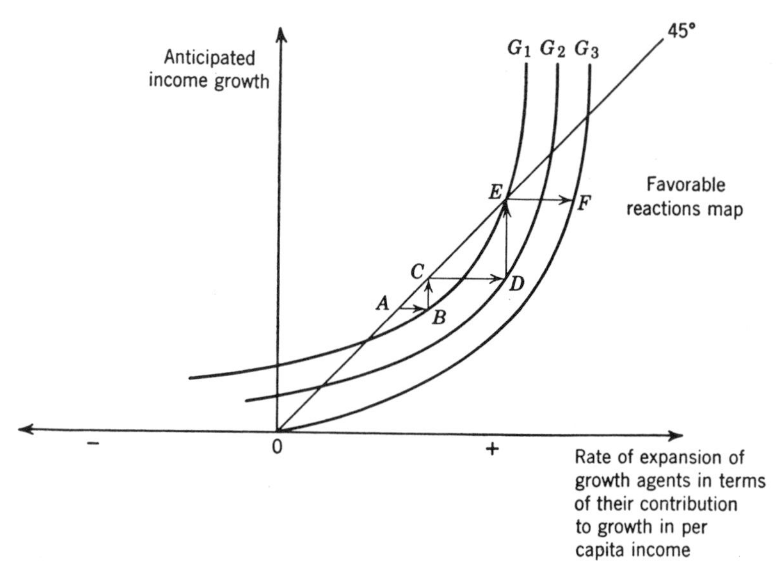

FIGURE 9–2

Also, the nature of the growth agent expansion curve and, hence, the extent of the increase in the growth agents depend not only on the anticipated rate of income growth but also on the stimulant to growth. In figure 9–3, we depict the effects of stimulants of varying size. The growth agent expansion curves marked S_1 to S_4 reflect the effects of larger stimulants as we proceed from S_1 to S_4. For very small stimulants the curves do not cross the 45-degree line at all, whereas for large ones they do. This fact reflects the critical minimum effort thesis elaborated previously. The point C represents the critical minimum effort as measured by the size of the stimulant and the minimum anticipated rate of growth required. S_2 is a curve where the stimulant has been too small for development. Points on S_2 reflect the fact that no matter how high the anticipated rate of income growth, it is a rate that cannot be achieved. The stimulant has not been sufficiently strong to generate sustained growth. Eventually, a decelerating process must set in. Compare the two points *D* and *F*. In both cases the anticipated growth rate is the same. In the case of *F* the stimulant has been sufficiently strong, that is, it has provided from an exogenous source sufficient new resources so that, given the generated expansion of the growth factors, the anticipation is realistic. On the other hand the point *D* implies that the new resources provided by the stimulant are so small that the anticipation is unrealistic.

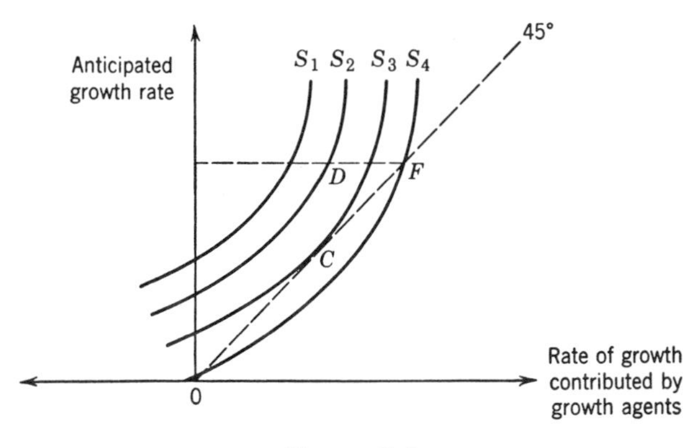

FIGURE 9–3

What is being said is that not all possible levels of anticipation will lead to activities that will provide just the opportunities implied by the anticipations. There is some range of levels of anticipation where the necessary opportunities are more likely to be forthcoming than for others, and the range where adequate opportunities are likely to be created, will be, for reasons already indicated, where aggregate anticipations are neither very low nor very high. But high anticipations are certainly not enough to create adequate opportunities.

Inventions and Innovations

An innovation represents the application of knowledge, hitherto unused, to the production process. The knowledge involved need not be a recent invention, although it is often of this nature. Thus innovations can come only from the existing stock of knowledge, and the extent of the existing stock of knowledge is clearly a determinant, although not necessarily the most important one, of innovations.

1. The meaning of "the stock of knowledge." Phrases like "the state of the arts" and the "stock of knowledge" are very vague and ephemeral in nature. Knowledge as such does not exist apart from human carriers, that is, apart from individuals capable of interpreting and communicating ideas and observations. But the sum total of records, books, libraries, etc., is the repository of knowledge. Additions to such records represent additions to the stock of knowledge in our repository. We must, however, distinguish between private and public knowledge. By private knowledge we refer to information available only to circumscribed entities such as specific individuals and institutions, either because the repositories are open only to such individuals or because it is carried only in the heads of such individuals. Public knowledge is knowledge that is available to everyone willing to pay the price or expend the effort for it. Knowledge may be public because the repositories are public or because the individuals in whom it resides are willing to sell the information. Certain types of additions to this stock of knowledge we call inventions. These presumably represent ideas different from those that can be found in the existing stock. Strictly speaking, these are the only true additions to the stock.

The stock of knowledge forms the resource base of innovations. Like other resources, it may or may not be used. Whether or not it is used depends on circumstances other than the stock itself. When we apply previously unapplied knowledge to economic activities, we call this act an innovation. It is important to note that private knowledge can become an innovation without going through the intermediate step of becoming public knowledge.

A peculiarity of knowledge worthy of note in contradistinction to other economically valuable stocks is that the use of it does not diminish it in any way. This may explain why so much of it is really a free good, although by monopolizing pieces of it, it can acquire considerable economic value. Thus, except for holocausts like wars and book burnings, only accretions to the stock of knowledge usually occur.

2. Growth of the knowledge base. We usually conceive of the growth of knowledge via inventions, namely, the discovery of new facts or new ideas. But from the standpoint of economic significance, the growth in the *availability* of the stock of knowledge may be much more important. Therefore, such activities as translating, publishing new editions, and duplicating existing records really do add to the knowledge base. Similarly, the superior organization of the repositories of existing knowledge adds to its availability. Also, the training of individuals to organize, transmit, and utilize knowledge adds to knowledge in the broad sense. In sum, any activity that helps to bring knowledge to the attention of entrepreneurs or to other users of knowledge in economic activities, adds to the *effective* knowledge base.

3. Innovations and entrepreneurship. Knowledge has economic meaning only through the activities of the entrepreneur and the skills of the labor force. An increase in the stock of knowledge changes the environment in which the entrepreneur decides whether or not to engage in a given entrepreneurial activity. New knowledge may enable the firm to produce a commodity by combining resources in a new way or to produce a new commodity. Thus, it is part of the entrepreneurial function, as part of his exploratory behavior, to determine whether or not the enlarged knowledge base opens up new economic opportunities.

Whether or not new knowledge is used is determined in a way similar to other entrepreneurial decisions. The accretions to the knowledge stock enlarge the range of possible production functions. Out of this enlarged set of production alternatives there may be one (or more), given the new cost and price constellation, that implies the possibility of a profitable venture. In this way entrepreneurial opportunities are created that otherwise would not have existed. Conversely, changes in the supply of factors or demand for commodities may enable the use of an invention that previously could not so be used. Similarly, an increase in the perceptiveness of entrepreneurs may lead to the use of knowledge that previously could not be used.

In view of the potential favorable effect of knowledge on entrepreneurial opportunities, it is clear that it is a desirable activity to invest in the expansion of the knowledge base. But, of course, there is an obverse side to this coin. The new knowledge and the consequent innovation may make the going concerns no longer profitable. Hence there is often an incentive to transform public knowledge into private knowledge, to engage in zero-sum activities and in this way avoid the adverse effects on the going concerns.

The extent of innovations depends on three factors: (*a*) the knowledge that is unused that could be used; (*b*) additions to the knowledge base; (*c*) changes in the values of the economic variables that determine whether or not it is economically desirable to use a "knowledge alternative" or whether or not it is desirable to suppress "knowledge alternatives."

The amount of usable knowledge that remains unused also depends on the level of per capita income. First, there is an investment cost involved in the use of knowledge. The investment in capital, and in "human capital," necessary in order to employ advanced techniques is hard to come by if incomes are low. Second, low wages keep out many types of potential labor-displacing innovations.

Similarly, additions to the knowledge base depend to some extent on the level of income. Additions to knowledge require investment in "human capital" as well as in research facilities. Furthermore, the incentive to engage in research and related activities depends on a market for such activities. There is little incentive to become a physicist if there are no employment opportunities for physicists. Of course, there will be a hard core who will engage in scholarly and research pursuits—pursuits that lead to intellectual discoveries—almost regardless of cost. But surely a higher level of income is more conducive to the *expansion* of such pursuits than a smaller one. In addition, the prospect of rising levels of income is likely to be of considerable significance, for it is the response to the anticipated opportunities generated by an expanding economy that leads to greater efforts.

4. Knowledge, innovations, and the entrepreneurial growth curve. We have seen that knowledge becomes an economic factor through the activities of the entrepreneur, that is, through the effect it has on changing the entrepreneurial prospects, opportunities, and horizons. Diagrammatically, we can show the effects of additions to the knowledge base by showing what it does to the entrepreneurial growth curve. We can distinguish three types of effects (illustrated in figure 9–4) that the impact of an initial addition to the stock of knowledge may have:

(*a*) The most direct effect is on the opportunities and prospects of the entrepreneur, which we may call the "opportunity effect." The new knowledge increases the production alternatives available and, hence, the profit opportunities available to the entrepreneur. For every level of anticipations new potential opportunities are created that did not exist before, and, as a result, the chances of having anticipations that can be fulfilled are increased. We show this effect by a shift in the original entrepreneurial expansion curve to the right.

(*b*) For every level of anticipated growth in per capita incomes and the consequent entrepreneurial activities there will be some further additions to knowledge because of the stimulus these activities may have on those that promote knowledge. For purposes of identification let us call this *the reaction effect*. The basic idea is that, in part, knowledge feeds on itself, and the initial increase in the knowledge base may open opportunities for promoting and developing further knowledge if the rewards are there. But such rewards depend indirectly on the anticipated income growth. Simultaneously, the entrepreneurial activities demonstrate the utilization of such knowledge, the rewards possible, and in this way they indirectly stimulate the agencies that "produce," spread, and promote knowledge. Hence the anticipated growth rate will determine, in part, what happens with respect to the increase in knowledge during that period.

(*c*) Finally, the introduction of new knowledge into the system may influence the entrepreneur's ability to forecast the outcome of his own activities. This is an effect that may work in either direction. If the new production alternatives made possible by the new knowledge are of a kind that reduce the extent of interdependence in the productive process or reduce the losses that may be involved in the poor synchro-

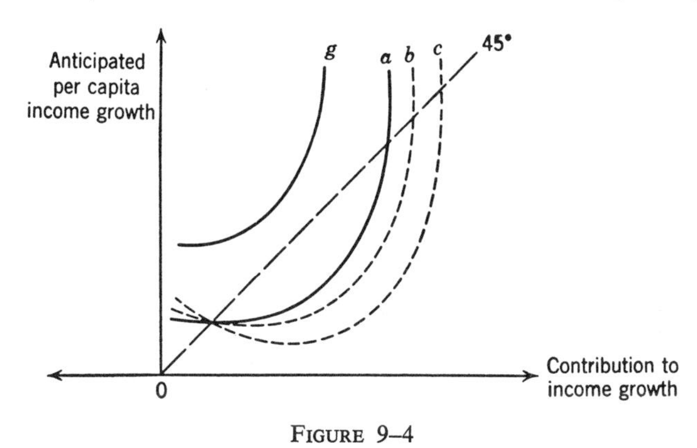

FIGURE 9–4

nization in the growth of the various factors, results are more likely to approximate anticipations and the entrepreneurial expansion curve will parallel more closely the 45-degree line than otherwise. If, on the other hand, as is more likely to be the case, the new knowledge increases the possibilities of specialization and therefore increases the significance of interdependence, forecasting may then become more difficult, the importance of correctly anticipating the simultaneous expansion of other factors of production may become greater, and the net result will be a "deepening" of the entrepreneurial expansion curve. It is this last effect, let us call it *the interdependence effect,* that is illustrated in figure 9–4. The curve marked *g* is the original entrepreneurial expansion curve. The curve *a* indicates the "opportunity effect." It is the same as the curve *g* but shifted to the right. Curve *b* shows the reaction effect, and the curve *c* shows the interdependence effect.[12]

Skills

In many respects the analysis of the development of skills is similar to the problem of developing knowledge and innovations. Skills are a

[12] Nothing we have said in this section should lead the reader to infer that knowledge-promoting activities will be pursued only in anticipation of economic gains. We do not mean to imply anything of the sort. Much knowledge-promoting activity will, of course, be pursued for its own sake, and in some cases, and at some point, the results of such activities may serve as stimulants to growth.

quality of the population. They are a potential resource and, like knowledge, they need not be fully employed. Whether or not skills are fully employed depends on whether entrepreneurs believe it profitable to do so.

The development of skills depends on the investment that is made in "human capital," for example, investment in education and training. But education is a consumption good as well as an investment in a factor of production. It is as a consumption good, and one that attaches to itself an honorific and prestige value, that education often manifests itself in backward economies. The level of education is in great part a function of income. But we must note that the type of education valued as a consumption good is not necessarily valuable as an economic good. There is surely some carry-over but exceedingly little wherever specialized skills are concerned. As a result, usually two types of costs are involved in the development of economically valuable skills. There are, first, the money costs in acquiring the skills as well as the income that may be lost during the period of acquisition. But there is also the cost of foregoing the classical and literary education that has a prestige and honorific value. With very low levels of income, very little education of any kind will be obtained; but with higher levels, the desire to emulate the established prestige class will lead to the demand for education of the traditional, honorific variety.[13]

1. Creating the demand for skills. The growth of skills depends on the creation of a demand for skills. There will, of course, be a supply of some skills always available since some of the education and training obtained as a consumption good will be transferable and utilizable as production skill, but to expand the pool of skills there is the prior necessity of creating an *observable* demand and anticipated rewards for such skills. The demand must come first.

But the demand for skills is created by entrepreneurial activities. Unless there are new entrepreneurial opportunities there will not be an increase in the demand. But not all entrepreneurial opportunities imply an increase in demand for new skills. We may distinguish between those activities that represent a widening of the economy and those that represent a deepening. By a widening we refer to those activities that involve an expansion of the same kind of activities, that is, activities that leave the proportions of goods produced the same but simply increase the scale. By a deepening we refer to increases in the other factors utilized per man employed, including investment in man. It is the deepening type of activities that involves the need for new skills.

[13] On this point see the interesting article by Thomas Balogh "Oxbridge Rampant," *The Universities Quarterly,* May 1955, pp. 263–272.

New types of capital may be either "skill-displacing" or "skill-using." These last two terms are self-explanatory. Therefore, only to the extent that entrepreneurial opportunities involve the utilization of capital that is skill-using will there be created a demand for additional skills.

A constant per capita income level requires no more than investment activities of the widening type but need not involve the deepening type of activities. Also, when skills are scarce the price of skill is high. Therefore, there is an incentive in backward economies, whenever technologically feasible, for the entrepreneur to employ skill-displacing rather than skill-using capital. We have already argued that the expansion of entrepreneurial activities depends on the extent of economic growth. It, therefore, appears that the development of the demand for additional skills depends all the more on, at least, anticipated growth in per capita income.

2. Determinants of the supply of skills. The demand for skills is a derived demand that depends on the extent of entrepreneurial activities, which, in turn, depends on the supply of entrepreneurship and the creation of entrepreneurial opportunities. But we would expect a lag in the response of supply to demand. Apart from the time lag, the derived increase in demand will have to be sufficiently large so that the increased reward for skills is made sufficiently attractive to overcome a number of obstacles. Among such obstacles are: (*a*) the usual inertia and immobility of the labor force in backward economies; (*b*) the direct costs of transfer of the labor force as well as the social costs of transfer; (*c*) the cost of training; (*d*) the risk involved in committing oneself to training prior to knowledge of demand for the skill at the end of the training period; (*e*) the competition of skill-displacing capital. Also, rewards for new skills may have to be sufficiently above the average wage so that their attractiveness can be observed in areas where communications are at best inadequate.

But high wages may not be enough to induce the desired expansion of skills. An additional obstacle, often inhibiting the development of the wage incentive as a force that can induce the expansion of skills (as well as the expansion of effort), is the lack of experience with a developed monetary economy. Higher wages can be attractive only if the recipients have acquired the tastes and desires for the goods that higher wages can buy. A lower per capita level of income implies a limited variety as well as a limited supply of goods available. Where variety is limited, higher wages may be used to purchase leisure.

The higher the income level and the greater the variety of goods, the more pronounced is the climate of acquisitiveness and the greater the responsiveness of the labor supply to wage differences. These considerations seem to imply that at low income levels the wage differentials necessary to induce the expansion of certain skills may have to be proportionately higher than at higher levels.

The consequence of some of these ideas is illustrated in figure 9–5. The solid curve marked *S* indicates the expansion in the supply of skill in response to alternate increases in wages above the initial wage level *OA*. The initial backward bending portion of the curve reflects the

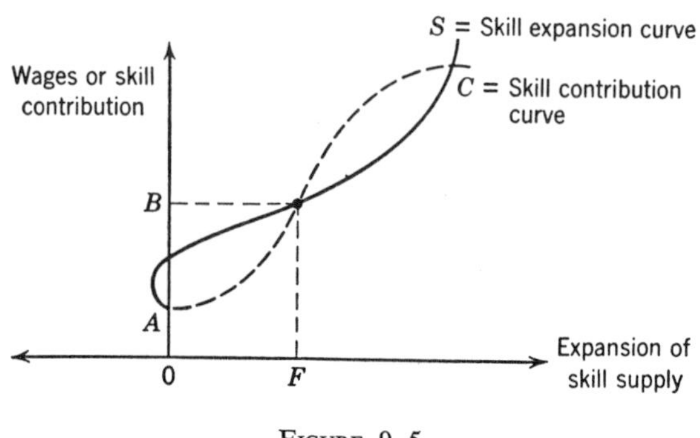

FIGURE 9–5

belief that very small increases in wages will entice no new entrants into the skill but instead will induce those already in it to trade some of their increased wages for leisure. There is obviously a limit to the extent to which the supply can be expanded within any period, and hence beyond some point the skill-expansion curve approaches a vertical line. The skill-contribution curve *C* indicates the additional net contribution to output per man for alternate amounts of the additional supply of skill.

As drawn, the diagram implies that it would not pay to expand skills by very small amounts, let us say, by amounts less than *OF*. It also implies that for skills to expand at a profitable rate it is necessary for per capita income to grow sufficiently so that it is consistent with a wage increase of *AB*.

The increasing net contribution (as shown on the broken-line curve *C*) as labor skills expand (an increasing-returns sort of phenomenon) is explained by such things as the very high cost of training small numbers and the lower costs per unit as the number to be trained each period increases. In part, it is also explained by the fact that the expansion of skills must be synchronized with the expansion in entrepreneurial activities. It would therefore seem reasonable to believe that for some very small increases in skill supply, the new skills cannot be used very effectively, whereas the larger the supply, up to some point, the more effectively they can be used and, therefore, there is a more than proportionate growth in their contribution to income.

In sum, we see that although the supply of skills depends in part on the initial cultural and social conditions and on the initial level of income, it may depend in a crucial way on the rate of increase in per capita income.

3. Effect on the entrepreneurial expansion curve. The connection between the development of skills and the entrepreneurial expansion curve is similar to that between the development of knowledge and the entrepreneurial expansion curve. A sudden growth in skills may have an "opportunity effect," new entrepreneurial opportunities created

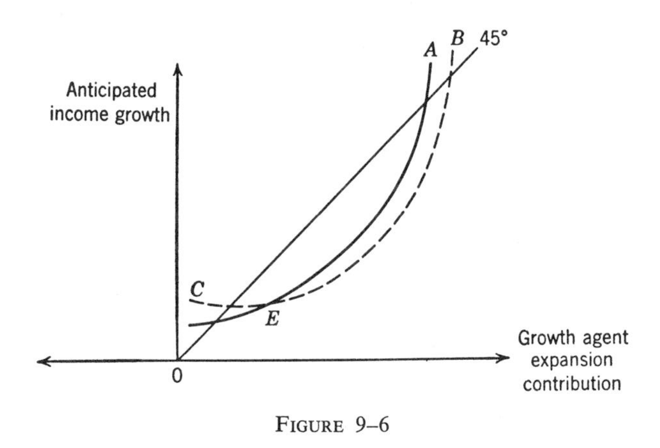

FIGURE 9–6

by the increase in skills, and we have, therefore, a consequent shift of the entrepreneurial growth curve to the right. But the important effect is likely to be the "reaction effect." This last is illustrated in figure 9–6. The curve marked *A* is the entrepreneurial growth curve on the assumption that the stock of skills is constant. *CEB* is the new curve that takes account of the reactions of skills as a consequence of entrepreneurial activities. The portion *CE* reflects the fact that for small increases in income, skill supply may actually be backward bending rather than constant.

Summary and Conclusions

We have considered matters that are more elusive than those usually dealt with in economics. Yet such matters as the creation and spread of knowledge, the tendency to innovate, the acquisition of skills, and the development of entrepreneurial perceptiveness may well be at the very heart of our problem.

The stress in our analysis is on the relationships between entrepreneurial activities and the other growth agents. We emphasize the following four connections between them: (1) The expansion of the non-entrepreneurial growth agents influences the environment in which entrepreneurial decisions are made, hence determining the extent and *choice* of the entrepreneurial activities. (2) The expansion of the non-entrepreneurial growth agents influences and, in part, determines the *results* of entrepreneurial acts. (3) In turn, the entrepreneurial decisions and their outcomes determine the expansion of the non-entrepreneurial growth agents. (4) The interaction between entrepreneurial anticipations and results determines the rate of expansion or contraction of entrepreneurship itself. It can readily be seen that (3) and (4) start the cycle of interaction all over again *ad infinitum.*

In order to draw conclusions, we must go beyond a mere statement of the related elements that are involved. We have, therefore, tried to say something about the probable nature of the relationships and their implications. Specifically, we have argued that the rate of growth will depend on the interaction between the plans for expansion of the various growth agents, their simultaneous attempts to carry out these plans based on anticipations about the economic environment in the future, and the actual rate of growth that results from these simultaneous activities which, in turn, determine the plans and activities of succeeding periods.

Our main point is that not all anticipated rates of growth will have equal power to induce a sufficient expansion of the growth agents so that anticipations materialize. For some rates of growth, results will be greater than expected and, for others, less than expected. Results greater than expected will stimulate a further expansion in the growth agents, and results less than expected will stimulate either no expansion or a contraction of the growth agents. The outcome will depend on the synchronization of entrepreneurial plans for expansion and on the simultaneously induced expansion of the growth agents. But it is quite likely that not all actual rates of growth will induce an equally felicitous synchronization of these factors.

Indeed, we offer reasons why very low rates of growth are unlikely to induce that synchronized expansion of all factors so that the interactions between anticipations and results generate sustained growth. Among such reasons are the necessity to overcome the proclivity toward zero-sum activities, general inertia toward the expansion of certain agents of production and the inertia and fear of undertaking new types of activities, the nature of the risk of new types of activities and their connection to the gestation period involved in the expansion of economic resources, the likelihood that at lower rates of growth more of the inexperienced will fail at the new activities and, as a result, stimulate a contraction of such activities which, in turn, will have an adverse effect on future anticipations and plans, etc.

At very high rates of growth anticipations may also not be realized because there are technical "bottlenecks" that cannot be foreseen. After all, there are physical limits to the rate of growth that can be achieved within any period. Hence, there is some middle growth range which is probably most conducive to sustained growth. In general, these

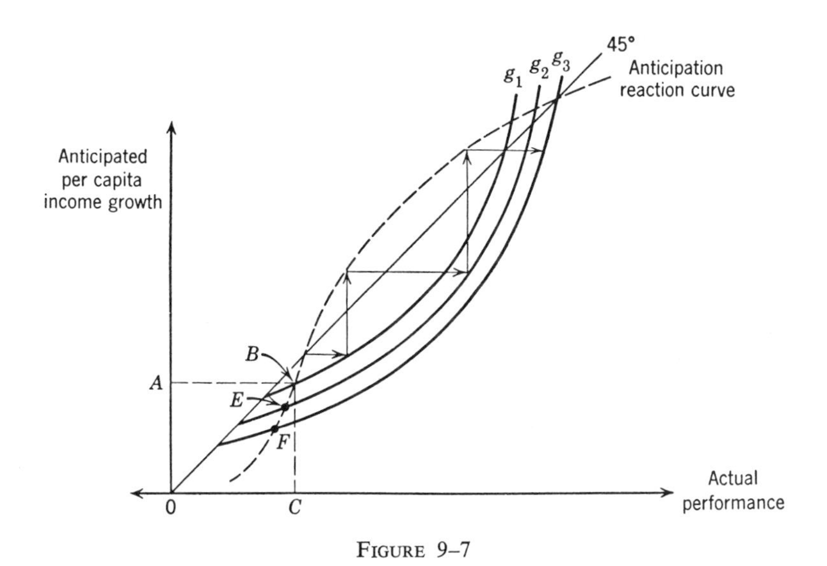

FIGURE 9–7

ideas fit in with our minimum effort notion. On the other hand, the initial stimulants have to be sufficiently large so that some growth can be achieved. And, in addition, the rate of growth that is achieved must be a sufficiently large rate so as to engender sustained growth.

Before closing, we must add something about some of the implicit assumptions that underlie our graphical illustrations.

In our main figures we used a 45-degree line to explain the interaction between anticipation and performance. But a 45-degree line reflects a particular kind of anticipation pattern. Such a line seems to say (see figure 9–7) that the actual past performance in growth will be the one anticipated in the future. In other words, people always believe that the existing trend will continue. There may be some rates of growth for which anticipations are such that people believe that the trend will continue. For very low rates of growth, however, they may be less optimistic than the trend seems to warrant, and, for higher ones, more optimistic than the trend seems to suggest. Such an anticipation reaction pattern is depicted by the broken line in figure 9–7.

The general result is the same. There is still a level of anticipated growth (OA) above which we can expect sustained growth—otherwise not. We make this point and illustrate the possibility of drawing the more complicated anticipated reaction curve in order to show that our results do *not* depend on the simple reaction curve that reflects the belief that the current trend will always continue.

We may conceive of a family of growth agent expansion curves (for example, g_1, g_2, g_3 in figure 9–7) where each curve assumes a different level of per capita income at the outset. The pattern of change can then be depicted by showing movements to different growth agent expansion curves as the results in one period imply a higher initial per capita income for the next period. Other complications can probably be introduced so that the anticipation reaction curve (or curves) depends on more than just the previous rate of per capita income growth. However, more complicated, and perhaps more realistic, reaction and adjustment mechanisms *need not* change the general picture. Anticipations will still depend in some way on past experience. And it is certainly likely that past experiences involving higher rates of growth will, up to a point, imply higher growth anticipations than past experiences involving lower rates of growth. We can still argue that, for the reasons previously elaborated, the growth agent expansion curves will, in a manner of speaking, cut the anticipation reaction curve (or curves) from above (see points B, E, F in figure 9–7) so that the need of a minimum initial growth rate (or growth pattern) in order to generate sustained growth still holds.

CHAPTER 10

Population Growth Theory and Economic Development

Some Erroneous Approaches to the Population Problem

The attitudes of economists toward the demographic aspects of their problem has shifted from time to time. To the classicists like Malthus and J. S. Mill, it was an integral part of economic theory. As theory refinement shifted the focus of attention to short-run problems, the population growth variable fell out of the picture since in the short run it could not be very important. During the nineteen-thirties when the major economic concern was the unemployment problem, the population growth aspect came back in a curious manner as part of the stagnation thesis. This time it was the *lack* of a sufficient rate of population growth to which the adverse economic conditions were, in part, attributed. But the return of the population factor was through the back door, and it was tolerated only if it agreed to remain an outsider. At best, population growth was looked upon as an independent variable that conceivably had something to do with the determination of effective demand. It certainly did not become an integral part of the "general" theory of employment.

Thus, over the years, population was gradually banished from the province of the economists' studies. It seemed that population growth had something to do with marriage and the family and, therefore, the exile was admitted to the realm of the sociologist. But once we return, as economists, to such longer-range problems as the problem of economic growth, the existence of that foreign element, once completely banished from our studies and thoughts, must again be recognized. There is still little evidence of sufficient recognition in current economic literature to imply an award of first-class citizenship privileges of acceptance as an endogenous variable. The best that most economists would seem to offer to population growth are the second-class rights of an independent variable. And the less tolerant confer no more than the third-class recognition of a factor to be mentioned *en passant.*

Of course, there are some who go to greater extremes. Socialist and Marxist writers have either denied the existence of the population element as a significant determinant or claimed that it was a bourgeois fiction that deflects attention from the real culprits responsible for poverty.

The position that we shall take is that the population variable is of importance, and that it can be properly understood and evaluated only if it is examined in the light of an endogenous variable. In order to help persuade the reader that this is the proper way to view the matter we first examine what we believe to be three erroneous approaches in handling the population variable: (1) the error of thinking in terms of current comparative densities of population, (2) the error of considering "population pressure" as an independent problem that can be handled apart from the general problem of economic development,[1] and (3) the error of considering population growth as an independent variable whose path can be forecast. Of course, there is no end to the erroneous approaches that can be considered, and to consider many of them would be to set up "straw men" to no purpose. But those that we shall discuss are chosen because, on the surface, they appear rather reasonable. Also, they are certainly "more defensible" than many other approaches to the problem. All are, in a sense, non-dogmatic and have at least this virtue: they all recognize the possibility that there can be a population aspect to the more general problem of economic backwardness.

1. The comparative population density approach. This approach appears to be the most reasonable of all. It involves a comparison of the man-to-land ratios between countries and attempts on this basis to come to conclusions about the significance of "population

[1] In a later chapter we also present computations based on empirical evidence that are intended to suggest the magnitude of the population growth variable as a factor in development.

pressure" in different areas.[2] Refinements of this approach lead to such designations as "overpopulation," "underpopulation," "overpopulated areas," etc. To begin with, there is the often-recognized statistical difficulty of finding arable equivalents. If we are to compare resources per man, we must have some way of translating different natural resources or pieces of land that are subject to vast differences in rainfall, temperature, type of soil, etc., into homogeneous equivalents. But even if the difficulty of converting varied resources into common resource equivalents is overcome the error of the approach remains. Such comparisons of degrees of underpopulation or overpopulation usually make very interesting reading and are often highly suggestive of the extremity and urgency of the problem. But it is their very suggestiveness that leads to the danger of misinterpretation.

Let us see what meaning we can give to such density comparisons at their best. Suppose we find that country *A* has, say, 400 men per square mile, country *B* has 300 men per equivalent square mile, and country *C*, 200 men per square mile of equivalent land units. We would be tempted to conclude from such a table that if any country suffers from population pressure it is *A*, and that certainly *C* cannot be said to be more overpopulated than *A*. Now suppose that the three countries are in very different stages of economic growth, *A* being the most developed country and *C* the least. We might then be tempted to argue that whatever the cause of *C*'s lack of development, it can certainly not be attributed to population pressure. But this conclusion might be quite wrong and the reverse assertion be correct.

The difficulty lies in the meaning we give to population pressure. The reader will recall that we assumed that the statistical problem of expressing population in terms of comparable resource or land units can somehow be overcome. But in order to do so we have to assume a given level of technology. In other words, we assume that the power to exploit a given bundle of resources is the same in all three countries. Thus, what the comparison means is that if all three countries had the same capacity to exploit their resources *at the time the comparison was made*, *A* would be the most overpopulated, *B* less so, and so on. But if the countries are in different stages of development, they certainly do not have the same capacity to exploit their resources. Nor is it legitimate to assume that, if a time ever came when the three countries were equally capable of utilizing their natural resources, the population density figures would then be the same.

---

[2] See Wilbert Moore, *Economic Demography of Eastern and Southern Europe*, League of Nations, 1945.

The point that must be made clear is that we do not argue that population density figures are meaningless. Far from it. It is simply that we must be very careful to see what type of questions they do and what type they do not answer. What such figures *do not* tell us is the significance of the population hurdle for the country involved. For example, it is often argued that the problem of economic development is one thing for the presumably densely populated countries of the Far East and Middle East but something else again for the presumably sparsely settled countries of Latin America and Central Africa. But this is not necessarily true. In principle, population growth may be a more significant hurdle for the more sparsely settled countries. The former assertion can be true only if it can be shown that the so-called sparsely settled countries have the same capacities to utilize resources and the same potentialities for population growth.

Let us return to our countries *A, B,* and *C,* of which *C* is the most sparsely settled. Three factors that may be said to be significant in determining the extent of the obstacle that population growth presents are: (*a*) the extent to which the economy may be subject to diminishing returns, (*b*) the potentialities for population growth, and (*c*) the nature of the potential capital growth. Suppose that country *C* is most subject to diminishing returns. Now, it is certainly possible that to a given stimulant, *C* responds with a much greater rate of population growth than the others. It is also possible that the additions to capital in country *C* necessary to raise national income may be of such a nature that the extent of diminishing returns remains much greater than in country *A*. Compounding these circumstances, we can see that the consequences of population growth are more significant in *C* than in either *A* or *B*. Current differences in the extent of settlement really tells us very little about the real obstacles to development.

We suggest, essentially, that it may not be meaningful to compare the population densities of different areas if the production techniques are at different levels. Suppose that country *C* uses technique *gamma* appropriate to its knowledge and capital stock, while *A* employs the more advanced technique, *alpha,* appropriate to its capital stock and knowledge. The proper comparison to make in order to get some idea of the relative "population pressure" in the two countries is between the population density of *A* and that of *C* when *C*'s technique develops to *alpha* and *C*'s capital stock increases accordingly. This is, of course, a very different sort of comparison from the usual one. A case in point is that of the population density of the American Indian, as compared with that of the white settler that succeeded him. The crude population density was unquestionably in favor of the American Indian, but given their level of technique, it is not unlikely that the American Indian population was subjected to considerable population pressure while that of the European settler, given his more advanced techniques, was not.

2. The independent population problem approach. It is not uncommon to find writers on the development problem paying a sort of lip service to the population aspect but not handling it as part of their general analysis. As previously stated, the virtue of this approach is that it does recognize population growth as an aspect of the development problem. Often, the focus is on one or more recommendations to the effect that something should be done about reducing fertility. What this approach seems to say is this: "Control the rate of population growth and there is a good chance that economic growth can be promoted by introducing the other measures we have indicated." On the surface this appears to be a reasonable attitude to the problem and yet the underlying assumption is erroneous. More important, it can lead to perverse policy recommendations. For what must underlie this view is the supposition that the control of population growth and the promotion of economic growth can be handled separately. The point missed in such a procedure is that the two sets of recommendations may be contradictory. The proposed measures for fostering economic growth may increase population growth and, conceivably, reduce the capacity of the economy to control population expansion, whereas measures that can diminish the rate of population growth may imply or lead to a retardation of economic growth.

The missing link of this "independent approach" is the connection between the institutional setting created by and conducive to economic growth and the consequence of that setting on population growth. For example, the *sustained* reduction of fertility rates has never[3] been achieved in a predominantly agricultural setting. Yet one finds time and again the advocacy of agricultural development in the absence of industrialization. Barring emigration, to the extent that agricultural development is successful, it must result in a greater rate of population growth than otherwise, which, in turn, may hamper further per capita income growth. In sum, this approach seems to recognize the connection between population growth and the prospects for development, but not the equally significant relationship between the effect of economic development on the rate of population growth.

3. The error of assuming an independent rate of population growth. A third type of error, but one that is somewhat easier to see

---

[3] The French experience in the early nineteenth century is sometimes cited as an exception to this generalization.

through than the others, is the assumption that the rate of population growth is independent of the rate of economic growth. This differs from the error considered in the last section in that in the previous case we argued against the belief that we could *influence* the rate of population growth apart from economic growth. In this section we are concerned with the belief that population growth will continue at some specified rate or in some specified pattern irrespective of what happens in the economic sector. There is no argument here about reducing the rate of population growth independently of economic developments. There is merely the assumption, in plans for development, of a given rate of population growth depending, if it depends on anything, on current or recent experience.

This position is based on a half truth that can be easily overstated. The basis of the half truth is that *some* of the factors that affect the rate of population growth are independent of economic conditions. This is especially true of medical and biological discoveries which, if applied, can lower mortality rates. Furthermore, such discoveries can, *to some extent,* be applied regardless of the rate of economic development by shifting some government resources to public health measures. In the instances where such measures have been taken, and have been successful, they have resulted in considerable short-term reductions in the death rate. Whether such, in a sense, "artificially" induced low death rates can be sustained, in view of very low levels of nutrition, has yet to be determined.

But granting this last point does not at all prove the proposition that the rate of population growth is independent of changes in economic conditions. In the first place, it should be noted that the demonstrated possibilities for influencing the rate of population growth are in the direction of expanding it rather than the reverse. Also, the greater the rate of income growth per head, the greater the possibilities of plowing investment funds into public-health measures. At the same time, greater incomes permit better nutrition and greater private health measures. Thus, to the extent that declines in the mortality rates determine population growth, we can see, and this point will be demonstrated in greater detail as we proceed, that economic growth is very much more likely to influence the rate of population growth.

But what about the fertility side of the picture? There is very little evidence that fertility rates can be reduced by direct measures in the absence of economic changes. Indeed, almost all the evidence seems to be in the other direction. What we do know is that in some cases fertility rates fell considerably after the inception of economic development, and in those cases the decline has usually been a concomitant of urbanization.[4]

The Properties of a More Adequate Theory and the Shortcomings of the Demographers' Contribution

We employ figure 10–1 as an aid in specifying those aspects of the inadequate. It is, therefore, of interest to determine some of the properties that a theory of population growth should possess if it is to be of greater use in the solution of economic development problems. We suggest at least two criteria that an adequate theory should satisfy, criteria the necessity of which appears to be sufficiently self-evident so that we anticipate their acceptance without detailed argumentation on their behalf. (1) Since the population variable is significant in economic development, an adequate theory should be formulated in such terms that it may readily be integrated into economic theories of development. (2) The theory should be able to explain the crucial events in the growth of the population either during the course of economic development or during attempts at development, whether or not such attempts are successful.[5]

We employ figure 10–1 as an aid in specifying those aspects of the problem that a successful theory of population growth should try to explain. The line marked y_0 shows the locus of the underdevelopment equilibrium points. We have already expounded on the nature of this type of equilibrium in earlier chapters. Each point represents the equilibrium condition of the equality of high fertility and high mortality rates at a level of income that just permits the population to replace itself.

The line marked y_m represents the locus of minimum effort points. These points are, of course, related to the minimum effort thesis developed in earlier chapters. The shape of the minimum effort curve is based on the notion that the larger the population size, the larger the necessary minimum effort required to escape the near-subsistence conditions. The minimum effort, in terms of an initial boost in per capita

---

[4] See United Nations, *The Determinants and Consequences of Population Trends,* Population Studies No. 17, New York, 1953, Chapter V.

[5] Of course, the theory should enable us to make predictions in the scientific sense of the word. But this is really an ultimate test that comes after other criteria have been met in the process of theory construction. For if, as we have claimed, the demographic variables are so linked with economic variables that the two types of variables cannot be completely determined separately, we can hardly hope for a theory that enables us eventually to make adequate predictions if in the construction of that theory the first criterion above is not met. Hence, the priority of that criterion.

income, can be viewed as the difference between the subsistence equilibrium income and the related point on the minimum effort locus.

An adequate theory of population growth should explain the points marked *A, B, C,* and *D,* in figure 10–1. They represent the following aspects of the problem:

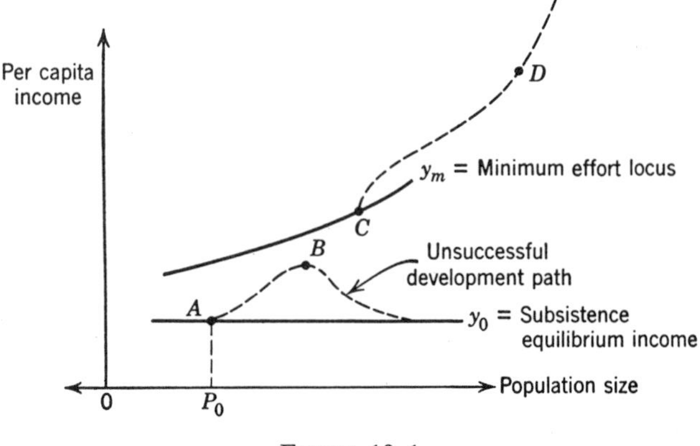

FIGURE 10–1

A. This is the subsistence equilibrium position where an equality between high fertility and high mortality rates exists. These are the maximum rates consistent with the survival of the population. Since we have already examined the question of initial equilibrium positions in earlier chapters, we shall only touch on it here.

B. This represents an early stage in population growth at which mortality rates fall, and during which there is a lag between the inception of the drop of mortality rates and the decline in fertility rates. This point may or may not be a point on the path toward ultimate economic development. Whether it is or not depends on the nature and magnitude of the stimulants to per capita income growth. The theory should explain the lag between mortality and fertility rates during early attempts at development or during periods when temporary boosts in per capita output do not generate development. Of course, all such explanations should be in terms that are connected with the rest of the theory of development.

C. This is a crucial point where the destiny of the economy is balanced precariously between progress and retrogression. It is probably not a point where any substantial fertility decline has begun. But it is likely to be a point where the gap between fertility and mortality rates is considerable. Ideally, the theory should help to explain this gap, as well as the relationship between the size of this gap and the minimum effort point. The existence of such a gap has, of course, been observed by numerous demographers, and attempts at what are unquestionably reasonable explanations have been made. We consider the nature of such explanations in the next section.

D. This point represents a case in which the economy is well advanced on the road toward sustained economic development. It is a point where the gap between fertility and mortality rates is steadily closing. Beyond this point the rate of population growth should decline as per capita incomes grow. We shall see that in explaining point *C* above, we explain, to a considerable extent, what needs to be explained under *D*. For, in grappling with our attempts to explain why the gap exists, we throw considerable light on what it is that causes the gap to close.

Those conversant with some of the theories of present-day demographers are aware that current generalizations about population growth do, in fact, go some of the way toward explaining the four points just enumerated. Nevertheless, the existing theories are in such a form that they are not as useful as they might be for economic development problems. Although it would be of interest to examine all existing theories in the light of our two criteria, limitations of time and space force us to restrict our remarks to the widely accepted notions that emanate from the "theory of demographic stages" propounded by Thompson, Notestein, Blacker, Landry, and others. There are three aspects of this amalgam of generalizations. There is, first, the doctrine of the stages of demographic evolution. Second, there is an explanation of the lag of fertility rates behind mortality rates. And, third, we are offered a series of vaguely related explanations of the secular decline in fertility rates. A summary of these ideas can be found in the recently published United Nations compendium of demographic doctrines and facts.[6]

C. P. Blacker, writing in the *Eugenics Review* in 1947, divided population into five types: high stationary, early expanding, late expanding, low stationary, and diminishing. The high stationary is our subsistence equilibrium population and it refers to a population characterized by the approximate equality of the high mortality rates and fertility rates. The others can most readily be characterized by the use of a simple diagram. In figure 10–2 the solid line represents the descent of mortality rates whereas the broken line represents the fertility rate. The five stages are designated *HS, EE, LE, LS,* and *D* from the initials of the approximate name of each stage. The stages are almost self-explanatory.

[6] See *The Determinants and Consequences of Population Trends,* pp. 44, 73–97.

In the early expanding stage, fertility is roughly constant while mortality declines. In the late expanding stage, the fertility decline has set in and the gap between mortality and fertility closes. We need not concern ourselves too much with the last two stages, since they go beyond our particular problem, and their empirical basis, which appeared to be reasonably evident in the nineteen-thirties, is now very doubtful.

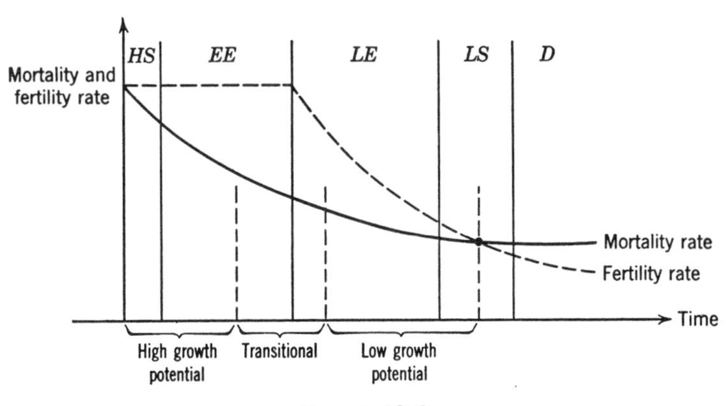

FIGURE 10–2

W. S. Thompson,[7] and F. W. Notestein[8] use only three stages in their summary of types. Blacker's stage one and the early part of two become countries of high growth potential. At the other extreme are countries of low growth potential. In the first case fertility is entirely uncontrolled; in the second it is fairly well controlled; in a third, or transitional state, the populations are in the process of changing from one type to the other. On the basis of such classifications it is possible to divide the various countries of the world in accordance with their population type.

The difficulty with the stages of demographic evolution doctrine is that it does not explain any critical aspect of the problem. At best, it is a broad description of past demographic events. But it does not shed light on the crucial question as to why some countries developed while others did not; nor does it indicate how the nature of population growth is related to the vast differences in per capita incomes that are to be found in different countries.

The explanatory parts of the "theory" are more in the nature of broad historical generalizations and insights rather than "in" a theory, in the usual sense of the word, that is, a system of related deductions derived

[7] *Plenty of People,* New York, Ronald Press Co., 1948, Chapter 6.

[8] "The Population of the World in the Year 2000," *Journal of the American Statistical Association,* September 1950, pp. 335–345.

from initial premises and relationships. There are three aspects of the problem which are touched on in the scattered writings of the demographers: (1) the decline in mortality rates, (2) the lag of fertility decline behind mortality decline, and finally, though not necessarily independently, (3) an explanation of the decline in fertility rates.

On the first, the following summary section taken from the recent United Nations review of the problem is indicative of the nature of such explanations.

> The spectacular decline of mortality in western countries, beginning at a slow rate during the first half of the nineteenth century and gathering momentum by the end of the century, has been traced to the general improvement in economic and social conditions of the populations concerned. The agricultural and industrial revolutions led ultimately to a higher level of living, including larger incomes, and better housing and clothing. Although the early effects of industrialization may possibly have had an unfavourable effect upon morbidity and mortality conditions among the factory population, the role assumed by governments had a salutary effect in correcting the abuses which developed. The by-product of increased prosperity was improvement in sanitation and other public health measures, advancement of medical knowledge, and the spread of general education—all important determinants of mortality levels. While during the eighteenth and the first part of the nineteenth century progress was due more to the rising standard of living than to the development of medical sciences, the reverse has probably been true during the last hundred years.[9]

On the fertility lag this summary statement from one of F. W. Notestein's[10] well-known articles is very much to the point:

> The more rapid response of mortality than of fertility to the forces of modernization is probably inevitable. The reduction of mortality is a universally acceptable goal and faces no substantial social obstacles. But the reduction of fertility requires a shift in social goals from those directed toward the survival of the group to those directed toward the welfare and development of the individual. This change, both of goals and of the social equipment by which they are achieved, is at best a slow process. As a result, the period of modernization is virtually certain to yield rapid population increase.

A major element in many theories of population growth is an explanation of the secular decline in fertility. A host of ideas and speculations, suggested by such terms as urbanization, industrialization, social mobility, the changed status of women, decline in religious interest, etc.,

---

[9] United Nations, *op. cit.*, p. 69.

[10] "Population—The Long View," in Theodore W. Shultz (Editor), *Food for the World,* Chicago, 1945, pp. 40–41.

has been advanced. From the recent United Nations report[11] we find such ideas summarized in these terms:

> Whereas certain writers have held that modern life has tended to reduce reproductive capacity, most recent writers have emphasized that the decline in family size has been brought about by the practice of family limitation. Related to this changing attitude towards family limitation are a complex of inter-related economic and social factors, such as the shift of the population from country to city, the desire to improve one's own social and economic position or that of one's children, the changes in the status and role of women in society, the improvement of the level of living, the increasing expenses of rearing children, a decline in religious interest and a decline in mortality.

The shortcomings of the explanatory parts of the demographers' theories are of a methodological nature. These and other explanations are not incorrect, but they do *not* possess a unified and distinct logical structure. Also the generic terms used are sometimes on different levels of abstraction. Some refer to very particular historical instances, others are much more general.

A major difficulty with the list of factors given in the last quotation is that it does not contain any unifying or integrating concepts. There is no way of knowing whether the various factors listed are separate explanations of the same phenomena, whether or not some of the aspects are the necessary concomitants of others, which are significant and which are not, whether they are competing or complementary explanations, or whether they are all really necessary in order to achieve fertility decline. In short, the various factors are not formulated in such a way that they can be related in some manner to a unified system. As a consequence, it is not possible from this sort of theory to deduce the set or sets of conditions necessary and sufficient to achieve secular fertility declines. Indeed, it is very difficult to know what can and what cannot be deduced from explanations in this form.

For the reasons just stated, the next section outlines a scheme of analysis in terms of concepts that are familiar to the economist, and one that can also be related to the categories utilized in our investigation of the development problem. We shall then apply these ideas to an explanation of the critical points indicated in figure 10–1. Our purpose in attempting to develop such a conceptual scheme is to show that the population aspect of the development problem can be seen in terms of a set of unified and integrated ideas, in the hope that such a scheme may eventually lead to a theory that avoids the methodological pitfalls condemned in this section.

---

[11] United Nations, *op. cit.*, p. 96.

Elements of an Economic Theory of Population Growth

Although it may appear on the surface that it is equally important to explain both mortality and fertility decline, an examination of the problem, as it has been treated in the demographic literature, suggests that the real crux of the matter is to explain the onset of the fertility decline.

Compared to the other components of population change, the factors that determine mortality trends are reasonably well understood. For our purposes we can divide such factors into two sets: those that are autonomous of the economic aspects of life and those that are functions of income. The autonomous factors, apart from "acts of God," such as floods and storms, are mostly scientific discoveries that reduce the incidence of certain diseases. The often-mentioned effects of DDT and the clearing of the swamps to combat malaria are of this nature. But medical and chemical discoveries require economic resources to put them into effect. Therefore, on the whole, mortality rates seem to depend on the "standard of life," that is, on the level of consumption. Hence, it is quite reasonable to posit that mortality rates are a monotonically decreasing function of per capita income, *given the state of public health measures in existence.* But in view of the simultaneous operation of the autonomous factors, we have to keep in mind the fact that there are forces, apart from income changes, that may lead to a secular decline in mortality rates.

It is not going too far to say that the essential element to be explained is the incentive or rationale behind the desire to have larger or smaller families. We have to visualize various contraceptive techniques as merely facilitating factors the utilization of which involves an economic or emotional cost of some sort. But the major burden of any theory must be on the explanation of the forces that create the necessary motivations for the creation of smaller rather than larger families.

A distinction has to be made between the knowledge of alternatives and the choice among known alternatives. It seems reasonable to suppose that as incomes increase, the knowledge of the alternatives pertinent to family limitation also increases. But we still have to explain what determines the choice from among a range of known alternatives. The basic idea behind our theory is that motivations with respect to family size are, to a considerable extent, rational; that, on the whole, parents will want an extra child if the satisfactions to be derived from that child are greater than the "costs" that are involved—where "costs" are to be interpreted rather broadly.

But why should we try to concoct a rationalistic explanation of fertility decline? Can we not simply say that people in backward economies are irrational; that they subject their women to a needless number of conceptions simply because it is conventional to do so, and, furthermore, they have neither the information nor the means to do otherwise? If that is the case, could we not then argue that economic progress results in the spread of rationality, information, and the means to limit fertility? There can be little doubt that the three factors just mentioned have been significant determinants of fertility trends. However, it is doubtful that they could account for the entire picture in the absence of appropriate changes in motivations.

In the first place, there is no evidence that the people in backward economies are irrational. Although it may be true that for the economy as a whole a smaller population size would be advantageous, it does not follow that this fact provides the appropriate motivation for any individual to limit his family size. For what may be appropriate when viewed from the standpoint of the economy as a whole may be most inappropriate when viewed from the position of an individual within that economy. This error involves something that is akin to the fallacy of composition. We shall see that it may be quite rational for individual family units to be interested in as large a number of births as possible in an economy where life is lived close to the subsistence level, while the consequent high birth rate may be quite detrimental to the economy as a whole.

Second, one might argue that those cultures that did not place great stress on child bearing simply disappeared in view of the recurrent high mortality rates. The surviving societies placed such a high value on children that fertility rates were maintained at sufficiently high levels to overcome recurrent high mortality. But can we explain the fact that Western economies gave up such values in the late nineteenth and early twentieth centuries if there is no rationale whatsoever behind such a change? Surely our case is strengthened if we can show that there is some rationality behind the values conducive to high fertility in backward economies and that the same type of rationality enables people to respond to economic changes so that the motivations conducive to the establishment of what has been called the small family system can arise during the course of economic development. Of course, the rate at which attitudes change will depend, in part, on the historical, cultural, and social conditions that determine the tenacity with which traditional views are maintained.

In this section a conceptual scheme is presented that explains two central aspects of the problem: (1) the rationale behind the high birth rate in the subsistence stage and (2) the rationale for the change in motivations as economic development occurs. Of course, it is recognized that changes in motivation are only one aspect of the problem. Appropriate changes in motivations are necessary, but never sufficient, conditions for other changes to take place. Given the appropriate motivations it is also necessary to have the spread of information and the availability of means with which to make the appropriate choices to fulfill the new desires.

And now to the theory proper.

The object is to formulate a theory that explains the factors that determine the desired number of births per family. Of course, family size depends also on how many of the births survive. Our central notion is that people behave in the same way as they would if they applied rough calculations to the problem of determining the number of births they desire. And such calculations would depend on balancing the satisfactions or utilities to be derived from an additional birth as against the "cost," both monetary and psychological, of having an additional child. We distinguish among three types of utility to be derived from an additional birth and two types of cost. The types of utility are: (1) the utility to be derived from the child as a "consumption good," namely, as a source of personal pleasure to the parents; (2) the utility to be derived from the child as a productive agent, that is, at some point the child may be expected to enter the labor force and contribute to family income; and (3) the utility derived from the prospective child as a potential source of security, either in old age or otherwise.

The costs of having an additional child can be divided into direct and indirect costs. By direct costs we refer to the conventional current expenses of maintaining the child, such as feeding and clothing him at conventional standards until the point is reached when the child is self-supporting. By indirect costs we refer to the opportunities foregone due to the existence of an additional child. These are represented by such lost opportunities as the inability of mothers to work if they must tend to children, lost earnings during the gestation period, or the lessened mobility of parents with large family responsibilities.

We may discern three changes that occur during the course of economic development that affect the utilities and costs of an additional child. It is convenient to refer to these as (1) the income effects, (2) the survival effects, and (3) the occupational distribution effects. That is to say, economic progress is characterized by increases in per capita income, increases in the chances of survival, and changes in the occupational distribution, and each tend to alter the motivations toward having additional children. To analyze our problem, we examine what happens to the utility and cost aspects as these three effects play their roles during economic growth.

Consider each of the effects in turn. The income effects are summarized in figure 10–3 below. It depicts the relations between alternate levels of per capita income and the utilities and costs of an additional child. The curves marked *a, b,* and *c* depict how the three types of utility to be derived from a child are likely to change as per capita

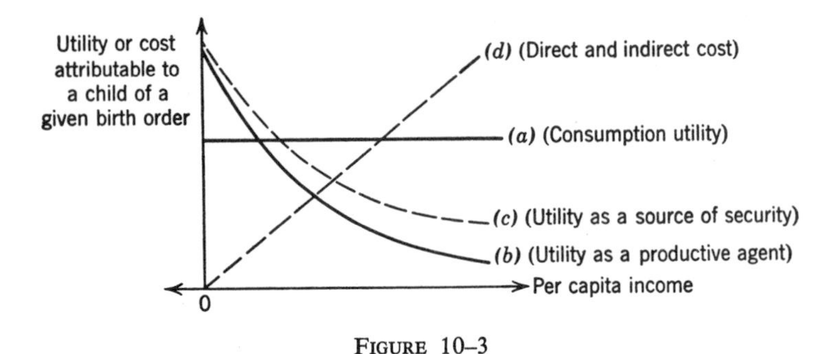

FIGURE 10–3

income increases. The relation (*a*) between the consumption utility and per capita income is difficult to determine, since it is hard to say whether parents get greater or less satisfaction out of an additional child if their income is greater rather than smaller. Arguments can be found for both views. If other sources of satisfaction and direct possibilities for personal fulfillment are exceedingly limited, it seems reasonable to suppose that a great deal of satisfaction is to be derived from a child. Usually an exceedingly high prestige is attached to the bearing of male children in backward economies. On the other hand, the complementary goods necessary for a child's development (and hence the satisfaction derived from observing such development) are more readily available with higher incomes. It is possible that with respect to children of the higher birth orders, greater utility is derived at lower income levels rather than at higher ones, but in the absence of more definite information, it is assumed that the consumption utility does not change in any significant way with changes in income.

The relation (*b*) between the value of a child as a contributor to family income and changes in per capita income is fairly clear. As per capita income increases, there is less need to utilize children as sources of income. At the same time the level of education and the general quality of the population implied by a higher income per head mean that more time must be spent on child training, education, and development, and therefore, less time is available to utilize the child as a productive agent. Therefore, the higher the income, the less the utility to be derived from a prospective child as a productive agent.

As incomes rise, the possibilities for parents to provide for their own old age, to insure themselves, and the ability of the state to provide adequate insurance unquestionably increase. As a result, the need for children as a source of security declines. Hence, the shape of the curve marked *c*.

The conventional costs of child maintenance increase as per capita income increases. The style in which a child is maintained depends on the position and income of the parents; therefore, we expect such costs to rise as incomes rise. The indirect costs are likely to behave in a similar manner. Opportunities for engaging in productive or in various time-consuming consumption activities are likely to grow as income increases; therefore, the opportunity costs of having to tend to an additional child rise accordingly as income increases.

The survival effect is, of course, closely related to income expenditures and costs. In a sense it is not a unique aspect of the situation. It is a consequence of the increased expenditure for the maintenance of children. However, we would not expect the relationship between increased expenditure and survival to be either a proportional or a linear one. First, not all direct costs result in increased survival. Second, when mortality rates are high, decreases in mortality are easier to attain. As mortality rates decline further improvements can be achieved only at progressively greater costs per unit increase in the expectation of life.

The survival effect on the three types of utility curves depicted in figure 10–3 is of special interest for our purposes. In general, increased survival rates raise the utility curves, since for each birth there are more prospective years of life and, therefore, more expected years of satisfaction. This is true also with respect to the utility of children as a source of family income and as a source of old-age security. It is important to note, however, that the survival effects will not be in proportion to the increase in the survival rates, a fact that turns out to be exceedingly important for our theory.

Indeed, what we have here is something that may be called "overcoming the infant mortality hump." Infant mortality rates are very much higher than average mortality rates, sometimes as much as fifteen times above the average rate. As mortality rates decline the infant mortality rate declines, at first, much more rapidly than the others. The initial survival effect is a considerable increase in the number of children per conception who conquer the high infant mortality hurdle. The economic costs of children decline since a higher proportion reaches the productive age groups where they make at least some contribution toward their maintenance. Therefore, the initial survival effect is to enhance the productive value of an additional birth. However, as mortality rates continue to decline, the relative impact on the infant age group lessens compared with the impact on the higher age groups. The decline in mortality rates in the relatively high age groups will have less effect on the prospective utility of a child than similar declines in the low age groups. As a source of parental income, increased survival in the higher age groups is unimportant since in those age groups the children have their own family financial responsibilities. Also, as a source of parental old-age security, increased survival in the high age groups is unimportant since most parents cannot hope to live to the point where their children fall into the very high age groups. Thus we see that beyond some point the survival effect must become progressively smaller as a force that motivates the desire for additional children.

The occupational distribution effect consists mostly in adding to the direct and indirect costs of children. As incomes increase, so do the degree of specialization and the degree of economic (and possibly social) mobility. The number entering narrower, more specialized, and more urban activities also increases. The new occupational environment limits opportunities for child labor, requires more costly training for children, and necessitates smaller family obligations on the part of the parents so that they can take advantage of the new and different economic opportunities.

This last point is related to the "social capillarity thesis" about which much has been written in demographic literature. As summarized in the United Nations report, this theory is roughly as follows:

> The desire to improve one's position in the social scale has been stressed as an important motive for family limitation. The argument is particularly associated with the name of Dumont, who in the latter half of the nineteenth century devoted an extensive series of studies to this phenomenon, which he termed "social capillarity" (*capillarité sociale*). Just as a column of liquid must be thin in order to rise under the force of capillarity, so also must a family be small to rise in the social scale. He and many others have argued that during the period when family size declined, the mobility between social classes increased greatly, and new attitudes toward social mobility developed. Whereas formerly most men took their social position for granted, concern with improving one's own position or that of one's children became an ever-pressing preoccupation in those countries where family limitation spread. The effect of social mobility on fertility appears to be attributed in general to the fact that rearing children absorbs money, time, and effort which could otherwise

be used to rise in the social scale. Social mobility is thus more feasible with one or two children than with a larger number.[12]

The "social capillarity" theory is, of course, only part of the picture. But it illustrates well the notion that the increased specialization implied by the growth in per capita output and the consequent changes in the occupational distribution imply concomitantly a set of social and economic circumstances in which the opportunity costs (that is, the economic opportunities foregone as a result of having to tend to children) of a large family increase rapidly. It is worth noting that the "social capillarity" type of opportunity costs probably depends more on the rate of growth of per capita income than on the *level* of per capita income. The greater the rate of per capita income growth, the greater the extent of the new economic and social opportunities that open up, and the more attractive the possibilities of economic and social mobility. Therefore, the more rapid the rate of growth, the more of a burden children and family responsibilities are likely to be. Hence, if this were the only factor at work, we would expect that the more rapid the rate of growth, the greater the motivation for family limitation.

Explanation of the Four Critical Points

Having spent some time developing the major parts of our analytical apparatus, we now turn to the task of trying to explain the four critical points, *A*, *B*, *C*, and *D*, in figure 10–1 with the aid of the notions just developed.

A. This point is characterized by very low income and very high mortality rates. An examination of the utility and cost factors indicates that they all work toward the creation of motivations conducive to very high fertility rates. For, in this case, the three types of utility to be derived from children are all quite high whereas costs are very low. Since mortality rates are high, a large number of conceptions is required to rear enough children so that two of them survive to an age when they replace the parents. The utility attached to two surviving children is likely to be very high while the direct costs in the agricultural environment are likely to be low. Actually, what we have called the survival effect is likely to be the dominant one where life is lived near the subsistence level. Although the birth rate is quite high, the number surviving will be just enough for replacement. In a sense, the law of diminishing marginal utility is as likely to hold in this case as it does in other types of satisfaction. The parents are likely to attach a greater

[12] United Nations, *op. cit.*, p. 79

value to a second surviving child than to a tenth. It is to be expected that two surviving children will have a very high utility since these, at least, are necessary for the survival of the family unit and the family name. Therefore, if mortality is at a maximum, the motivations will be conducive toward maximum fertility. All the potential parents are aware of is that the chances of survival are very low, and therefore only through maximizing the number of births can they be sure of a reasonable chance that they will have children to survive them.

B. This point is a critical one in any explanation of the fertility aspect of the problem. Here we have to explain why fertility rates do not fall whereas mortality rates do; we have to explain the fertility lag. We can attribute the existence of the fertility lag to two factors: one is what we might call the "realization lag," and the other is the influence of the survival effects of this juncture. Either would probably be a sufficient explanation for the mere fact of a lag, but both help to reinforce each other. The first point simply involves the fact that realization of a change in conditions takes time. The impact of the improvement in the chances of survival is not likely to be felt immediately. The more gradual the rate of change, the less the impact of the change at any point, and the more than proportionate time necessary for the realization that a change has taken place. We can see in this familiar phenomenon a reason for *some* lag in the creation of the motivations conducive to fertility decline.

The other aspects that help to explain the fertility lag depend on a number of factors that work in opposite directions at this juncture. First, the old birth rate now has quite different implications for family size or for the average number of children of a given number of births that survive to a certain age. If under the previous subsistence conditions (point *A*) only two children, on the average, survived, say, to the age of thirty, parents would have to consider whether there was some advantage in having a third child to survive to the age of thirty. Given a law of diminishing utility per additional child, we would expect that the "consumption utility" to be attributed to the third child would be less than that attributed to the second surviving child. And, if this were the only factor involved, and all the other factors were the same as before, we would expect the creation of motivations conducive to fertility decline. But all the other factors change in such a way that their influence is in the opposite direction. (1) The fact of more income means that parents can afford more surviving children as consumption items. (2) Furthermore, the net direct costs of child maintenance decline although at first blush this might appear to be a rather surprising fact. This decline is due to the way the survival effect works out at first. Although it is true that gross costs of maintenance per year rise, the net costs of maintenance (derived by deducting the child's prospective contribution to the family coffers from the direct maintenance cost and averaging this over the expected life of the child) will fall at first, because the initial mortality decline will reduce drastically the proportion that die in the early years as compared to the proportion that die in the productive years. We have already touched on this point when we considered the phenomenon of "overcoming the infant mortality hurdle." As a consequence, the ratio of the productive years to non-productive years per child will at first increase; hence, the value of a child as a source of family income and as a source of old age security increases at first. As a result we cannot expect that the motivations conducive to fertility reduction will be developed in the very early stages of improvement. Indeed, quite the reverse motivations might be established at first.

C. Here we explain why some point is likely to be the crossroad between progress and retrogression and how this point is related to the pattern of fertility rates. There are, of course, both a demographic and an economic aspect to this question. In the interest of continuity, consider the demographic aspect first.

Let us look at some of the forces generated by income growth that work in the direction of creating motivations conducive to fertility decline. First, we have the diminishing "consumption utility" of additional surviving children. Second, there is the decline in the value of the marginal child as a source of family income because the survival effect becomes progressively less important, and the age up to which children are trained and kept out of the labor force gradually increases. Third, the parents' need for a child's earnings as a source of family income and the need for children as a source of old-age security progressively decline as incomes increase. The indirect effects of rising per capita incomes are likely to become progressively more and more significant. For example, the concomitants of rising per capita incomes are likely to lead to the kind of changes in the social structure and in the system of social organization, that result in the gradual disappearance of the child's value as a productive agent and as a source of security. That is to say, urbanization as a concomitant of income growth, later school-leaving ages, new systems of old-age security, the spread and use of insurance plans of various kinds gradually reduce the utility value of a child solely to that of a consumption good. Fourth, the indirect costs, in terms of greater economic opportunities for women, and the increased need for greater mobility are likely to rise continually as incomes grow.

It is of interest to note that some of the factors just considered involve decisions that are of an *all-or-nothing* variety, and, therefore, when such influences do manifest themselves, they are likely to have a considerable effect on "fertility motivations." For example, consider the case in which greater career opportunities are opened to women. Here the problem is not whether or not to have an additional child but whether to have some or none. The average age of marriage may be considerably affected by such considerations. Aggregating the effects of all of the factors, we can see that, beyond some point, the costs and disutilities per additional surviving child increase progressively per unit of income growth. Furthermore, as incomes rise, a point is reached at which the motivation toward more births generated by the survival effect becomes less significant than the motivations toward fewer births induced by the diminishing utility and the increasing costs of an additional child. At this point the balance shifts toward the creation of motivations conducive to fertility decline.

How are these considerations that determine the onset of the fertility decline related to point *C* in figure 10–1? Broadly speaking, the main connection between these demographic factors and the process of economic growth is the notion that the smaller the fertility lag, the smaller the initial minimum effort required, and hence the lower the per capita income at which point *C* occurs. That is, the more rapid the rate at which the fertility decline sets in, the lower the rate of induced population growth, and the less the extent to which population growth absorbs potential national income gains. Or we can say that the question of whether or not the rate of income absorption by population growth is more significant than the rate of capital accumulation will depend on the extent to which fertility declines lag behind the falling mortality rates. But the point *C* need not be a point at which the decline in fertility has already begun. It is quite possible for fertility decline to set in after the critical minimum income level has been achieved. Our argument is simply that the point at which fertility decline sets in will determine the height of the critical minimum income level.

It is of interest to note that this view of the relationship between fertility decline and economic development cannot be deduced entirely on the basis of historical evidence. The reason for this is that although fertility decline may be a necessary condition, it is certainly not a sufficient condition for economic growth. Sustained development may depend on the onset of fertility decline, but sustained fertility decline depends in turn on sustained development. Therefore, in the usual case either both occur or neither occurs. One cannot argue, as Josue de Castro seems to argue,[13] that, on the basis of historical evidence,

---

[13] Josue de Castro, *Geography of Hunger,* Boston, Little, Brown and Co., 1952. De Castro connects poverty with protein deficiency and protein deficiency with high fertility (pp. 70–72, 160–167). Hence, the implication that the elimination of poverty eliminates protein deficiency and its consequence, high fertility.

fertility decline is *a consequence* of economic development and if we can just take care of development, we need not worry about birth rates. The reason why this approach is fallacious is that the economy might not have experienced sustained development if fertility rates had not declined at some crucial stage during this experience. One need not impute the absence of a barrier simply because the race is of such a nature that the barrier cannot be seen when it is successfully overcome.

D. This point refers to the stage at which per capita output is quite high, considerably beyond the subsistence level, and where the economy has overcome the major obstacles to sustained growth. Usually, this is a point at which the gap between mortality and fertility rates closes gradually. In this situation the business cycle is likely to be a significant determinant of economic and social phenomena. Since we are not concerned, in this essay, with short-term fluctuations we shall not enter into an analysis of fertility determinants under such circumstances.

Before closing this section it is worthwhile to recall that our discussion throughout has been in terms of motivations and not in terms of the necessary conditions for fertility decline actually to set in. The creation of the appropriate motivations is just one aspect of the problem. The necessary conditions for fertility decline require in addition that information about alternatives to uncontrolled fertility and effective means to utilize such alternatives be made available. Income growth, technological changes, and all the concomitants that are implied therein, will most probably eventually make available the necessary information and the means. However, in view of the necessary conditions for fertility decline, it is quite likely that *actual* fertility decline sets in later, perhaps much later (depending on the sociocultural conditions at the outset) than the point at which motivations conducive to such decline have been established. It would also seem reasonable to believe that to some extent governmental intervention may, depending on the nature of the activities, either facilitate or hinder the spread of the necessary information and means that can accelerate or retard the onset of fertility decline. However, one cannot be too hasty in drawing policy conclusions from such considerations since ethical and religious values seem to be so very much tied up with these matters.

Summing up, we have seen that a rational and integrated explanation can be worked out to explain various aspects of demographic behavior. Also, the foregoing analysis does suggest, in generic terms, the type of conditions that lead to establishing the motivations conducive to the reduction of fertility rates. To the extent that the institutional and legal framework of an economy can be changed to promote development, it appears that such changes should be in the direction of decreasing the value of children both as productive agents and as sources of security, while simultaneously increasing the indirect opportunity costs of additional children.

The Proper View of the Population Problem

We began this chapter by discussing some incorrect approaches to the population aspect of economic development. One of the points that we tried to establish was that the significance of the population variable cannot be determined by analyzing the current rate of growth. The correct approach is a somewhat more complicated one, the nature of which is discussed with the aid of figure 10–4.[14]

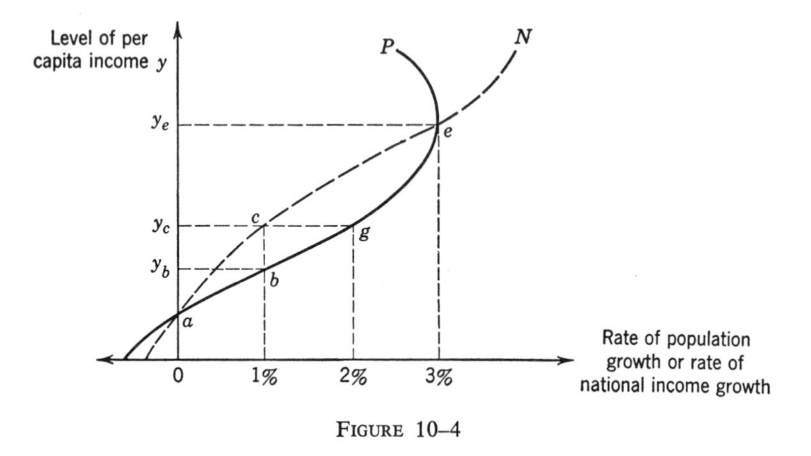

FIGURE 10–4

Under the assumption that the rate of population growth is a function of the level of per capita income, the curve *P* in figure 10–4 indicates, at each level of income, the rate of population growth that would occur if that level of income were sustained. The reader will note that at some per capita income level the rate of population growth is a maximum and beyond that point the rate declines. The shape of the curve *P* is in accordance with ideas we have already discussed. Other things being equal, the higher the level of per capita income the greater the rate of population growth until the maximum rate is reached at *e*.

The curve labeled *N* indicates the level of per capita income required to generate a level of national income growth equal to the rate of popula-

[14] Like other figures used in this book, this one abstracts some central aspects of the problem from a large number of the complications that exist in real situations, and like the others, it is intended only for illustrative purposes so that we may proceed with the argument. At most, the figures are intended as aids to *steps* in the argument, and not as summary pictures of the entire situation.

tion growth. For example, consider the point *c*. It shows that a per capita income of y_c will generate a 1 per cent increase in national income if the rate of population growth is 1 per cent. All the other points on *N* reflect similar combinations of per capita income and population growth such that, if they existed, the growth in national income would just equal the rate of population growth. Given these two definitions of the curves, we can readily see that the point *a* reflects the subsistence equilibrium point at which there is neither population growth nor income growth.

Consider for a moment the meaning of points between *a* and *e*. Suppose that the level of per capita income is y_c. Related to this per capita income we have the points *c* on the *N*-curve and the point *g* on the *P*-curve. These points signify that at the y_c level of per capita income the rate of population growth is 2 per cent whereas the rate of national income growth is only 1 per cent. Obviously, this is a disequilibrium state and cannot represent a level of income that can sustain itself. Returning to figure 10–4, we can see that it would be incorrect to argue that at the initial per capita income of y_b and the related rate of population growth of 1 per cent we need only increase national income by more than 1 per cent per year in order to overcome the population hurdle. The reason why such a view is erroneous, as is any argument based on only the current rate of population growth, is that at the higher level of per capita income, as a consequence of the creation of a rate of national income growth of more than 1 per cent, the related rate of population growth increases by more than the induced rate of national income growth. It is only at and beyond the point *e* that we reach levels of per capita income that generate rates of national income growth that are equal to or greater than the induced rates of population growth. Therefore, we may view per capita income y_e as the critical minimum per capita income that has to be achieved if we are to have sustained internally generated *per capita* income growth.[15] A more adequate way to look at the demographic aspect is to ask whether there is some level (and, if so, what level) of per capita income at which the economy will save and invest at such a rate that the additions to national income are greater than the rate of population growth that would be generated by that level of per capita income. Obviously, this is a very different approach from the one in which, say, a 1 per cent rate of population growth is observed and the conclusion that is drawn is that the population obstacle can be overcome by a more than 1 per cent rate of growth in national income. The real population obstacle, if we may view the

[15] Again this oversimplifies the matter. See the appendix to this chapter and especially Chapter 13.

matter in these terms, is (in the case depicted in figure 10–4) the maximum rate we can expect during the course of development, that is, a 3 per cent rate of growth, even though the current and past rates of population growth have been no larger than 1 per cent.

At this point a query that may have arisen in the mind of the reader must be considered. Does not the problem arise simply because of the way we have drawn the two curves *P* and *N*? Consider the very different situation illustrated in figure 10–5. In this case the *P*-curve is always

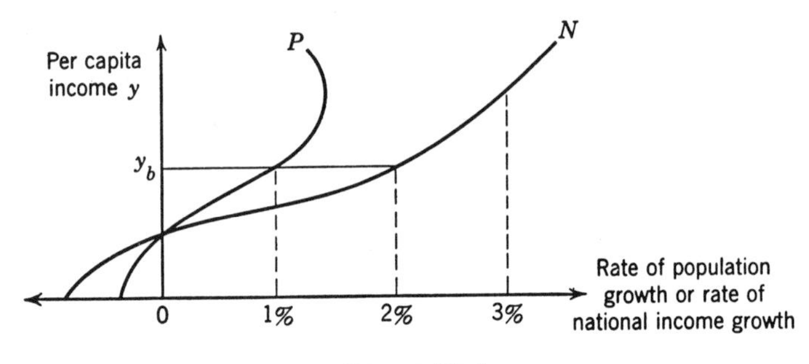

FIGURE 10–5

above the *N*-curve for all levels of per capita income above the subsistence equilibrium level. This implies that for every level of per capita income above subsistence, the rate of national income growth will always be larger than the rate of population growth. Obviously, this is an essentially progressive economy in which the critical minimum effort hypothesis does not apply.

There is no reason to reject the case depicted in figure 10–5 on purely logical grounds. However, we cannot believe it to be the typical case or the case that we are interested in given the nature of the problems that we have in mind. As we have already argued in previous chapters, this case represents a type of situation that cannot explain the persistence of economies at near subsistence levels for long periods of time, since the equilibrium position in this case is essentially an unstable one. That is, it depicts an essentially progressive economy that does not contain any distinctive properties that would enable us to rationalize the absence of growth. Yet it is the absence of growth in some areas, as against its persistence in others, that interests us primarily. The case shown in figure 10–5 implies that even at exceedingly low levels of income people in such an economy choose to augment their capital stock more than they would choose to increase consumption and, as a consequence, reduce mortality rates. Furthermore, it implies that at such low per capita income levels there is, nevertheless, a sufficient inducement to save, a sufficient incentive to invest, and a sufficiently efficient distribution of investment so that the resulting rate of national income growth is more significant than the impact on population growth that results from attempts to increase consumption above the initial near subsistence level. All this appears to go counter to our usual impressions of the conditions that exist in backward areas.

But we cannot entirely dismiss out of hand the situation depicted in figure 10–5. It may be representative of what may be called the "open spaces" type of situation, the sort of situation that we associate with the development of the United States, Canada, Australia, etc. It may be the sort of situation in which a people possessing very much more advanced techniques than the natives take over a country in which the application of the new techniques makes the availability of potentially cultivatable land exceedingly more abundant than the old ones. This is especially true of those cases in which with new techniques land becomes so exceedingly plentiful that it is almost a free good, for example, the American frontier during some periods. But this is certainly not the situation that we have to deal with in the present-day backward economies.

APPENDIX TO CHAPTER 10

We can, if we wish, consider somewhat more complicated systems than those depicted in figures 10–4 and 10–5 by introducing additional variables. Consider, for example, the important case where the *P*-curves and the *N*-curves depend also on the *rate* of per capita income growth. Figures 10–6, 10–7, 10–8, and 10–9 illustrate in compact form the type of complications we have in mind and indicate how we can add to our analytical tool box in this way. In chapter 13 similar relations are presented in a less compact manner.

In figure 10–6, we have a map of our *P*-curves which reflect the possibility that population growth may depend not only on the level of per capita income but also on the rate at which per capita income grows. On the curve P_0 each point indicates the alternate rate of population growth for alternate levels of per capita income on the assumption that the rate of growth in per capita income is zero. In a similar way the curve P_1 reflects the same kind of relationship except that the assumed rate of per capita income growth is 1 per cent. P_2, P_3, and so on, are defined in a similar manner for the given rates of per capita income growth implied by the subscripts. The greater the rate of per capita income growth, the greater the rate of investment and, hence, the lower the level of consumption per unit of income. On the presumption that lower levels of consumption imply higher mortality rates, we arrive at the conclusion that the greater the rate of per capita income growth the less the rate of population growth, other things being equal. Therefore,

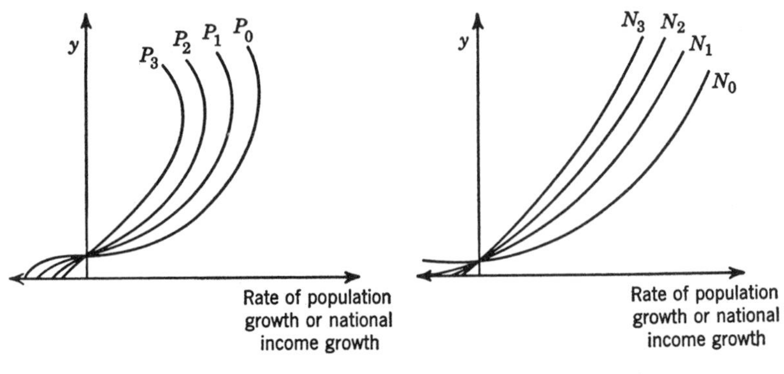

FIGURE 10–6 FIGURE 10–7

the *P*-curves with the higher subscripts are drawn to the left of those with the lower subscripts.

In figure 10–7, the map of *N*-curves is built up in a similar fashion. Consider the curve N_1. A point on that curve implies that for the given level of per capita income and the given rate of population growth, a level of national income will be generated that will result in a 1 per cent increase in per capita income. Similarly, the other curves suggest the same sort of thing for 0 per cent, 2 per cent, and 3 per cent growths in per capita income.

In figure 10–8 the maps developed on figures 10–6 and 10–7 are superimposed on each other. The intersection e_0 of the N_0 and P_0 curves reflects the point *above* which the economy will generate *more than* a 0 per cent rate of per capita income growth. Similarly, the intersection e_1 of the N_1 and P_1 curves is a point at which the economy will generate a 1 per cent rate of growth. The points designated by e_2, e_3, etc., could be similarly interpreted. It should be observed that none of these points are stable equilibrium points. Since once a rate of per capita income growth is generated, the level of per capita income rises to a new high which implies still different rates of per capita income growth. Note that in figure 10–8 the level of per capita income designated y_1 is the critical minimum per capita income level. It indicates that unless the economy can raise per capita income to that level, economic growth cannot be sustained.

In figure 10–9 an interesting possibility is illustrated. The curve

L_1L_1 is the locus of points e_0, e_1, e_2, etc., that we considered in figure 10–8. However, this curve need not take the shape indicated by L_1L_1. Some experimentation with the shapes of the population growth maps (P-curves) and national income growth maps (N-curves) will indicate that the locus of points e_0, e_1, etc., could take on the shape shown by L_2L_2 (given by the locus e_0', e_1', e_2', e_3', etc.). Now, what does such

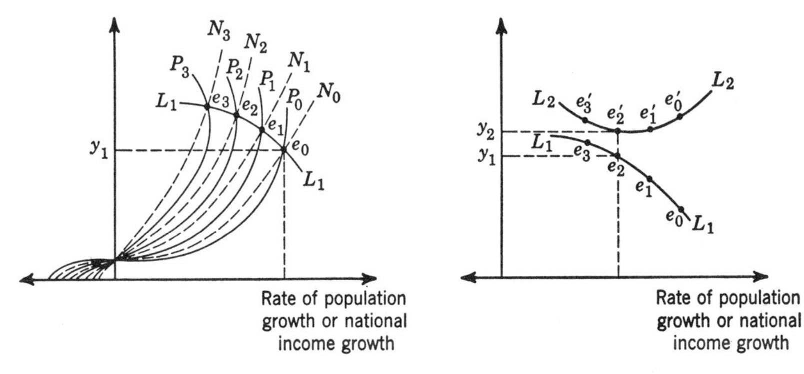

FIGURE 10–8

FIGURE 10–9

a curve reflect? Consider the point e_2' and its related level of per capita income y_2. This last point indicates that the critical minimum per capita income level is related to a 2 per cent rate of income growth rather than a 0 per cent rate of growth. It reflects the rather interesting, and entirely possible, situation in which the backward economy must somehow raise itself to a level of per capita income at which it can grow at, say, at least 2 per cent, or some other positive rate, or not grow at all. In other words, in the case illustrated, the structure of the economy is such that initial rates of growth of less than 2 per cent cannot generate sustained growth if the initial per capita income level is only y_2. That is to say, not only must the exogenous stimulant raise the per capita income level up to some minimum, but the minimum per capita income level must also be one that can generate at least a certain minimum rate of per capita income growth if growth is to sustain itself.

CHAPTER 11

Some Notes on Capital-Output Ratios

Introduction

In chapter 13 we shall use the incremental capital-output ratio as part of a summary view of our theory of development. To set the stage for that chapter we consider here the relation between capital-output ratios and the level of per capita income.

The use and development of capital-output ratios, or variants thereof, stem, in part, from the well-known models of Harrod, Hicks, Domar, and others. Although these writers seem initially to have had the business cycle problem in mind, it is clear from the nature of the concept that it is easily transferable to growth problems in the underdeveloped areas. For an aggregative income growth theory, the role of the capital-output concept can be readily seen from the simple connection between the *incremental* capital-output ratio and the rate of national income growth.[1] By "incremental capital" we really mean investment, and,

[1] The exact role that the incremental capital-output ratio plays in our theory is indicated in chapter 13. As the reader might expect, the capital-output ratio will be employed in the determination of the current *rate* of national income growth. In its simplest form this last is obtained by multiplying the current investment rate (proportion of net national income invested) by the reciprocal of the incremental capital-output ratio. Let Y be net national income, ΔY the absolute increase in net national income, and let I be net investment, that is, the

unless we indicate otherwise, we shall mean net investment.[2] Roughly speaking, the incremental capital-output ratio tells us the rate at which investment is turned into additions to net income per year for the economy as a whole. For example, if net investment is 15 per cent of national income, and if we know that the rate at which investment is turned into net income per year is 5 to 1, we infer that the rate of national income growth will be 3 per cent per year. But this is really too simple an approach to the problem.

The helpfulness of the capital-output concept can be easily exaggerated. It is probable that the incremental capital-output ratio would be a powerful tool of analysis if it could reasonably be assumed that the ratio is independent of the behavior of the other variables in the system. But, as we shall see below, there is really no reason to believe in the independence of the capital-output ratio from the behavior of other variables. Therefore, it seems appropriate at this juncture to consider some of the possible relations that may exist between changes in the capital-output ratio and our index of development, per capita income. However, a few distinctions are called for before we get into more substantive matters.[3]

One difficulty with incremental capital-output ratios is that their value is indeterminate since the circumstances under which they are to apply are not specified. Capital-output ratios can have little meaning if factors completely unrelated to additions to the capital stock can cause great variations in output. The major factor that will change the value of the capital-output ratio is the extent to which other agents of production are utilized in the productive process but which, for various reasons, are not counted as part of the increment to the capital stock. There are several possibilities. There may have been unutilized capacity prior to the addition to the capital stock which for some reason or other, uncon-

---

increment to the capital stock. We therefore write I/Y for the investment rate, and $I/\Delta Y$ for the incremental capital-output ratio. It then follows that the rate of net national income growth is

$$\frac{I}{Y} \cdot \frac{\Delta Y}{I} = \frac{\Delta Y}{Y}$$

[2] The "investment-output ratio" would probably be a better term, but in deference to what appears to be current usage, we shall employ the term "capital-output ratio."

[3] When we speak of the "capital-output ratio" we shall always mean the *incremental* capital-output ratio, unless otherwise indicated. There are obvious expository advantages to the shorter form.

nected with capital accumulation, is employed after the investment takes place. Another obvious factor is the increase in the labor force that can occur, and indeed usually does occur, simultaneously with the addition to capital. Still another influence, one that is usually unnoticed, is the change in the nature or availability of "free factors" that are important in the production process. We have in mind such elements as climatic conditions, the availability of space or air, or any other physical attribute of the production process which, because of its abundance or the nature of its availability, bears no economic cost. The most obvious items, such as sunshine and rainfall, may influence output significantly in some industries. In all such cases the capital-output ratio is lower than otherwise because the other factors that come into play increase output to an extent that cannot be accounted for by the increase in capital. The reverse might also take place, so that decreases in the labor force or changes in some other factors, unrelated to changes in the capital stock, decrease output.

The quality and the energy of the labor force are other factors that will obviously have some bearing on the capital-output ratio. A highly skilled labor force, and one that becomes increasingly energetic as well as one that is highly flexible and mobile, will quite naturally produce more output per unit of capital than a phlegmatic, immobile, and tradition-bound labor force.

Our enumeration of the possible factors that may influence the value of the capital-output ratio has only begun but enough has been said to suggest that if the incremental capital-output ratio is to be used in a meaningful way then we must always keep in mind the changing circumstances that may occur when additions to the capital stock are made. In this connection it may be well to distinguish between the incremental capital-output ratio as it actually occurs *ex post facto,* that is, and what we might call the *net* incremental capital-output ratio (NICOR) and the adjusted incremental capital-output ratio (AICOR). By the net incremental capital-output ratio (NICOR) we have in mind the capital-output ratio as it would be on the assumption that the supplies of all other factors are held constant. By the adjusted incremental capital-output ratio (AICOR) we have in mind what the capital-output ratio would be if it were adjusted to a *given* increase in the supply of other factors, for example, a 1 per cent increase of the labor force. Thus, in the NICOR we try to visualize the capital-output ratio net of any changes in other factors of production whereas in the AICOR we visualize the ratio for a given specific change in other factors. Although we shall not make use of these distinctions directly it is well to keep them in mind as we proceed with our considerations.

The Relationship between Capital-Output Ratios and Per Capita Income

Do capital-output ratios remain constant, increase, or diminish as a country becomes more developed economically? This is the question we must face if we intend to use the capital-output ratio as part of a theory of income growth. Of the three possibilities suggested by the question we shall employ the hypothesis that capital-output ratios decline as a country becomes more developed economically.[4] It is important to observe that neither this hypothesis nor its alternatives can be proved on *a priori* grounds on the basis of existing economic theory. However, it seems that the hypothesis just mentioned is more likely to hold generally, and therefore we shall advance in this section arguments that support this belief.

Unfortunately, some of the arguments that are pertinent are of the "on the one hand, on the other hand" variety. At the very least, we can point to some factors that increase capital-output ratios as a country develops and to others that suggest the opposite tendency. As a consequence, the arguments in defense of our hypothesis can never be conclusive. At some point we have to strike a balance and indicate which of the factors we consider more important.

As we proceed with our discussion, we will observe that there are two broad aspects to the question. That is, as development occurs the overall capital-output ratio may change because (1) the capital-output ratios change for some or all of the commodities produced, or because (2) the aggregate output bundle shifts in its composition from commodities that utilize more capital in their production to those that utilize less, or vice versa. In actual practice both influences are likely to operate simultaneously.

Let us now consider some of the specific arguments. One of the first that comes to mind is that as an economy develops, the wage rate will rise and, as a consequence, there will be a tendency to substitute capital for labor. The result is that in those industries where factor substitution is possible, the methods of production will be less labor-intensive than in the less-developed stage, and capital-output ratios will rise with development. But, as we shall see later, this is only a small part of the picture. An interesting study by an Indian economist V. V. Bhatt[5] is suggestive in this connection. Bhatt's computations and

---

[4] Note that our theory (see chapters 12 and 13) does not depend on this hypothesis, although we shall see that the hypothesis developed here does help to support our general theory.

[5] V. V. Bhatt, "Capital-Output Ratios of Certain Industries: A Comparative

data indicate that the empirical evidence for a number of countries, both developed and underdeveloped, does not support the expectation that capital-output ratios are lower (for the *same* manufacturing industries) in the less-developed than in the more-developed countries. For some manufacturing industries, the more advanced countries do indeed have higher capital-output ratios, but for a great many manufacturing industries (indeed, in the list studied, which may not be representative, it seems to be so for most of them), quite the reverse appears to be the case.

Another argument that supports the case for increasing capital-output ratios as a concomitant of economic development is related to the fact that exhaustible, non-replaceable resources per man will decline as both income and population grow. As a consequence, the supply of the exhaustible resource declines and its price rises. To the extent that this resource enters into the production of capital goods, the capital-output ratio will rise accordingly. But on this point we can easily get into a controversy as to whether *known* resources do or do not in fact decline over time. The optimistic attitude is that for many, many decades we have heard about the possible exhaustion of some specific resource in the very near future, and yet, as time goes on, resource discoveries are such that we always seem to have as many resources as we had in the past. What this approach amounts to is that what really counts is the number of known resources, and that the rate of resource discovery has always been greater than the rate of utilization. Consequently, the optimistic argument runs, there is no reason to believe that this happy state of affairs will not continue in the future. It is impossible to argue for or against assertions about future discoveries. The point of the matter is that most of these discoveries would have probably been made in any event, and the supply and accessibility of any given resource would quite clearly have been greater if the rate of utilization in the past had been less. Thus, with respect to cost per unit of resource, it does appear likely that costs are higher than otherwise if the population size is greater than formerly.

On the other hand, Colin Clark[6] has argued that the capital-output ratios should diminish as a country develops economically because the capital-output ratios are lower in tertiary industries, and the composition of output shifts away from the primary and toward the tertiary industries as per capita income grows. But there may be some significant excep-

---

Study of Certain Countries," *The Review of Economics and Statistics,* August 1954, pp. 309–320.

[6] Colin Clark, *Conditions of Economic Progress,* 2nd Ed., London, Macmillan and Co., Ltd., 1951, Chapter XI, especially pp. 500–504.

tions to this general view. For example, in medical care the capital-output ratio is quite high compared with the capital-output ratio in some secondary industries. Furthermore, some more advanced countries have higher capital-output ratios than some (but not all) seemingly less advanced countries.[7] Also, the data are often of such a quality that it would be most hazardous to draw reliable inferences from them. Nevertheless, there may be some good reasons for accepting the Clarkian hypothesis on grounds other than the empirical data to which Clark appeals.

A number of factors in conformity with this hypothesis readily come to mind. We have already mentioned the effect of the change in the composition of output. The quality of the labor force and the energy with which the labor force applies itself in the production process is likely to increase as income grows. One reason for this, among others, is the fact that increased consumption expenditure from the increased income is likely to improve the vitality and knowledge of the labor force.[8] This is not an exogenous change in the quality of the labor force which we have in mind but one that is directly attributable to the growth in per capita income itself. At the same time, as we argued in a previous chapter, the increased capital should facilitate the division of labor and, hence, bring about higher labor productivity due to the fact that the productive activities are being carried out where they could be carried out most efficiently.

A number of other arguments could be advanced that would favor the diminishing capital-output ratio thesis. Some of the possibilities in this direction are the facility with which indivisibilities of certain capital goods can be overcome as output increases, and, in a similar vein, the likelihood that external economies may become more significant as output increases. In any event economies of scale are likely to be very important.[9] Also, as output per head increases, the variety of commodities also increases, hence, the greater the possibility of utilizing capital-saving innovations. All of these reasons are very similar to those usually used in arguments that suggest the possibilities for increasing returns as income per head rises.

An especially interesting aspect of the problem is the relationship between the durability of the capital and the capital-output ratio. The

---

[7] See Bhatt, *op. cit.*, among others. Also Clark, *op. cit.*

[8] The reader will recall that the arguments in chapter 6 were based on this notion.

[9] As a country develops, the scale of output of various firms is likely to increase. Bhatt's calculations suggest that for the ten Indian manufacturing industries for which he presents the data, the capital-output ratios are always lower in the large scale than in the small scale firms. See Bhatt, *op. cit.*, p. 317.

first notion that comes to mind is that the more durable the capital, other things being equal, the higher the capital-output ratio. But the relation is somewhat more complicated. Let us assume for a moment that value of output is equal to cost of output. It is clear that the fixed costs of depreciation, depletion, and obsolescence that stem from the capital costs are not the only costs of production, and hence not the only factors that enter into the determination of the value of output. Other current costs may also be involved. But it follows from these considerations that the more significant these fixed costs are as a proportion of the value of output, the more important is the durability of capital in determining the capital-output ratio. If capital is the only agent of production, durability is the only determinant. Therefore, when the other operating costs are small, durability is likely to be highly significant.

Consider the relations between these variables in the case of low per capita incomes and heavy population pressure as compared with the situation in which the reverse conditions hold. In the low income situation, capital is the very scarce factor and labor the ample one. For those industries in which the coefficients of production are fixed, the capital cost will be high and the labor cost low. If the durability of the capital used is the same in the earlier as in the later stages of development, we would expect the capital-output ratio to be larger in the earlier stages. But when the coefficients of production are not relatively fixed, the situation is indeterminate. On the one hand, in the low per capita income situation, labor will be substituted for capital as compared with the high per capita income case. But, on the other hand, the relative price of a unit of capital, as against a unit of labor, will be higher in the low income situation. As development proceeds, the relative price of a unit of capital declines, but at the same time the capital to labor ratio increases. Which factor will be the more significant is difficult to say.

The durability of the capital is not likely to remain constant as development proceeds. There is some reason to believe that the durability of the capital is likely to be greater in the earlier stages of development because of the nature of some of the necessary construction projects in the initial stages. This is especially true of such factors as the provision of initial transportation and storage facilities as well as the so-called overhead costs of urbanization that may be necessary in the early stages. The durability of such structures as roads, railroads, public buildings, is certainly likely to be longer than various types of light industrial machinery that may form a greater proportion of investment in the later stages of development.

An additional point in the same direction is that the rent component of total cost (and of total value of output) is likely to be less in the earlier stages of growth. Rents on the fixed factors of production are likely to increase as development proceeds, because as output increases, the competition for the fixed factors will increase accordingly. Therefore rent, as a proportion of the total cost of output, is likely to be less in the early stages, the capital component will be relatively greater, and the importance of the durability of the capital as a determinant of the capital-output ratio will be greater accordingly.[10]

Probably the most important force working in the direction of declining capital-output ratios is the "non-capital investment" aspect of the development process. We have already alluded to this factor previously, but it may be worth repeating since it so often goes unnoticed. Among the concomitants of per capita income growth are increased expenditures per capita on what might be called "human investment." These are expenditures which increase the productive capacity of the labor force, and which come about as a consequence of the usual operation of the economy as such, but which we do not classify as additions to the capital stock. Expenditures on education and on the learning of specific skills are of this nature. As the labor force is gradually improved in this manner, the value added by labor per unit of output increases accordingly. Hence, the same quantity of labor without any increase in capital yields a greater output. This is obviously a factor that contributes toward declining capital-output ratios.

In sum, we have seen that quite a few factors contribute toward declining capital-output ratios as a consequence of per capita income growth. Among those we have mentioned are the probabilities that income growth will be accompanied by: (1) an increase in the capacity of the labor force, (2) an increase in the size of the labor force, (3) an increased ability of the economy to overcome capital indivisibilities, (4) a shift in demand toward services that require little capital per unit of output, (5) a shift away from the need for highly durable capital so necessary in the early stages of industrialization, (6) an increase in the rate of obsolescence, and (7) increases in rent per unit of output. On the other hand, there may be the need to replace depleted natural resources by man-made resources during the course of development. But at the same time economic development may increase the capacity of the economy to discover some of its potential natural resources. Of course, the nature of the inventions that may occur during the process of development cannot be foretold. Discoveries of

[10] Of course rents may decline as a result of the discovery and introduction into the economy of man-made resources that replace fixed natural resources.

more economic but more durable types of capital goods, or the invention of economic production processes or commodities that are more highly capital-using than the average can result in increasing capital-output ratios. But all in all, it seems that, in the general case, there is some reason to expect declining net incremental capital-output ratios as development proceeds.

It is especially interesting to note that our general hypothesis of diminishing capital-output ratios as growth increases reinforces our critical minimum effort hypothesis; for once the initial high capital-output ratio is overcome, the obstacle to economic growth is reduced, since a smaller rate of saving is necessary in order to induce further growth.

CHAPTER 12

A Summary View

This and the next chapter complement one another. Here we consider in brief the more general ideas developed thus far, while in the next chapter we tie together the basic relations with the use of a specific model.

In reading these paragraphs it is important to keep in mind that no attempt has been made to consider every aspect of economic growth. Rather, we have tried to present a broad thesis whose purpose is to shed some light on central aspects of the development problem. We have also examined elaborations on our general hypothesis and applications of it to various aspects of the growth process. Of course, some aspects not considered, such as, the role of the monetary mechanism and the influence of international trade, are of considerable significance. By limiting the scope of our considerations we were able to go a little more deeply into the general problem. The facets of economic growth are much too numerous to be treated in their entirety.

What follows is a summary view of the general theory, not an outline of all the chapters. In the interest of brevity many concepts and ideas previously introduced are not redefined.

Basic Distinctions

We began our analysis by distinguishing between two general sets of circumstances under which an economy may appear to be operating. One is an equilibrium or quasi-equilibrium system under which the variables of the system, or at least some of them, possess equilibrium values. In the other, the non-equilibrium system, the values taken on by the variables change, period after period, without any tendency to approach a specific set of values. In other words, the non-equilibrium system is characterized by constant flux. Employing per capita output as an index of economic development, we indicated some of the major properties of specific equilibrium states in which per capita output (or income) is at a subsistence level. One variant of such an equilibrium state is the stationary state in which per capita income is at subsistence, and under which there is no expansion of either the capital stock or of the population. Although it is simpler to keep the stationary equilibrium model in mind as an illustration of an extreme state of economic backwardness, we have seen that we need not limit ourselves to models of that nature. We can also visualize quasi-equilibrium states in which the absolute magnitudes of some of the variables, such as capital and labor force, expand constantly, whereas the relation between the expanding variables is such that their interaction with the other variables in the system manifests itself in a tendency of the resulting per capita income to approach or fluctuate near and about a subsistence level. Thus, per capita income may have an equilibrium value even if some of the other variables in the system do not. In both models our index of development, per capita income, possesses a subsistence equilibrium value, and it is the extent and the nature of the stability of the actual or near equilibrium per capita income level that are our major concerns.

Our non-equilibrium state is one in which there is continuous secular growth. That is to say, in the long run we visualize constant increases in the capital stock, in population, in the labor force, in technique, and in per capita output. Under these circumstances there are no definable equilibrium values for the variables. From time to time there may be some temporary fluctuations due to lapses from "full" employment during which per capita income may decline. But, on the average, the economy's capacity to produce goods and services per head increases in the long run.

Finally, we suggested that the quasi-stable subsistence equilibrium system characterizes the underdeveloped areas whereas the non-equilibrium system characterizes the developed ones. This is not meant to suggest that the underdeveloped areas are necessarily in a *state* of equilibrium, but simply that their state is such that, if no exogenous influences intervened, they would return eventually to a state characterized by a near subsistence level of income. The problem for the backward economy is to transform its situation in such a way that it may escape from the subsistence or near subsistence equilibrium state.

The Critical Minimum Effort Thesis

The crucial aspect of our theory has to do with an explanation of why the subsistence equilibrium state should possess stability in the small but not in the large. There are two parts to this problem. First, we must be able to explain why, at low levels of per capita income or at levels not very much above subsistence, the *dynamics* of the economy are such that income per head eventually returns to its subsistence level. The other is to indicate the sets of relations which imply that for some sufficiently large displacements from equilibrium the economy will shift from the equilibrium to the non-equilibrium type. Thus, we visualize that for the typical underdeveloped economy there is some crucial level of per capita income, and a related level of per capita income *growth,* above which the economy ceases to be of the equilibrium type and changes into the non-equilibrium type.

Specifically, our aim is to show that a certain minimum per capita income level has to be achieved in order for the economy to generate sustained growth from within. In order to demonstrate this we distinguished between endogenous or induced events, that is, events that are explained by the behavior equations of the models, or less technically, events that can be expected to spring from the day-to-day economic processes of the economy, and exogenous or autonomous events that originate outside the economy or are exceptional in the sense that they could not be expected to arise from the day-to-day economic processes. We are especially concerned with a specific type of exogenous event which we referred to as a stimulant, that is, an exogenous event the initial impact of which is to *raise* per capita income above its former level.

Briefly, this is the general argument that leads us to expect that the subsistence equilibrium per capita income level will possess stability in the small: Every per capita income-raising force brings into play income-depressing forces. At low per capita income levels the income-depressing forces are more significant than the income-raising ones. However, at high per capita income levels the reverse may be true; the income-raising forces generated by the stimulant may be and usually are more significant than the income-depressing ones. From this we derive what we have called the critical minimum effort thesis. This states that if sustained development is to be generated, it is necessary that the initial effort or the initial series of efforts[1] must be above a certain minimum magnitude. That is to say, not all efforts to raise per

[1] The minimum effort need not be made all at once. It may be more effective if it is broken up into a series of smaller efforts of which the applications to the economy are optimally timed. On this and related matters see chapter 15.

capita income lead to economic development. There are some that are too small to do so.

Growth Agents and Growth Activities

The rationale of our thesis rests on the notion that certain favorable economic conditions have to exist in order that the "growth agents" may expand at a sufficient rate to render their contribution more significant than the depressing effects of the retardation factors. By growth agents we mean the quantum of capacities residing in the members of the population to carry out growth-contributing activities. The outcome of such growth-contributing activities is to increase the quantum of productive capacities of the population, their entrepreneurial capabilities, their skills, their stock of knowledge, etc. But it is important to note that while the growth-contributing activities expand the capacities of the labor force, they may, and usually will, in part, expand the magnitude of the growth agents themselves.

Whether or not the growth agents (and the activities by which they manifest themselves) expand will depend on the anticipated outcome of such activities, the actual result, and on the incentives for further expansion or contraction generated by the interaction of the anticipations, the activities, and the results. In discussing motivations and incentives we contrasted two types: those that led to activities that yield increases in national income (positive-sum incentives) and those that did not (zero-sum incentives). We also argued that in stagnant backward economies the incentives, at the outset, are by and large of the zero-sum type. Also, some of the activities set in motion by positive-sum incentives lead to their degeneration and to the creation of counteracting, zero-sum incentives. But at the same time there will be some members of the economy who will have invested in capital or in the development and expansion of their own economic skills and abilities, whose anticipated gains are fulfilled. Quite naturally we expect that activities that result in at least their anticipated gains would give rise to further positive-sum incentives of a similar nature. Also, it seems reasonable to posit, and there are certainly many reasons that can be advanced for the belief, that the greater the actual rate of growth, the greater the extent to which such anticipations are fulfilled. Hence, our contention that in the general case, only a fairly rapid rate of growth, as a consequence of the appropriate stimulants, could lead to an economic environment in which the continually created positive-sum incentives are more important than those that are degenerating as well as more important than the counteracting, zero-sum incentives.

The point is that not all anticipated rates of growth will have equal power to induce a sufficient expansion of the growth agents enabling anticipations to materialize. For some rates of growth results will be greater than expected and for others less than expected. Results greater than expected will stimulate a further expansion in the growth agents, and results less than expected will stimulate either no expansion or a contraction of the growth agents. The outcome will depend on the synchronization of entrepreneurial plans for expansion and on the simultaneously induced expansion of the growth agents. But it is quite likely that not all actual rates of growth will induce an equally felicitous synchronization of these plans and events.

We concentrated especially on three growth-contributing activities: the creation of entrepreneurship, the expansion of productive skills, and the increase in productive knowledge. In this connection we argued that the expansion of the growth agents responsible for such activities requires at the outset (*a*) a minimum level of per capita income above the subsistence level and simultaneously (*b*) a minimum rate of growth. The first condition (*a*) is necessary because expansion in the growth agents comes about, in great part if not entirely, through "investment in human beings," that is, in a state of affairs in which consumption is for more than merely subsistence. Since there is bound to be a lag between the "investment in human beings," and the application of the new non-capital resources to productive activities, there must be a rate of growth sufficiently large to generate enough new economic opportunities to allow the purpose of, benefits from, and inducements for this type of non-capital investment to be seen.

Furthermore, the critical minimum income at which the required rate of growth can be achieved must be sufficiently large to overcome many influences hostile to change as well as those that have the direct effect of decreasing resources per capita. We can point to a number of such influences, prominent among which are: (1) the zero-sum entrepreneurial activities directed toward the maintenance of existing economic privileges through the inhibition and curtailment of potentially expanding economic opportunities; (2) the conservative activities of both organized and unorganized labor directed against change, such as featherbedding, security regulations, and the maintenance of existing techniques; (3) the resistance to new knowledge and ideas and the simultaneous attraction of classical knowledge and old ideas; (4) increases in "essentially non-productive" conspicuous public or private consumption expenditures that use resources that could otherwise be used for capital accumulation; and (5) population growth and the consequent labor force growth that has the effect, other things being equal, of diluting the amount of capital available per worker. (6) An additional supporting strand in this connection is the hypothesis developed in the last chapter to the effect that the incremental capital-output ratio is likely to be higher in the less-developed than in the more-developed stage.

At the same time consider the major concomitants and effects of sustained growth. (1) Per capita income increases usually imply an expansion of economic opportunities and an environment conducive to the success of past economic ventures. As a result, the expansion of the productive capacities of the economy in previous periods appear to be justified and serve, at the same time, as incentives for the further expansion of the agents of production. (2) Economic growth tends to penalize the economically retarding and conservative forces in the economy, since sustained growth usually occurs in an environment under which the rewards of success go, generally, to those who make a contribution toward growth. (3) But at the same time economic growth creates some incentive for some of the potentially retarding forces to inhibit further growth. There will always be some who will be displaced by change and, therefore, the greater the rate of change, the greater the incentive for such people to fight against change. However, the greater the rate of growth, the easier it is for marginal firms and other factors of production to maintain themselves, and hence the less significant become the efforts, compared to the rate of growth, of those who find it in their interest to struggle against further change. (4) The greater the rate of economic growth, the greater the rate of population growth—but only up to a point. This last assertion is more significant for the earlier rather than the later stages of development. Furthermore, there is always a biological maximum to the rate of population growth, so that a sufficiently large rate of economic growth can always overcome the population hurdle. In sum, we see that the perception of, belief in and experience of per capita income growth above some minimal rate, and the consequence of such growth, may itself be a necessary condition for further growth.

With regard to the demographic aspect of per capita income growth, we saw that a crucial element is the length of the lag of fertility decline behind mortality decline, that is, the timing of the onset of sustained fertility decline after the development process has begun. The timing depends on the creation of motivations conducive to fertility decline. The earlier such motivations are established, the earlier fertility decline sets in, and the less the consequent rate of population growth. But the creation of the appropriate motivations depends on forces generated and sustained by per capita income growth and its concomitants.

As income rises, the desire for additional children falls, in part, because of what we have called the survival effect of income growth, the fact that conceptions result in more live births that mature to adulthood. Also, the value of children as sources of additional income and security decline in importance as parental incomes rise. In addition, the indirect effects of economic development (for example, urbanization, higher school-leaving ages, etc.) often lead to such changes in social structure and social organization as to decrease gradually the availability of children as productive agents. At the same time other indirect burdens of large families created by such concomitants of per capita income growth as the widening of economic opportunities for women, the growing ease of and advantages from geographical and economic mobility, etc., further engender motivations toward fertility control. To some extent the "high-fertility" motivations that exist in the less developed stage will persist as development proceeds among some sectors of the population, but at some point in the process the balance will shift toward the predominance of motivations conducive to fertility decline. (And should the means be available, it is most likely that such motivations will be implemented.)

The main link between the demographic and economic aspects considered lies in the belief that diminishing returns with respect to labor typically exists in the early stages of development—"in the general case." Therefore, the more rapid the rate at which per capita income growth induces the onset of fertility decline and the greater the *rate* of fertility decline, the lower the rate of *induced* population growth and the less the extent to which population growth absorbs potential national income gains.

Small-Growth versus Large-Growth Stimulants

But why cannot per capita income growth begin at any level, say, the subsistence income level? An answer suggests itself if we look at the nature of the likely aggregate income expenditures at various income levels. We may divide such expenditures into five classes. These are expenditures: (*a*) on capital replacement as capital wears out, (*b*) on the subsistence needs of the population, (*c*) on luxury consumption, (*d*) on new capital, and (*e*) on "human investment." During the near-subsistence income stage the expenditures are mostly for current subsistence and to some extent for capital replacement. Of course, even in backward economies there will usually be a small wealthy group that enjoys a very high level of conspicuous luxury consumption. But consumption of this sort does not increase the productive capacity of the population. We have seen that development requires an expansion of the productive skills and capacities of the population as such, that is, what we shall call, for want of a better term, "human investment."

But note that human investment does not take place immediately upon an increase in per capita income above the subsistence level. Indeed, the initial expenditures from incomes above subsistence will generally be toward the maintenance of a larger population and toward an increase in the consumption standard of the current population. At the same time, the capital stock will not, at the outset, expand as rapidly as the increase in the labor force. This last is largely an empirical matter that depends on the fact that, at near subsistence levels, the potential reductions in mortality rates as a consequence of expenditures on improved nutrition and on public health are exceedingly great, whereas the prospects of increasing the per capita level of savings and investment are exceedingly small. Therefore, only at a certain minimum per capita income level considerably above the subsistence level can we expect the expenditures to flow toward the expansion of the growth agents and toward investment in new capital at a rate greater than the simultaneous increases in the labor force.

We must remember also that at every level of income, the desire for expenditure on "luxury" consumption, as a result of what Dusenberry and Nurkse called the "demonstration effect,"[2] may compete with expenditures on capital accumulation or on "human investment." Furthermore, the minimum level of per capita income may have to be rather high in order to generate a *rate* of growth that permits the payment of relatively high rewards for the expansion of productive capacities as compared with the gains from alternative expenditures, especially in view of the nature of the risk element that appears to be involved in, say, new manufacturing activities as compared with, say, the traditional commercial or agricultural activities. The reason is that "human investment" involves an investment in knowledge, capacities, skills, and other activities where the returns from such investments are not always evident, since they often come at a considerable time after the investments are made. The investor in the growth agents, and in new productive capacities, invests in essentially unknown elements as compared with expenditures on the traditional, the known, and therefore, the apparently safe. In sum, we may say that at low income levels the basic non-capital expenditures are on the maintenance of life and not on the expansion of the human productive capacities, nor are they expenditures that lead to the creation of an environment in which such capacities can flourish, increase, and reap their rewards.

On the other hand, let us look at the consequences of a stimulant

---

[2] R. Nurkse, *Problems of Capital Formation in Underdeveloped Areas,* New York, Oxford University Press, 1953, pp. 63 ff.

sufficiently large to raise per capita income above the critical minimum necessary to foster sustained growth. The first and most obvious effect will be an increase in the capital stock as a result of investment from the higher per capita income. But less obviously, although equally important, the stimulant and its consequences will lead simultaneously to the following effects: (*a*) an expansion of the growth agents and, therefore, an expansion in the ability of the economy to take advantage of new productive opportunities; (*b*) a possible increase in the contribution of the growth agents per unit of capital because of possible declines in the capital-output ratio; (*c*) an eventual decrease in the effectiveness of the retarding factors by increasing the rationality of the population, increasing the gains from change, and decreasing the fears from insecurity that may arise because of perspective changes; (*d*) the creation of social and environmental conditions that can promote physical and economic mobility necessary for development; (*e*) the expansion of the degree of specialization and especially the expansion of the secondary and tertiary industries; and finally (*f*) the development of an atmosphere that leads to changes in mores conducive to economic and social changes, and especially an environment that leads to eventual fertility decline and an eventual decline in the rate of population growth.

CHAPTER 13

Basic Relationships—A Diagrammatic Summary

We now continue our summary by weaving our argument around diagrammatical illustrations that suggest the nature of and connections between the major relationships. First, we shall look at the problem from the short-run point of view, from the viewpoint of those aspects and relationships that determine the outcome for a single period. Second, we shall concentrate on the long-run problem.

Although we find it convenient to gather the various strands of the argument through the medium of two-dimensional graphs, there are some dangers in this procedure, and a few words of caution may be in order. Not all aspects of the theory can be put in terms of such diagrams. Also, such diagrams must be looked upon simply as illustrations and not as representing the theory in its entirety. The theory itself is broader, more flexible, more amenable to elaboration and change than can usually be suggested by the graphs employed in economic theory.

Our concern with the single-period problem is derivative rather than primary. The relationships that determine the short-period outcome are a necessary step that enables us to see the connection between the short-period results and the nature of the long-run problem. To this end we present a simple single-period model. The model is by no means unique. Other models in which some of the relations vary from ours may be equally suitable as theories of short-run output determination. But this one, apart from being simple, does point up the basic connections between the major strands of our theory.[1]

The Single-Period Model

The single-period analysis is built on the interactions between four relationships: (*a*) the capital-output relation, (*b*) the investment demand schedule, (*c*) the savings supply schedule, and (*d*) the population growth relation. We will consider each briefly and then combine some of them in various ways in order to compare the alternate possible outcomes.

1. The incremental capital-output relation. In the model to be developed here we assume that the values of the variables depend, in part, on the state of the economy prior to the period under consideration, and, more specifically, on the level of per capita income at the outset. Since income is a flow concept, this means that our variables depend on the level of per capita income achieved in the previous period. For example, we shall postulate that the rate (percentage of current national income) of savings supplied depends on both the per capita income level of the previous period and on the current increase in net national income. Of course a host of other past events may influence the current situation, but for the single-period analysis history is given.

The reader will recall that in chapter 11 we upheld the thesis that the incremental capital-output ratio falls as the per capita income level rises. Wherever necessary, we shall reflect this notion in our graphical illustrations. With this in mind, consider the curves shown in figure 13–1.

On the horizontal axis in figure 13–1 we indicate alternate amounts of net investment as a percentage of current net national income, that is, the current increment to the capital stock as a percentage of national income. On the ordinate we indicate alternate current rates of increase in net national income. The curve $C–O_1$ depicts the incremental capital-output relationship for a given initial[2] per capita output of y_1. Each point on $C–O_1$ relates the percentage of national income invested

---

[1] In this connection it is probable that representativeness is more important than either uniqueness or universality. In other words, our model is probably representative of a class of possible models that are consistent with the ideas that we have discussed. What we are trying to do, essentially, is to present a model that illustrates the general theory that we have in mind.

[2] We employ the terms "initial" and "last period's" interchangeably when the parameters involved are flows rather than stocks.

(shown on the abscissa) to the percentage of increase in national income (shown on the ordinate) that would be created by that investment. Thus, on $C\text{–}O_1$, the relation illustrated indicates that if the rate of investment is 15 per cent, the related increase in national income would be 3 per cent. This last, of course, reflects an incremental capital-output ratio of 5 to 1.

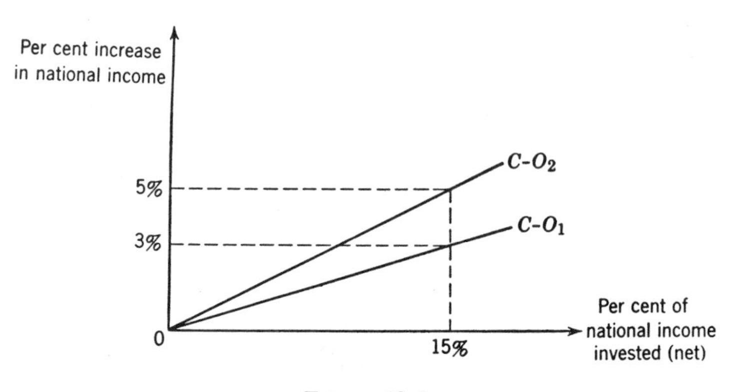

FIGURE 13–1

The curve $C\text{–}O_2$ in figure 13–1 illustrates a lower incremental capital-output ratio than $C\text{–}O_1$ as a result of a higher initial level of per capita income of y_2. This last statement is in conformity with the thesis developed in chapter 11. For simplicity of exposition we have drawn the capital-output relations as linear functions. But, of course, in actuality this need not be the case. The incremental capital-output curve may rise at an increasing rate at first in order to reflect possible advantages of complementarities in investment that may take place. Beyond some rate of investment, the curve may rise at a decreasing rate, thus reflecting the growing significance of the fact that at alternately higher rates of investment, increased competition for scarce resources may make capital goods more expensive. It seems reasonable to expect that beyond some point increased growth rates can be achieved only at higher capital-output ratios at the margin. (But we need not complicate the picture by excessive concern with these details at this juncture.)

For the single-period model the important thing to observe about the capital-output curve is that the actual rate of national income growth that materializes must be determined with reference to some point on this curve. We shall see that whatever it is that determines the actual investment rate, it is the incremental capital-output relation in connection with the actual rate of investment that determines the actual rate of national income growth.

2. *The investment demand schedule.* The demand for investment will depend on the amount of investment opportunities that arise at any time and on the supplies of entrepreneurship, labor skills, and knowledge that can be utilized for economic purposes. The first set of factors, that is, the supply of economic opportunities, will depend on the increase in national income, whereas the second set of factors will depend on the level of living of the economy at the outset, although it may depend also, in part, on past rates of growth. Combining these

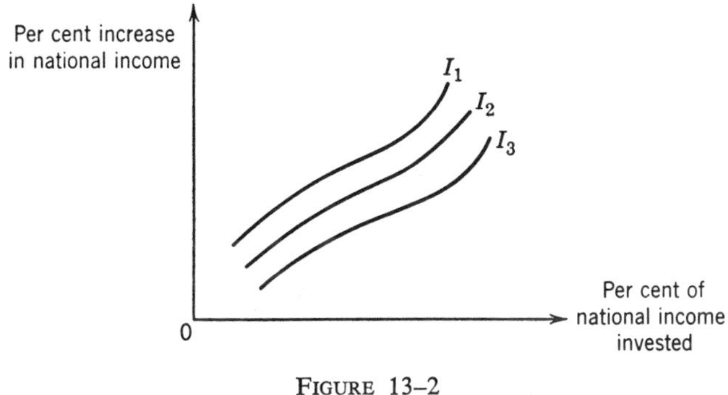

FIGURE 13–2

two ideas, we can say that the demand for investment depends on the expected rate of increase in national income and on the level of per capita income at the outset.

We illustrate the investment demand schedule on the same type of diagram that we used for the capital-output relation, as we shall find it convenient to illustrate all of our single-period relations.

The curves marked I_1, I_2, I_3, in figure 13–2, indicate the percentage of national income invested for different rates of increase in national income. In other words, the rate of growth in national income is the independent variable (shown on the ordinate) and the rate of investment demand is the dependent variable. The subscripts indicate the different initial rates of per capita income. The higher the subscript, the higher the initial level of per capita income, and the greater the rate of investment, other things being equal. (This statement may be true only up to some point, but more on this later.) The general shapes of the curves in figure 13–2 are based on the notion that the higher the current rate of income growth, the greater the investment opportunities that occur, the greater the feeling of optimism about future growth possibilities, and, therefore, the greater the investment demand. However, beyond some point there may be a fear that existing rates of growth cannot be sustained and also that the existing entrepreneurial capacities may not be able to discover all of the possibly expanding investment opportunities, so that eventually investment demand is likely to expand at a decreasing rate with respect to increases in the rate of income growth. In figure 13–2 this last possibility is reflected by the upward turn that the investment demand curves take.

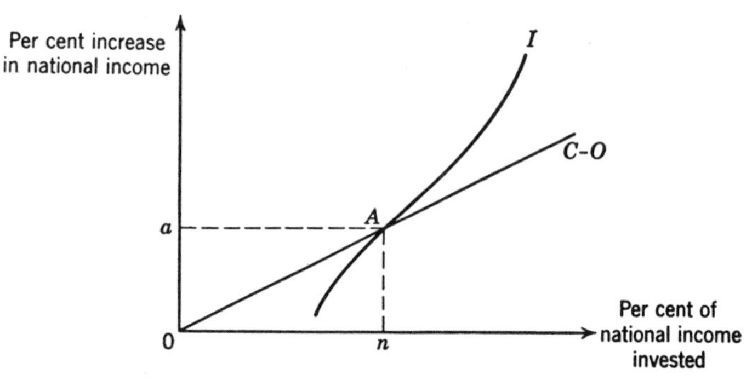

FIGURE 13–3

3. The intersection of the investment demand schedule and the capital-output relation. The interaction of the capital-output relation and the investment demand schedule is of interest. In figure 13–3 both curves are shown simultaneously, and the point A marks the intersection between them.

What does the point A signify? The point A is on both the capital-output curve $C–O$ and on the investment demand curve I. On the curve $C–O$, the point A indicates that if the rate of investment were On, the rate of income growth would be Oa. The point A on the I curve indicates that an investment rate of On is possible, but one larger than On is not. But On is not the rate of investment that will necessarily result. The outcome depends on the availability of an adequate savings rate. If savings are available to satisfy at least the investment demand rate of On, the diagram indicates that the rate of national income growth that results will be Oa.

4. The savings supply schedules. In a closed economy, consumption plus savings equals national income. Therefore, we can choose between examining our problem in terms of the level of consumption or its obverse, the level of savings. For our purposes it happens to be more convenient to employ the savings relation. Thus, we postulate that the rate of savings (percentage out of current national income that is saved) depends on the per capita income level of the previous period and on the current increase in national income. The nature of the relationship is illustrated in figure 13–4. Points on the curve marked S_1 indicate the percentages of national income saved (at a given initial level of per capita income) for alternate increases in national income. The greater the rate of increase in national income, the greater the percentage saved, since consumption is bound to depend, to a considerable extent, on past habitual patterns.

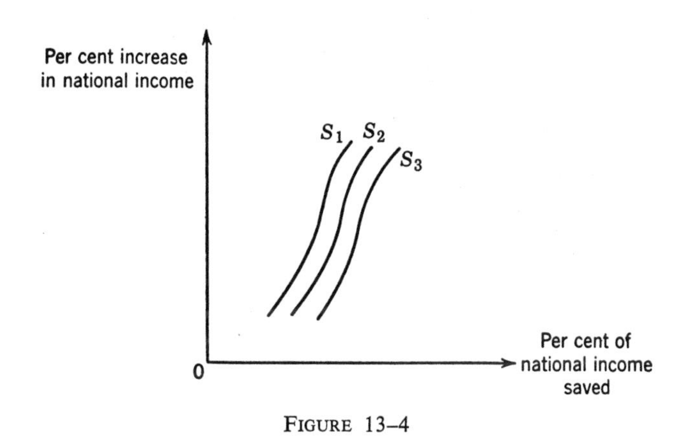

FIGURE 13–4

The curves marked S_2, S_3, etc., are similar savings-income growth relations for different initial per capita incomes. The higher the subscript, the higher the level of initial per capita income, and the greater the savings rate for given levels of national income growth. This last fits in with previously discussed and generally accepted notions about the relation between the level of per capita income and the rate of savings.[3]

5. The interaction of savings supply and investment demand. A significant point to observe with respect to our single-period model is that it is not an equilibrium model, it does not depict the equilibrium situation, and therefore the interaction between the supply of savings schedule (S) and the investment demand curve (I) (see figure 13–5) does not determine the actual rate of investment. Rather, savings supply and investment demand play limiting roles in such a determination.

[3] Our model would be simpler still if we did not assume that the rate of savings varied with per capita income. But the usual differences in the savings rates between advanced and underdeveloped countries suggest that this is not an unreasonable assumption. Certainly the capacity to save is greater, the greater the level of per capita income.

Points on the *S* curve in figure 13–5 should be interpreted as rates of savings that would occur if there were adequate demand for such savings, and similarly points on the *I* curve imply rates of investment that would occur if there were adequate savings available for such a rate of investment. As the curves are drawn, investment demand is shown to be more sensitive to changes than savings supply with respect to the income growth rate. The basic notion here is that the consumption rate is more likely to depend on the initial level of per capita income whereas investment opportunities are more likely to depend on

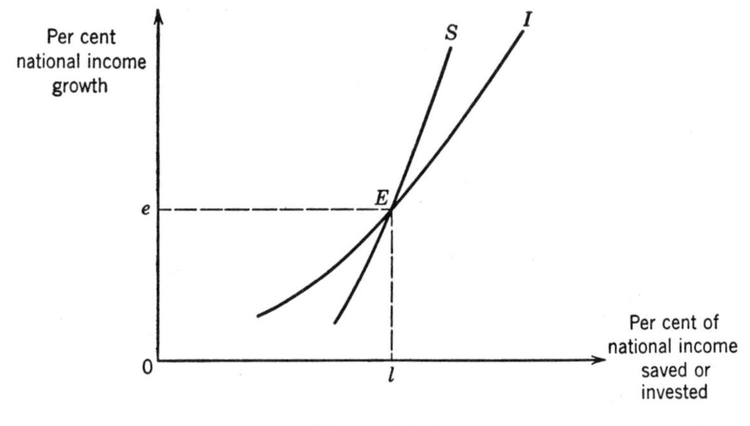

FIGURE 13–5

the current rate of income growth. That is to say, the perception of investment opportunities expands more rapidly than that of savings with respect to national income growth. As a result, the *S* curve cuts the *I* curve from above.

Consider the point of intersection *E* in figure 13–5. The point *E* and its related rate of investment *Ol* are the equilibrium rate of investment, but it need not turn out to be the actual rate of investment that materializes *ex post*. *Ol* is an equilibrium rate in the sense that if it occurred, savers' expectations would be satisfied, and conversely, there would be no known investment opportunities missed for lack of available "funds," that is, for a lack of release of sufficient resources from current consumption enabling the investment to take place.

The equilibrium rate of investment *Ol* could materialize only if this rate of investment did in fact lead to the rate of national income growth *Oe,* that is, that rate of national income growth that would be sufficient to induce the equilibrium rate of investment, *Ol*. This means that the capital-output curve must pass through the point *E* for the equilibrium investment rate to occur. Otherwise the rate of income growth that actually materializes will be either too high or too low to bring forth the equilibrium rate of investment. But more on this point as we proceed.

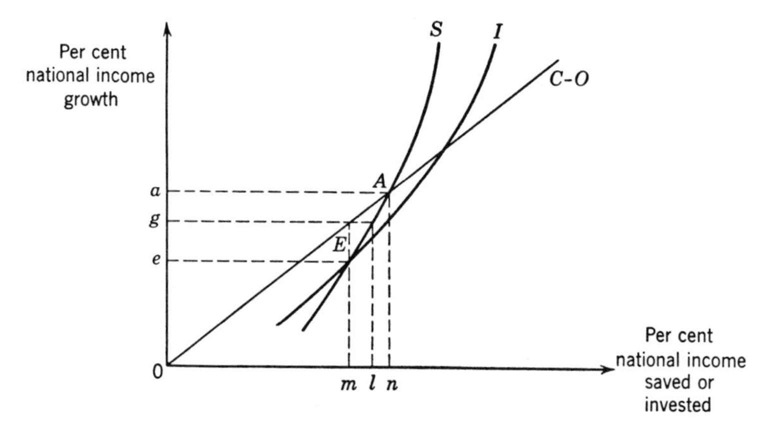

FIGURE 13–6

6. Determination of the rate of investment. Let us suppose that the capital-output curve does not pass through the point *E*. How is the investment rate determined? Two broad possibilities are illustrated in figures 13–6 and 13–7. As might be expected, we shall see that the incremental capital-output relation is one of the determining factors in this situation.

Consider first the situation illustrated in figure 13–6. The point *E* is the intersection between the *S* and *I* curves, but a moment's reflection should indicate that the related rate of investment, *Om,* cannot be the actual rate of investment. For if actual investment were *Om,* the income growth rate would be *Og,* for the rate of income growth is determined by actual investment and the incremental capital-output relation. Consequently, savings would rise to *Ol.* But at a rate of investment of *Ol,* the rate of income growth would rise above *Og,* and actual savings and investment must rise to a still higher level. Only a rate of savings and investment of *On* is consistent with the simultaneous rate of income growth *Oa.* Of course, at the point *A* there will be an excess investment demand, but in the short period there is no reason to assume the existence of a mechanism that equilibrates the investment demand (that is, the investment opportunities seen by entrepreneurs) and the supply of savings. Indeed, the excess investment demand in one period is one of the dynamic factors that stimulates the expansion of the economy in future periods.

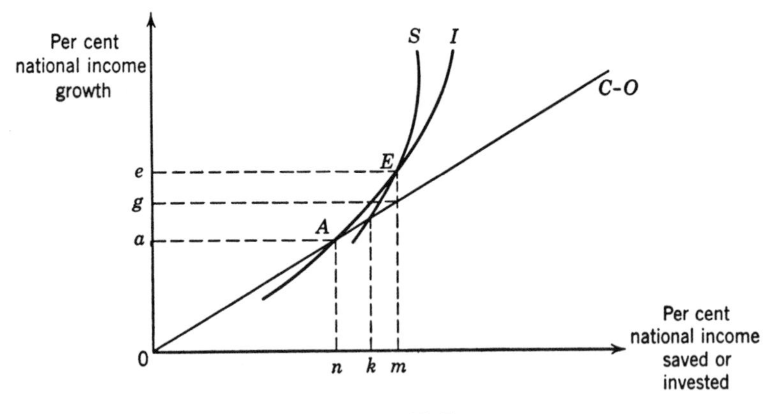

FIGURE 13–7

In figure 13–7 we depict a situation in which there is a deficiency of investment demand. By an argument parallel to that used with respect to figure 13–6, we can see that *Om* cannot become the actual rate of investment. The consequent rate of income growth *Og* would be too low to sustain that high a rate of investment. Also *Ok,* determined by the intersection of the *S* and capital-output curves, cannot be the actual rate of investment, because at the related income growth rate, there is insufficient investment demand to absorb savings of *Ok*. The actual investment rate must be *On,* determined by the intersection of the investment demand curve and the capital-output curve. The real savings rate is also *On* in this case. As a rule we see that the actual rate of investment is determined by the intersection between the capital-output curve and the *S* or *I* curve, whichever intersection yields the lower rate of investment.

7. Population growth. We now turn to a consideration of the role of population growth in the single-period drama. Although population growth is probably of greater significance in the long run, it is of some importance even in the short run since it enters into the determination of the current rate of *per capita* income.

The current level of population growth depends on the factors that determine current births and the mortality rate. But the current birth rate will depend on marriage rates and on the procreative activities in previous periods, which, in turn, may depend on past economic conditions. For the most part the current fertility rate is not determined by the positive procreative activities during the current short period. Past experience is the major determinant. But mortality rates will be affected by current experience, since to some extent mortality rates depend on the current level of consumption (or on its obverse, the current level of savings). The implied relationship is illustrated by the curve *r* in figure 13–8 where the rate of population growth is shown to depend, in part, on the rate of investment.

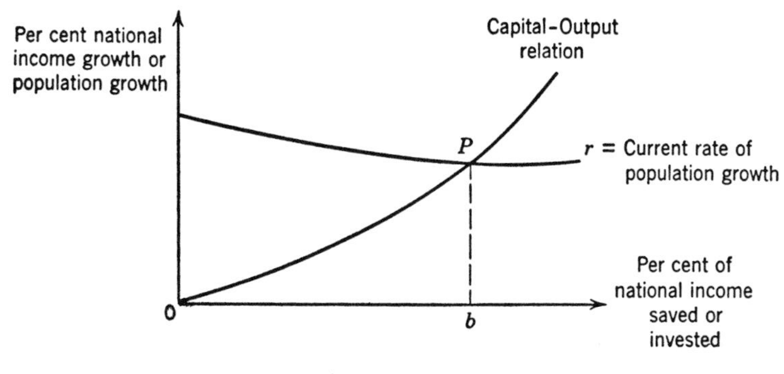

FIGURE 13–8

Examine for a moment the investment effect on population growth. The greater the rate of investment (or savings), the less the absolute amount of consumption; but the greater the rate of investment, the greater the increase in per capita income from which we might expect a greater absolute consumption level. Which effect is to predominate? This depends on the capital-output relation. As long as the adjusted incremental capital-output ratio is greater than unity, the amount of the decrease in consumption, as a consequence of a unit increase in investment, will always be greater than the increase in consumption out of the increased income. Therefore, every increase in investment implies a decrease in consumption and a mortality rate higher than otherwise, hence, a decrease in the rate of population growth. The short-run impact on mortality of greater versus lesser investment rates is not likely to be especially heavy, and, therefore, in drawing the curve *r* we have endeavored not to exaggerate its negative slope.

The related adjusted incremental capital-output ratio is also shown in figure 13–8. This curve shows how alternative increases in investment are related to alternative increases in national income. The capital-output relation at each point is adjusted to the rate of population growth for that particular rate of investment, since under many circumstances an increase in population and the related labor force growth will result in increases in output per unit of capital.[4]

[4] It may be argued that the rate of population growth and the capital output ratio could not be determined independently, since the greater the capital-output

The intersection of the two curves in figure 13–8 and the related point *b* on the abscissa tell us the minimum rate of investment necessary for the rate of income growth to just equal the rate of population growth. In other words, it tells us the minimum rate of investment above which there is a possibility of per capita income growth in the current period.

8. Review of the points of intersection. Before considering all of our single-period relationships simultaneously it may be well to go back for a moment and recall the interpretations given to the various points of intersection dealt with thus far. These were:

1. *Figure 13–3.* The point *A* is the intersection of the investment

---

ratio, the less the rate of population growth due to the lesser income produced out of the greater capital-output ratio. At the same time the smaller the rate of population growth, the greater the capital-output ratio since population now makes a smaller contribution to output. But, of course, it is quite readily conceivable that these two factors will be determined simultaneously so that for each level of investment there is a level of population growth and a capital-output ratio which are consistent with each other. This is illustrated in the figure 13–9

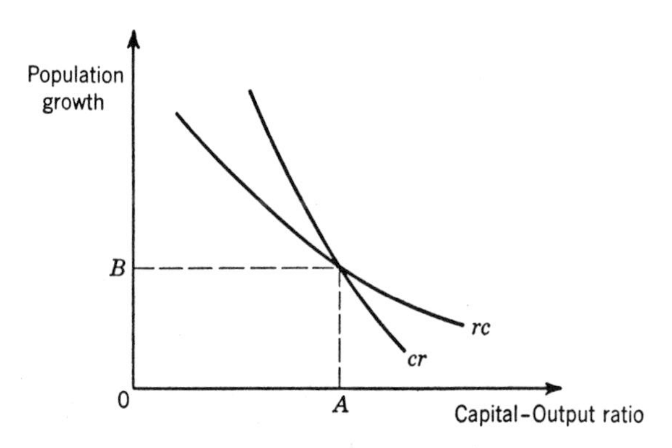

FIGURE 13–9

where ror a given investment we show by the curve *rc* the effect of changes in the capital-output ratio on the rate of population growth. Namely, the greater the capital-output ratio, the less output we get out of the investment, and the lower the rate of population growth. The curve *cr* shows the effect of increases in population growth on the capital-output ratio. The lower the rate of population growth, the higher the capital-output ratio because of the smaller contribution of additional population to output. The intersection of these two lines gives us simultaneously the adjusted capital-output ratio, *OA*, and the rate of population growth, *OB*. In the graph it is assumed that the effect of the population growth on the capital-output ratio is more significant than the effect of the capital-output ratio on population growth.

demand curve (I) and the capital-output relation C–O. The investment rate related to the point A indicates the rate of actual investment that would occur provided there were at least an equally large rate of savings.

2. *Figure 13–5.* The point E is the intersection of the savings supply curve (S) and the investment demand curve (I). The investment rate related to the point E is the equilibrium investment rate that would leave neither a deficiency of savings supplied nor a deficiency of investment demand. But the equilibrium rate of investment can become the actual rate of investment only if the capital-output curve passes through it.

3. *Figure 13–6.* The point A in this case is the intersection between the savings supply curve and the capital-output curve. At this point and at its related rate of national income growth there is an excess of investment demand, and, therefore, savings supply is the limiting factor that determines the actual rate of investment.

4. *Figure 13–7.* The point A in this case is the intersection between the investment demand curve and the capital-output curve. At this point and at its related rate of national income growth there is an excess supply of savings. Therefore, in this case, investment demand is the limiting factor that determines the actual rate of investment.

5. *Figure 13–8.* The point P is the intersection between the short-run population growth curve (r) and the capital-output curve. The investment rate related to the point P is that rate of investment which, if it occurred, would yield a rate of income growth just equal to the rate of population growth. In other words, the related investment rate to P is that rate of investment that will maintain the initial level of per capita income.

9. The single-period outcome. The outcomes for the period determined by the interaction of the four relationships are illustrated in figures 13–10 and 13–11.

In figures 13–10 and 13–11 we contrast the outcomes in two situations. Figure 13–10 depicts the set of related functions and results in the case of an economy that at the outset produces a very low per capita income, whereas figure 13–11 depicts an economy that has the capacity to produce a relatively high per capita income. The curves are drawn in such a way as to reflect the differences in the assumed productive capacities of the two economies. Thus the S and I curves in figure 13–11 are to the right of those in figure 13–10, and the incremental capital-output ratio is assumed to be lower in figure 13–11 (that is, the output-capital ratio is higher). Also, prior to the onset of fertility decline we expect the population growth curve to be somewhat higher for the country with the higher per capita income. Hence the curve *r* in figure 13–11 is above the curve *r* in figure 13–10.

Three points of intersection on each graph are of special interest. The points *A*, *P*, and *E*, and the related points *a*, *p*, and *e*, reflect the outcome for the current period. Their relative magnitudes tell us some-

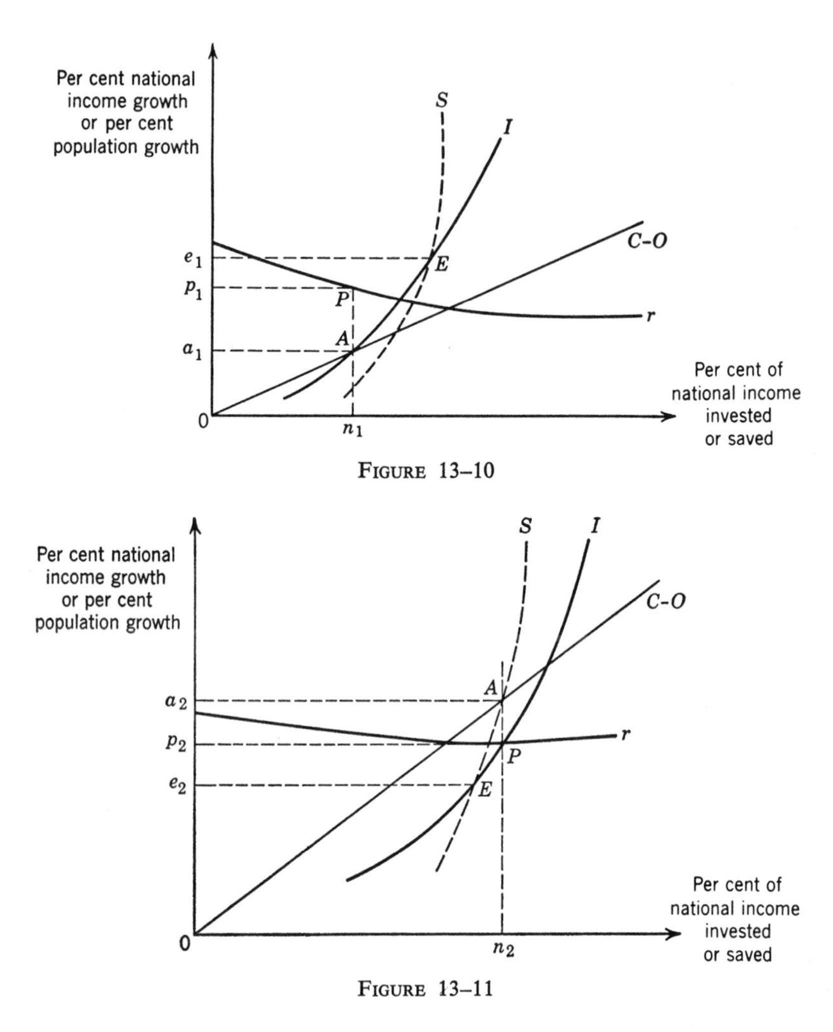

FIGURE 13–10

FIGURE 13–11

thing about the relation between events during the period and their influence on events in the future. In figure 13–10, the intersection *A* between the investment demand curve and the capital-output curve determines the current investment rate On_1 and the rate of national income growth Oa_1. The related rate of population growth is Op_1.

Since the rate of population growth is greater than the rate of national income growth (Oa_1) a decline in per capita income is implied.

In figure 13–11, the reverse possibility is shown. The investment rate On_2 results in an increase of national income of Oa_2, which is higher than the related rate of population growth of op_2. This last, of course, reflects an increase in per capita income—a factor that works in the direction of stimulating further growth.

Other points worthy of special notice are the point *E*, the related levels of national income growth e_1, and e_2 in figures 13–10 and 13–11, respectively. We assume that investment demand, that is, the perception of investment opportunities, expands more rapidly than savings with respect to national income growth. As a result, the *S* curve cuts the *I* curve from above. Above the point *E* (and related income growth e_1 or e_2) there is an excess of investment opportunities over savings, whereas below *E* there is a deficiency. We would expect that an excess of perceived investment opportunities would stimulate expansion in the future, whereas a deficiency would serve as a contracting force. Excess investment demand should raise interest rates, stimulate an increase in the savings rate, and simultaneously stimulate an expansion of the intangible agents of production, and the growth agents, in response to perceived but unfulfilled investment opportunities. A deficiency of investment demand works in the reverse direction.

In figure 13–10 the actual rate of income growth Oa_1 is less than that necessary to induce the equilibrium rate (Oe_1) of savings supply and investment demand. At the actual rate of income growth there is a deficiency of investment demand compared to savings available; it operates as a contracting influence. In figure 13–11 the reverse is true. The fact that Oa_2 is greater than Oe_2, should operate as an expansive influence in the next period.

In general, we see that the outcome in the present period influences the next period in two ways. Let *A* stand for the actual rate of income growth, *P* the rate of population growth, and *E* the rate of income growth necessary for the investment demand and the savings supply to be equal. If *A* is greater than *E*, there will be unfulfilled investment opportunities, which in turn will stimulate expansion in the next period. *A* greater than *P* implies per capita income growth which, other things being equal, also stimulates expansion in the next period. On the other hand, contraction is induced by the actual rate of national income growth being less than *E* and by the actual rate of national income growth being less than the rate of population growth. We employ these relations in the next step of our summary where we consider the long-run problem.

The Long-Run Aspect

The dynamics of the system depends on the relationship between present and past events. This is another way of saying that present events are, in part, determined by historical experience.

Our single-period analysis assumes a given historical experience and a given tempo of change. This experience cannot readily be expressed in the usual two-dimensional graph, but, if we employ a summary measure of the tempo of change, we can illustrate graphically the effects of past events. Let us use as a summary measure *the discounted average rate of per capita income growth.* That is to say, we envision

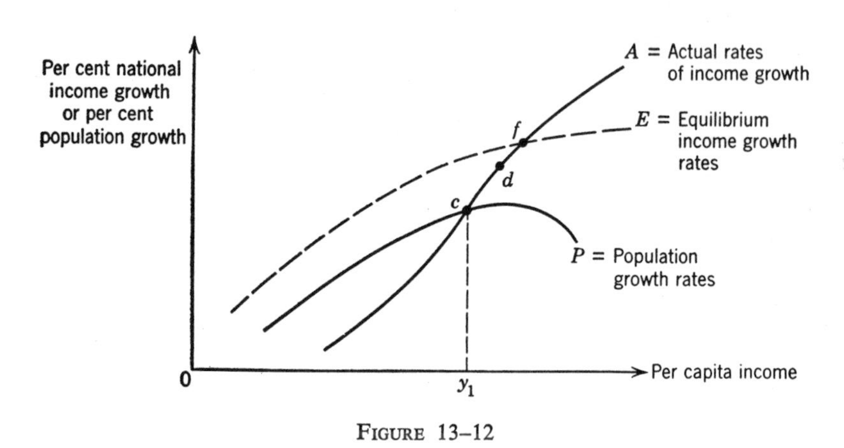

FIGURE 13–12

an average rate of growth for a number of periods in the past computed in such a way that the more recent rates of growth are weighed more heavily than those in more distant time periods. We shall use this summary rate as an index of the tempo of change.

1. Basic relations for a given tempo of change. Consider first the situation, *for a given tempo of change,* illustrated in figure 13–12. For alternative initial levels of per capita income we draw the alternative rates of population growth, *P,* the alternative actual rates of national income growth, *A*, and the alternative rates of "equilibrium" national income growth, *E*. We call *E* the "equilibrium" rates of growth, for want of a better term. A point on the curve *E* is that of national income growth that, if it occurred, would permit the fulfillment of *both* current investment and savings plans or one that would leave neither investment plans nor savings plans unfulfilled. Hence, we use equilibrium here only in this special sense. It follows that an actual rate of income growth above the equilibrium level implies some current unfulfilled investment demand and a potential expansion of investment opportunities in the next period. Conversely, an actual rate of income growth below the equilibrium level implies a current deficiency of investment demand, which in turn induces, other things being equal, a contraction in investment demand in the next period.

Each set of points on the curves *A, P,* and *E* for a given level of initial per capita income is the outcome for a single period as determined by the set of relationships illustrated in figures 13–10 and 13–11. Thus points on the curve *P* indicate the alternate rates of population growth that would result for the given alternate levels of initial per capita income shown on the abscissa, assuming for each point the *same* given tempo of change in the past. Similarly, the points on the curve *A* indicate the alternate actual rates of national income growth for alternate levels of initial per capita income, again on the basis of a given tempo of change. In the same way the points on the curve *E* represent the alternate equilibrium rates of income growth for alternate initial per capita incomes.

The point of intersection *c* (and later the point *d*) in figure 13–12 are of interest, but we must be careful in their interpretation to keep in mind the implications of the assumed tempo of change. The reason for this is that the current growth rate will affect the discounted rate of per capita income growth (our index for the tempo of change) in the next period, which in turn will affect the positions of the curves *A*, *P*, and *E*. For example, the initial per capita income level y_1, opposite the point of intersection *c*, should lead to an eventual *decline* in per capita income, if the past tempo of change is positive. At the point *c* the rate of population growth is just equal to the rate of national income growth, and hence the rate of per capita income growth is zero. But a zero rate of per capita income growth reduces the tempo of change, that is, the discounted rate of per capita income growth which in turn reduces the rate of national income growth in future periods.

2. *Maintenance of the tempo of change.* Consider for a moment the population growth curve *P* and the actual income growth curve *A* by themselves, as in figure 13–13. If the initial level of per capita income is equal to y_1, the rate of population growth (Oc_1) is equal to the rate of actual income growth (Oc_1), and the per capita income level just maintains itself. There is no growth. But we have argued that future growth is propelled not only by the per capita income level but also by the tempo of change. If the past tempo of change was positive, the current rate of per capita income growth must be positive in order to maintain the tempo of change. Clearly this cannot be done if the current rate of growth is only Oc_1. But there is some point, say the point d (above the point c on curve A), and a related level of initial

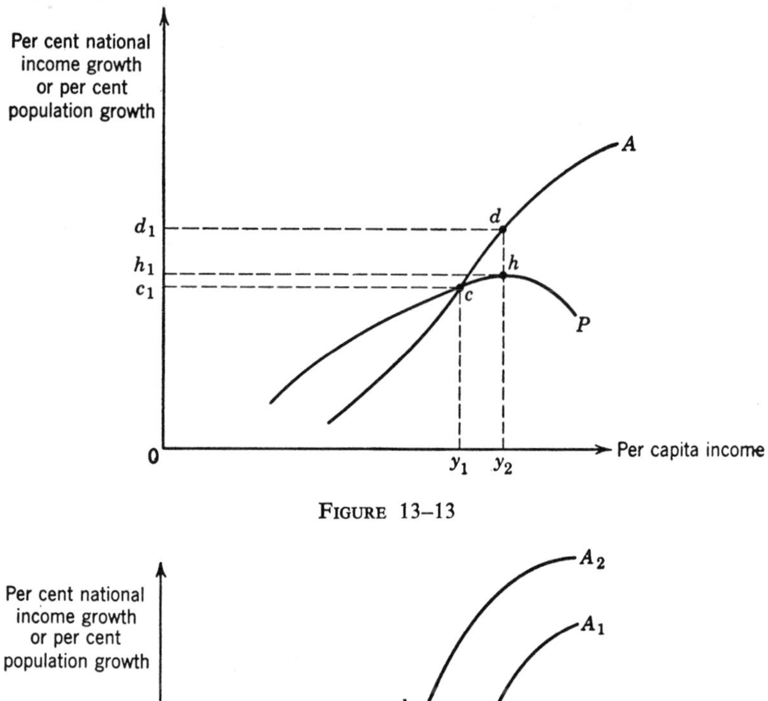

FIGURE 13–13

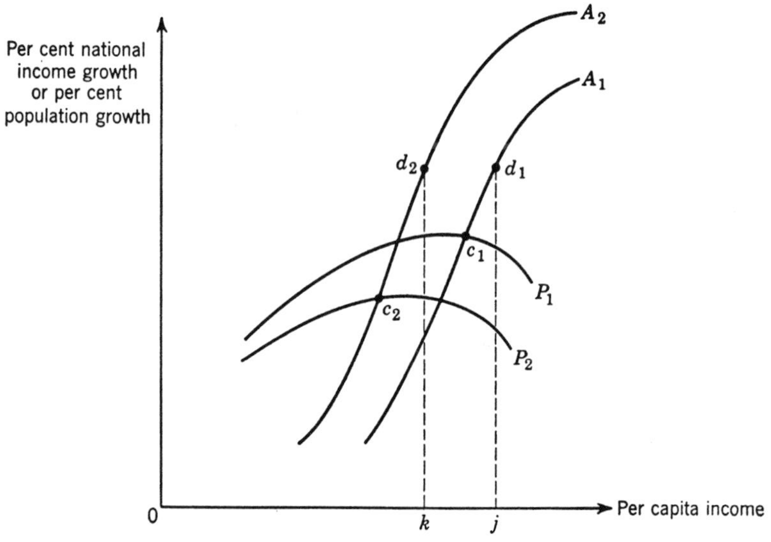

Per cent national income growth or per cent population growth
A_2
A_1
d_2
d_1
c_1
P_1
c_2
P_2
0
k
j
Per capita income

FIGURE 13–14

per capita income, say y_2, at which the rate of national income growth is sufficiently in excess of the rate of population growth (Oh_1), so that the resulting per capita income level exceeds its former level by an amount sufficient to maintain the discounted rate of per capita income growth. That is to say, the point d, with its related level y_2, is a position that sustains growth and maintains at least the past tempo of change. The significance of the point d will appear more clearly as we proceed.

For each tempo of change there is a related actual national income growth curve, as well as a related population growth curve. In figure 13–14 we show two sets of such curves. The assumed tempo of change behind each curve is designated by the appropriate subscript. The curve A_1 is the actual national income growth curve on the assumption that the discounted growth rate is, say, 1 per cent per year, and similarly the curve A_2 is the actual national income growth curve on the assumption that the tempo of change is 2 per cent. A_2 is drawn above A_1 to reflect the underlying notion that the greater the tempo of change, the greater the current rate of national income growth, other things being equal. The population growth curves P_1 and P_2 are to be interpreted in a similar manner. P_2 is drawn below P_1 to reflect the idea that the greater the tempo of change, the less the rate of population growth, since a rapid tempo of change is probably more conducive to declining fertility rates than a slow one.

As suggested before, the most significant points in figure 13–14 are not the points of intersection (c_1 and c_2), but rather the points d_1 and d_2. The point d_1 indicates that if the tempo of change is 1 per cent, the related initial per capita income level of Oj will generate a rate of national income growth above the rate of population growth sufficient to maintain the tempo of change at 1 per cent. In a like manner we interpret d_2 for a 2 per cent tempo of change.

3. Determination of the zero growth and sustaining tempo lines. Figure 13–15 illustrates the same points as figure 13–14 for a large number of population growth and national income growth curves. Again the assumed tempos of change are designated by the appropriate subscripts. Thus the curves $A_1, A_2, \ldots, A_n$ are the actual national income growth curves on the alternative assumptions that the discounted growth rates are, say, $1, 2, \ldots, n$ per cent, respectively.[5] As before, the relative positions of the curves reflect the underlying postulate that generally the greater the tempo of change, the greater the current rate of income growth. Therefore, the curve A_2 is to the left of the curve A_1, etc. But we also consider the possibility that beyond some point we may have a tempo of change so rapid that it has a disorganizing effect on current production activities. In this case, the curves for the very high tempos of change will

---

[5] For a zero tempo of change the points c_0 and d_0 would coincide.

be to the right of those for lower tempos.[6] The curves P_1, P_2, and P_n in figure 13–15 are the alternate population growth curves for different discounted growth rates. And, as before, the position of these curves reflects the notion that, at the higher per capita income levels, the greater the tempo of change, the less the rate of population growth.

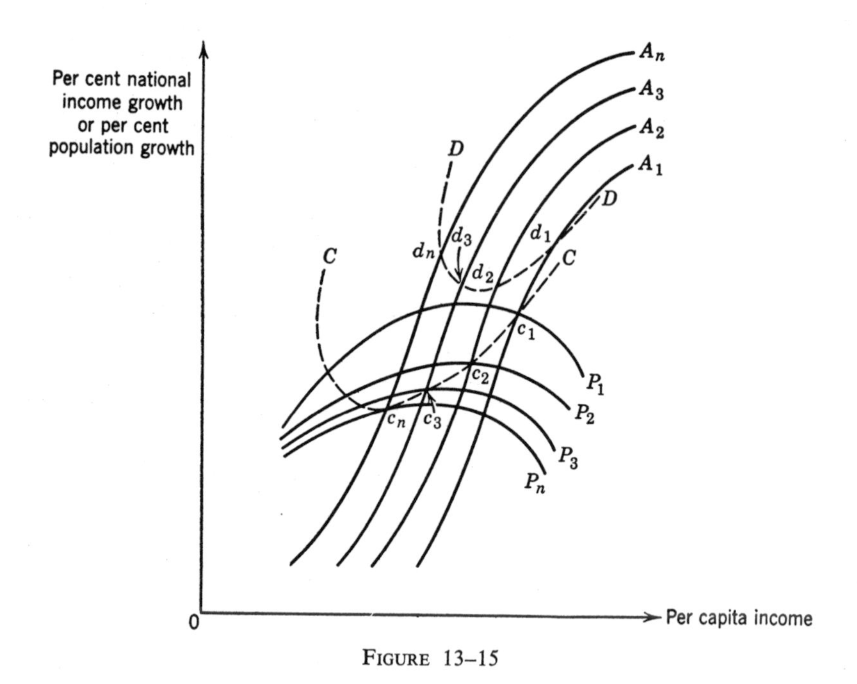

FIGURE 13–15

The intersections (designated by c_1, c_2, etc., in figure 13–15) of the appropriate A and P curves enables us to determine the alternate levels of initial per capita income for the given alternate tempos of change above which there will be a current per capita income growth and below which there will be a current per capita income decline. The locus of such points (CC) is reflected in the curve CC in figure 13–18.

Also, on each A curve there is a point at which the rate of national income growth is sufficiently above the rate of population growth so that the resulting *per capita* income growth maintains the tempo of change. The points marked $d_1, d_2, \ldots, d_n$ indicate the rates of national income growth on each of the A curves that imply rates of *per*

[6] Also, the derived curves CC and DD may bend back toward greater initial per capita incomes under such circumstances.

capita income growth that maintain their related discounted growth rates. The locus of such points will be reflected in the curve *DD* in figure 13–18.

4. Determination of the equilibrium growth line. And now we must take into account the influence on future growth of the current deficiency or excess of investment demand. The latter depends on the relation between the equilibrium national income growth rate and the actual national income growth rate. The nature of these relations is illustrated in figures 13–16 and 13–17.

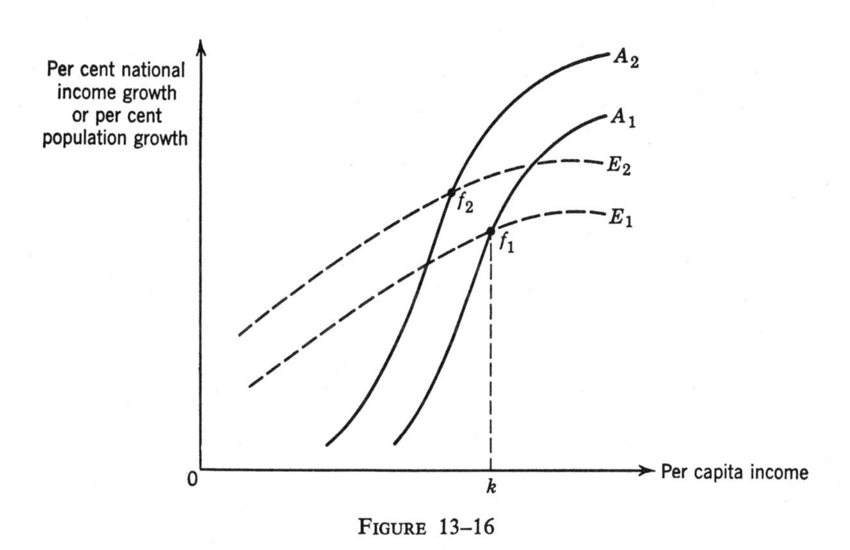

FIGURE 13–16

The curve E_1 (in figure 13–16) is the equilibrium income growth curve for a 1 per cent tempo of change. (The E_1 curve is defined in the same way as the E curve in figure 13–12.) Each point on this curve indicates, for each initial per capita income level, that rate of national income growth that would be generated if the capital-output relation passed through the point at which the savings supply was equal to the investment demand. But this happens only at the point f_1, and at its related initial per capita income level of Ok. For initial per capita income levels greater than Ok the diagram indicates that the actual rate of national income growth will be above the equilibrium rate, thus implying an excess of investment demand, whereas the reverse will be true for initial per capita income levels less than Ok. More on the implications of these relationships below.

The curve E_2 represents the equilibrium income growth curve for a 2 per cent tempo of change. We draw E_2 above E_1 to reflect the notion that the greater the tempo of change, up to a point, the greater the equilibrium national income growth rate. The point f_2 is interpreted in a similar fashion to f_1.

In figure 13–17 we show a whole series of curves E_1, E_2, . . . , etc., to E_n for progressively greater tempos of change of 1 per cent, 2 per cent, . . . , to n per cent, and simultaneously we show the related actual national income growth curves A_1, A_2, . . . , to A_n.

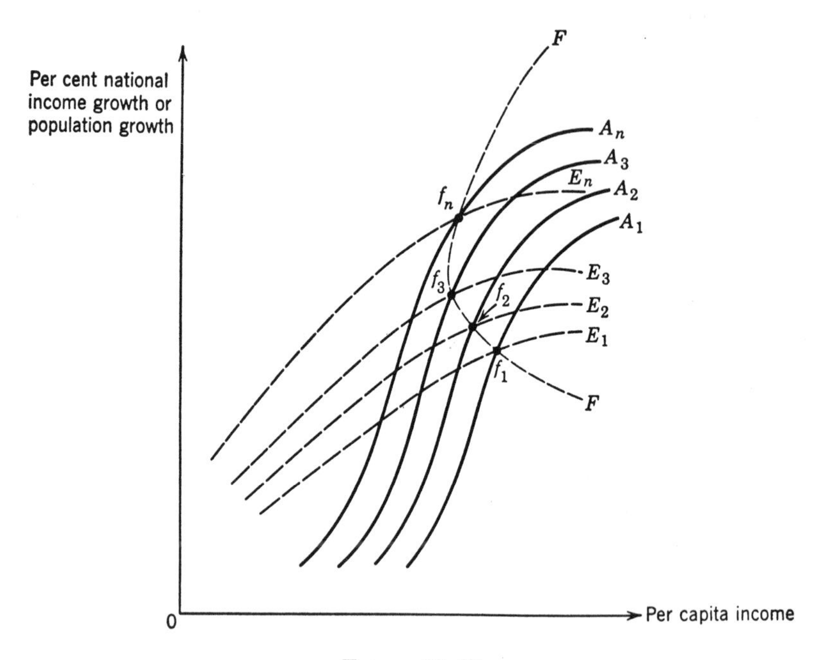

FIGURE 13–17

From figure 13–17 we obtain from the intersection of each set of curves A_1E_1, A_2E_2, etc., a set of points f_1, f_2, etc. The relevant information with respect to all the points discussed above is shown in a more convenient form in figure 13–18.

5. Derivation of the critical minimum per capita income level. The three solid curves in figure 13–18 are the loci of points that reflect information derived from figures 13–15 and 13–17. *CC* is the locus of initial per capita incomes for the related discounted growth rates above which there will be generated in the current period some per capita income growth and below which there will be per capita income decline. Similarly, *DD* shows the locus of points that indicate the initial per capita incomes for related discounted growth rates that would generate a level of per capita income high enough to at least maintain the related discounted growth rate for future periods, *other things being equal.* In a like manner the curve *FF* shows the locus of points reflecting a similar type of information for the intersections of the *A* and *E* curves, that is, above the designated initial per capita incomes for the related discounted growth rates there is an excess of current investment opportunities which in turn stimulates an expansion of investment demand in the next period.

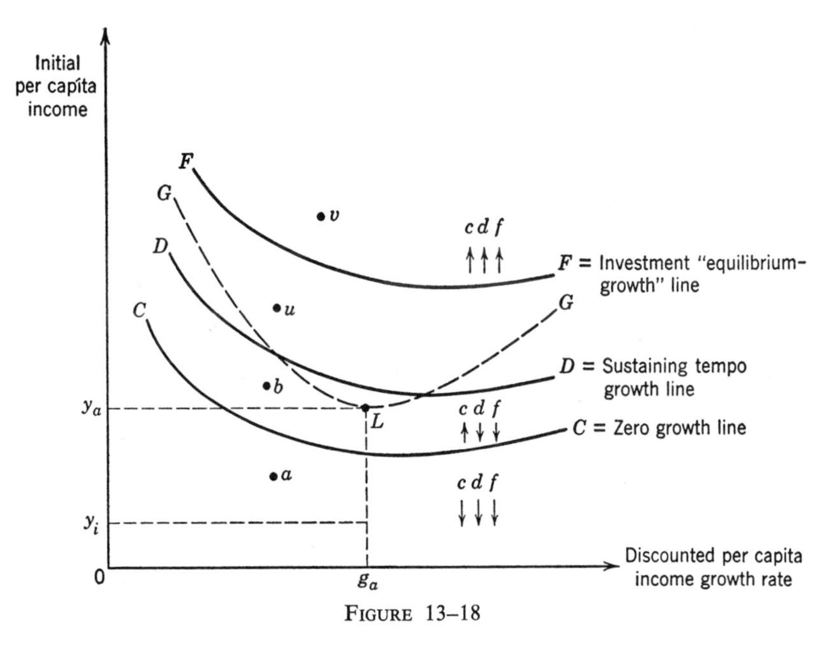

FIGURE 13–18

The three solid curves separate figure 13–18 into three distinct areas. It is clear that initial per capita incomes and related discounted growth rates that fall into the area below the curve *CC* cannot possibly lead to sustained growth, for a point *a* in the area below *CC* implies that the current rate of population growth will be greater than the rate of national income growth. Also, it means that the discounted growth rate cannot be maintained, and hence we would expect a per capita income decline on this score. Finally, since the point *a* is also below the line *FF*, we would expect the future investment rate to decline.

If we begin with a point *b* above *CC* but below *DD*, some initial per capita income growth is possible, but not necessarily sustained per capita income growth. The "tempo effect" (the fact that the past tempo of change cannot be sustained at this point) will be a retarding influence on the growth rate.

On the other hand, if we begin with a point v above the line *FF*, all of the influences that we have mentioned would appear to work in the direction of maintaining and increasing the rate of growth. In this case sustained growth is assured.

It is important to note that it is possible for *some* points that lie in the area between *CC* and *FF* to lead to sustained per capita income growth. In this area some of the influences promote growth in future periods whereas others retard it. Thus it is conceivable that for some point above *CC*, but below *DD*, the influence of current per capita income growth on the expansion of future investment opportunities and on the expansion of other activities may be more significant than the retarding effects that arise from the fact that the tempo of change falls, and also more significant than the effect of the current deficiency of investment demand compared to current potential savings. Having these opposing influences in mind, we can visualize a curve *GG* that forms a boundary between those points that *cannot* lead to sustained growth and those points that can. That is to say, if we begin with a point above *GG*, the economy will generate forces that, on balance, promote rather than retard per capita income growth in the succeeding periods. In time a point will be reached at which the per capita income level and the discounted growth rate will be above the curve *FF*, where all the influences stimulate further growth.

We can look upon the curve *GG* as the minimum initial per capita income curve, that is, for every discounted growth rate the curve tells us the related minimum initial per capita income level that will yield sustained growth. Consider the meaning of the point *L*, and suppose that the actual initial per capita income level is only y_i. The point *L* implies that it is necessary to inject stimulants into the economy at a rate sufficiently heavy so that the discounted growth rate becomes g_a by the time the per capita income level reaches y_a. Beyond that point no more exogenous stimulants are necessary, and thenceforth the economy will generate sustained growth on its own.[7]

The significance of some of these ideas will be made clear in chapter 15.

[7] Of course, we may wish to minimize the total magnitude of the exogenous stimulants necessary to bring about sustained growth. In this case it may, under some circumstances, be worthwhile to inject the stimulant in order to attain a lower discounted growth rate (than g_a) and a higher per capita income level at which the injections are discontinued.

CHAPTER 14

Population Growth, Investment Rates, and Related Magnitudes— Some Illustrative Projections and Calculations

It is a methodological commonplace that all economic and social theories involve a high degree of selectivity in the variables considered. Although it is often (and probably always) impossible to measure all conceivable variables, it is certainly of interest to determine whether the main variables that are included are likely to be of a significant magnitude or whether they really do not matter very much.

In this chapter we shall present data and the results of computations that suggest the magnitude of the population growth variable, as well as data on capital-output ratios, savings, etc., which, combined with population growth projections, suggest the relative magnitudes of these variables. Because the data available are often very scanty, what we shall present can only be suggestive of some aspects of the empirical nature of the problem and nothing more.

Patterns of Population Growth

At first blush it may be thought that the best way to estimate the probable rates of population growth under various circumstances, and therefrom obtain some idea of the population hurdles to development, would be to do so separately for each of the underdeveloped countries. But whether or not this can be done depends on two things: (1) the technique of population projection that is employed, and (2) the availability of statistics given the projection technique. The cruder the requisite data, the larger the number of countries that can be included. But any technique that employs even so limited a refinement as taking into account the age distribution of the population forces us to abandon the country-by-country approach. The difficulty with the country-by-country approach is that most of the existing underdeveloped areas do not publish sufficiently long statistical series to make the necessary projections. An alternative approach is to assume that underdeveloped areas have certain uniform demographic characteristics and to estimate the relevant magnitudes for what might be called a "representative" underdeveloped area. This is the approach that we shall employ.

Our use of a "representative" population area which reflects the experience and statistical data of a number of countries is justified on the basis of our limited objective. It will be recalled that our objective in this chapter is not a very ambitious one. It is merely to gather representative statistics in order to get some idea of what the magnitudes of some of the major variables are and to see what they look like when they are related to each other. That is, to give us some notion about "the orders of magnitude" of the things discussed.

We have argued previously that the current rates of population growth do not tell us very much about the nature of the population hurdle to development. The significant question is what the rate and pattern of population growth will be at various stages in the development process? In order to understand the nature of the population hurdle to growth we have to have an understanding of the entire complex of potential population growth rates. Toward this end, we have calculated a series of population projections based on alternative patterns of development, the results of which we present below. The basic sources of data upon which the projections were made, and the projection technique employed, are explained in the appendices to this book. The rationale upon which the following population projections are based is this: For purposes of estimating alternative patterns of population growth we find it statistically convenient to use the expectation of life at birth as our index of economic well-being. Later, we shall relate expectation of life statistics to per capita income statistics and consider how we have to interpret the results in the light of these facts. But for the time being, let us accept increases in the calculated expectation of life at birth as an index of economic betterment. The population of a backward economy generally has a low expectation of life, and a usual consequence of economic development is to increase longevity.

For a given expectation of life the age distributions of different populations are often very similar. One can speak of a typical age distribution for an underdeveloped area for which the expectation of life is specified. We begin our considerations by determining the typical age distribution for countries for which the expectations of life at birth are around 40 years.[1] We find also that reasonably high correlations exist between changes in age-specific mortality rates and changes in expectation of life. Hence, for every change in the expectation of life we have a related change in the age-specific mortality rates. On the basis of available empirical evidence we chose assumptions about the initial age-specific birth rates and changes in the age-specific birth rates during the process of development. By applying the appropriate set of mortality rates to our representative population, and by applying the postulated set of age-specific fertility rates to the female population in the child-bearing age groups, we can compute the growth pattern of the population for various patterns of increase in the expectation of life attendant upon industrialization.

Once we obtain the population projections, we can make comparisons that are suggestive and illuminating. To indicate the nature of the comparisons we have in mind consider these examples: (1) For some of the projections we assume an increase in the expectation of life[2] of 22 years over a 55-year period (which implies a rather rapid rate of growth) whereas for others we assume no increase in the expectation of life over the 55-year period. Comparing these projections should suggest the difference it makes to the rate and pattern of population between a rapid increase in the expectation of life attendant upon development and the absence of any increases in life expectancy. (2) European fertility rates prior to development have generally been lower than the fertility rates in the backward economies of the Far East, the Near

[1] Plans to determine the typical age distributions for countries for which the expectation of life at birth is below 40 years, say 35 or 30, had to be abandoned for lack of available, adequate data.

[2] Wherever we refer to the expectation of life we mean the expectation of life at birth unless we specifically state otherwise.

East, and Central and South America. We shall assume for some of our projections "low" and "high" fertility rate patterns that are roughly representative of the two fertility rate patterns we have just mentioned, and by comparing the resulting projection we should get some idea of the difference these initial distinctions make. (3) There is usually a lag between the onset of secular mortality decline and the onset of secular fertility decline. By assuming different lags in our projections, we should get some idea of the difference the speed of the onset of the fertility decline makes in the rate and pattern of population growth. Of course, these examples do not exhaust the comparisons that could be made or that we shall make.

Basic assumptions

We now turn to a brief discussion of the building blocks out of which our population growth projections were made.

The representative age distribution assumption. In table 14–1 we show the age and the sex distribution of our representative population among an arbitrary starting population of 1,000,000. The age distribution in table 14–1 was determined on the basis of an examination of eighteen age distributions for countries whose population had a male expectation of life of 40 years or below. Since the expectation of life for females is generally about two years greater than that for males, the representative age distribution for females was based on populations whose expectation of life was 42 years or below. The actual proportions shown in columns 2 and 4 of table 14–1 were obtained by averaging the observations available for the appropriate age groups and then rounding the results so that the total population would be equal to 100 per cent.[3]

The mortality assumptions. Although it is not especially surprising that age-specific mortality rates and the expectation of life are highly correlated, it is a convenient fact that we can put to good use in determining the pattern and extent of population growth that may occur in response to improvements in living conditions. In order to determine the mortality assumptions for our population projections we correlated the age-specific mortality rates of various populations with the expectation of life. In determining the relationship for each sex and age group an attempt was made to use as many observations as possible, and a special attempt was made to find observations for populations with relatively low life expectancies. For most of the age groups, over eighty

[3] In Appendix 1, table 1, we present age distributions for selected populations for which the male expectation of life is 40 or below. A comparison of these with our "typical" age distribution should suggest the extent to which our hypothetical population is representative of the usual case.

observations for a relatively large number of countries were used (see Appendix 2).

Since life tables are computed from age-specific mortality rates, there is some reason to expect some correlation between changes in age-specific mortality rates and changes in life expectancy, but there is no necessity for the correlation to be a high one. It is conceivable in principle for the age-specific mortality rate to decline in a more or less random fashion. But the correlations for most of the age groups being quite high would seem to imply that a specific pattern of mortality decline results from improvements in general living conditions.

TABLE 14–1. Age and Sex Distribution of a Representative Population of 1,000,000 of an Underdeveloped Economy

(For Which the Male Expectation of Life is below 40 and the Female Expectation of Life is below 42)

Age Group	Males		Females	
	Per Cent	Number	Per Cent	Number
0–4	13.8	69,000	14.0	70,000
5–9	13.3	66,500	12.9	64,500
10–14	12.1	60,500	11.1	55,500
15–19	9.8	49,000	10.0	50,000
20–24	8.5	42,500	9.0	45,000
25–29	8.0	40,000	8.4	42,000
30–34	6.9	34,500	7.1	35,500
35–39	6.2	31,000	6.0	30,000
40–44	5.4	27,000	5.3	26,500
45–49	4.2	21,000	3.9	19,500
50–54	3.6	18,000	3.7	18,500
55–59	2.4	12,000	2.3	11,500
60–64	2.4	12,000	2.5	12,500
65–69	1.3	6,500	1.3	6,500
70–74	1.0	5,000	1.2	6,000
75–79	0.5	2,500	0.6	3,000
80–84	0.4	2,000	0.4	2,000
85 and over	0.2	1,000	0.3	1,500
All ages	100.0	500,000	100.0	500,000

The nature of the relationships between age-specific mortality rates and expectation of life is illustrated by the scatter diagrams shown in figures 14–1 and 14–2. These are samples of the thirty-two correlations made for each of the sixteen age groups by sex. The extent to which the scatter diagrams shown are really representative of all the age groups may be gleaned from the correlation coefficients presented in table 14–2. Up to age 65 the correlations are very high. On the basis of the regres-

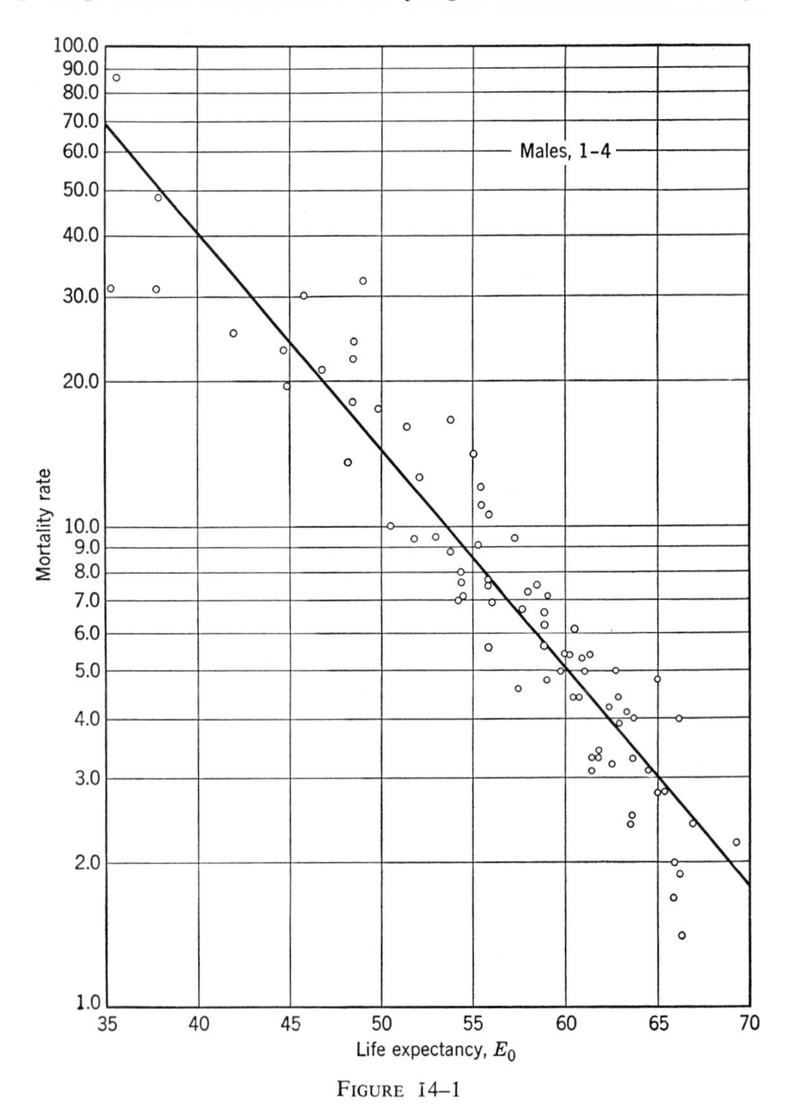

FIGURE 14–1

sion equations for each age group, we compute survival rates for each age and sex group so that for any presumed pattern of change in life expectancy we can determine the surviving population at any future point in time.

The initial fertility assumptions. In order to trace and observe the structure of the population as it changes in time we have to employ age-specific fertility rates in making our population projections. As

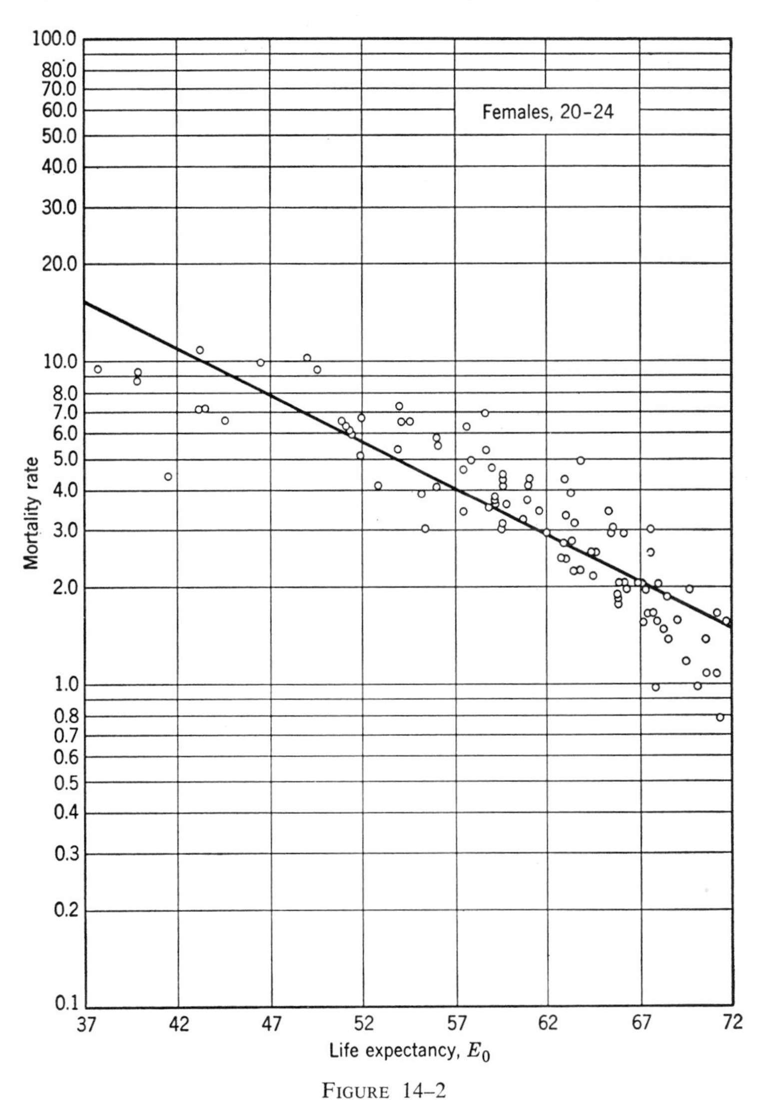

FIGURE 14–2

usual, it is most difficult to find observations for the underdeveloped countries of Asia and Africa since their statistical reporting systems are often equally underdeveloped. For the most part we have no choice but to use the available data on European populations for those periods when

TABLE 14–2. CORRELATION COEFFICIENTS

(Mortality Rates Specific for Age and Sex with Life Expectancy E_0)

Age Group	Correlation Coefficient: Males	Females
Under 1	−0.9080	−0.9688
1–4	−0.8171	−0.8177
5–9	−0.8692	−0.8226
10–14	−0.8674	−0.9035
15–19	−0.8394	−0.8833
20–24	−0.7542	−0.8966
25–29	−0.8620	−0.9825
30–34	−0.8992	−0.9251
35–39	−0.8997	−0.9357
40–44	−0.8673	−0.9246
45–49	−0.8675	−0.8646
50–54	−0.8541	−0.8652
55–59	−0.7773	−0.7943
60–64	−0.8067	−0.7711
65–69	−0.6832	−0.7409
70–74	−0.6463	−0.6863

the countries involved were still relatively underdeveloped. Once again we used life expectancy as our index. But we did not have to be quite so restrictive in the sets of fertility rates that we could use as in the sets of mortality rates since there is usually a time lag between mortality decline and fertility decline. As a result, we chose sets of age-specific fertility rates for populations whose life expectancy for males was 47 or less. In tables 14–3 and 14–4 we show a number of observations of such age-specific fertility rates.

To some extent our choice of the fertility-rate assumptions was arbitrary, as indeed such assumptions always must be, but it is based on historical magnitudes. Certain observations were omitted from our calculations on the ground that they were too low to be typical of present-day conditions in backward economies. For example, fertility rates in northwestern Europe, when that area was underdeveloped, were no doubt lower than in the present-day underdeveloped countries. The usual, crude fertility rate in England or Sweden was around 32 per thousand in the mid-nineteenth century whereas the rates in present-day backward economies are often above 35 per thousand, usually around 40, and sometimes above 45 per thousand.[4]

[4] On this point examine the statistics presented by W. S. Woytinsky and E. S. Woytinsky, *World Population and Production,* New York, The Twentieth Century Fund, 1953, pp. 138–151.

TABLE 14–3. AGE-SPECIFIC FERTILITY RATES FOR COUNTRIES WITH LIFE EXPECTANCY FOR MALES OF 47 OR LESS RANKED ACCORDING TO "TOTAL FERTILITY RATE"

Country and Year	Chile, 1940	Sweden, 1841–50	Sweden, 1861–70	Sweden, 1851–60	Bulgaria, 1925–28	Sweden, 1816–40	Austria, 1906–10	Chile, 1930–32	Japan, 1930	Finland, 1891–1900	Austria, 1901–05	Finland, 1886–90	Low Fertility-Rate Assumption
E_0 and Year	39.8 1940	46.60 1841–45	46.40 1861–70	44.64 1851–55	46.64 1925–28	43.56 1816–40	42.84 1906–10	37.7 1930	46.54 1926–30	45.6 1891–1900	41.06 1901–05	44.18 1881–90	Average of Last Eight Columns
Age Group	Fertility Rates												
15–19	60.1	8.0	8.8	7.8	36.6	13.2	28.4	63.5	31.5	17.3	27.4	18.3	29.5
20–24	166.3	97.8	101.7	97.7	225.0	120.8	173.2	177.0	200.2	154.8	176.4	155.7	172.9
25–29	194.7	206.5	201.9	202.3	240.7	223.3	244.9	211.3	248.6	211.4	260.1	236.8	234.6
30–34	187.6	237.1	229.3	235.3	187.8	240.6	228.9	216.6	217.0	237.8	245.2	240.5	226.8
35–39	138.8	198.5	200.9	203.3	130.1	195.3	160.2	152.3	163.1	192.7	171.7	204.4	171.2
40–44	73.1	108.9	118.3	116.0	62.8	107.1	80.3	79.7	71.6	115.6	85.0	121.2	90.4
45 and over	26.4	17.7	18.8	18.5	29.8	19.1	16.1	33.1	10.3	17.7	17.0	20.7	20.5
Total	847.0	874.5	879.7	880.9	912.8	919.4	932.0	933.5	942.3	947.3	982.8	997.6	945.9
Total × 5 = Total Fertility Rate	4235.0	4372.5	4398.5	4404.5	4564.0	4597.0	4660.0	4667.5	4711.5	4736.5	4914.0	4988.0	

TABLE 14–4. AGE-SPECIFIC FERTILITY RATES FOR COUNTRIES WITH LIFE EXPECTANCY FOR MALES OF 47 OR LESS RANKED ACCORDING TO "TOTAL FERTILITY RATE"

Country and Year	Germany, 1891–1900	Japan, 1925	Austria, 1895–1900	Germany, 1881–90	Mexico, 1929–31	Hungary, 1900–01	European RSFSR, 1926–27	Bulgaria, 1901–05	European Russia, 1896–97	High Fertility-Rate Assumption
E_0 and Year	43.97 1891–1900	43.20 1921–25	38.97 1895–1900	40.25 1881–90	34.07 1930	40.51 1900–01	45.61 1926–27	42.20 1900–05	33.36 1896–97	Average of First Eight Columns
Age Group	Fertility Rates									
15–19	21.7	43.2	28.4	20.0	117.4	56.8	40	23.5	30	43.9
20–24	192.2	227.8	181.1	188.8	228.5	259.0	275	288.6	309	230.1
25–29	289.9	259.3	265.2	295.6	242.9	280.0	286	312.2	334	278.9
30–34	243.4	228.3	260.3	253.8	217.0	230.5	233	309.4	331	247.0
35–39	175.1	174.0	182.2	194.0	156.1	161.4	177	204.3	219	178.0
40–44	73.3	74.8	88.0	85.5	83.4	69.3	87	121.0	130	85.3
45 and over	8.6	12.4	17.6	10.9	4.9	13.9	24	55.5	59	18.5
Total	1004.2	1019.8	1022.8	1048.6	1050.2	1070.9	1122	1314.5	1412	1080.7
Total × 5 = Total Fertility Rate	5021.0	5099.0	5114.0	5243.0	5251.0	5354.5	5610	6572.5	7060	

Two fertility-rate assumptions are used in the projections. The low fertility-rate assumption is based on and was obtained by averaging the age-specific rates of the eight populations (shown in table 14–3) whose "total fertility rates"[5] are between 4500 and 5000. The high fertility-rate assumption was obtained by averaging the eight populations (in table 14–4) whose "total fertility rates" are between 5000 and 6600, inclusive. The low rates are close to those of Chile, Japan, or Finland when these countries were less developed than they are today; the high rates are close to those of Mexico in 1930, Hungary in 1900, or European Russia in 1926. It is unlikely that any really backward economy today would have fertility rates much below those in our low fertility-rate assumption. It is probable that most of the backward economies have fertility rates closer to our high fertility-rate assumption, but, since they rarely collect and publish age-specific rates, it is difficult to check this assertion directly. But on the basis of their crude fertility rates compared to the experience of the countries included in our calculations, and taking into account certain biases in fertility-rate reporting, this last assertion would appear to hold, at least roughly.

The fertility decline assumptions. At some point it is important to consider the possibility of fertility decline as a factor that determines the size and nature of population changes. To take account of the consequences of this possibility we have introduced in six out of our twelve population projections an assumption about fertility decline. To determine reasonable rates of fertility decline we went once again to the available statistical evidence. In five of the projections we assume that fertility decline sets in about 30 years after the economy experiences sustained mortality decline. Historically, this is a rather short fertility gap reflecting the fact that most of our projections are probably on the conservative side.[6] This means that most of our projections are more likely to underestimate rather than overestimate the population hurdle

---

[5] By the "total fertility rate" we mean the sum of the age-specific rates.

[6] There seems to be general agreement among demographers about two facts: (1) There generally is a *delay* in the fall of fertility after mortality, and (2) after the fertility decline sets in it falls at some point at a faster rate than mortality decline. But from the literature it is not at all clear what the length of the fertility gap has been in different countries. One of the reasons for this is that it is rather difficult to date the beginning of the sustained decline in mortality in various countries. However, it is probably safe to guess that for most of the countries of Northern Europe (excluding France) the delay in fertility decline was greater than 30 years. See F. W. Notestein and others. *The Future Population of Europe and the Soviet Union,* Geneva, League of Nations, 1944, pp. 48–49. Also, R. R. Kuczynski, "The International Decline in Fertility," in Lancelot Hogben (Editor), *Political Arithmetic,* New York, The Macmillan Company, 1938.

to development. Some of the reasons for this will be considered later. In any event, if our representative population begins with a life expectancy of around 40 years for males and 42 years for females and increases its life expectancy by 2 years every 5-year period, the life expectancy of the population will be between 54 to 56 years at the time that the assumed fertility decline takes effect. Table 14–5 shows the computed average annual age-specific rates of fertility decline for countries that had experienced several decades of fertility decline and for which the population's life expectancy was roughly between 53 to 57 years.

On the basis of table 14–5, we chose three fertility-decline assumptions. The countries in this table are arrayed from left to right in terms of those that experienced the smallest rates of fertility decline to those that have experienced the largest rates of decline. The historical evidence seems to indicate that the experience of the countries of northwestern Europe is neither typical of what we might expect today nor typical of conditions in the recent past. Those countries that experienced their fertility decline in the late nineteenth century started with lower fertility rates than those countries that experienced their fertility decline later. Also their annual rate of fertility decline was significantly lower than those countries that experienced their fertility decline later.[7] Therefore, the fertility-decline experiences of Denmark, Norway, and Sweden have been eliminated from our considerations since their experience is most unlikely to be typical of countries that develop at a later date. We chose the average rates of decline of the next four countries as our low fertility-decline assumption. (See columns 4–7 and the averages shown in column 2.) The averages of each age group of the six countries (columns 4–9) having the largest rates of decline became our medium rate of fertility-decline assumption, and the rates of decline for Japan during the relevant period became our high rate of fertility-decline assumption. Both Italy and Japan have had high rates of fertility decline for the periods in question, although Japan represents the more extreme case.

Every population projection is, in an important sense, a statistical experiment. Starting with certain assumptions, the projections tell us both the short-run and the long-run implications of the assumptions. It is not at all difficult to invent small or large variations of any set of assumptions, and hence it is quite easy to increase the number of possible projections almost endlessly. As a result, there is, and of necessity must be, some selection and some degree of arbitrariness in the selection of projections. Nevertheless, we can claim that our projections are reason-

[7] Kuczynski, *op. cit.*, pp. 53 ff.

TABLE 14–5. AVERAGE ANNUAL RATES OF INCREASE OR DECREASE IN AGE-SPECIFIC FERTILITY RATES FOR COUNTRIES WITH E_0 = 53–57

Age Groups	Average Annual Rates of Increase (+) or Decrease (−).*									High Rates of Fertility Decline Assumption	Low Rates of Fertility Decline Assumption	Medium Rates of Fertility Decline Assumption
										Group Averages		
	Denmark 1878/84–1901/05 †	Sweden 1886/90–1901/05 †	Norway 1881/85–1889/1905	Finland 1911/20–1930/32	France 1908/13–1925/27 ‡	Spain 1930/31–1947 §	Portugal 1930/31–1947 ‖	Italy 1922–36 ¶	Japan 1937–1951	Columns (1)–(3)	Columns (4)–(7)	Columns (4)–(9)
	(1)	(2)	(3)	(4)	(5)	(6)	(7)	(8)	(9)	(10)	(11)	(12)
	%	%	%	%	%	%	%	%	%	%	%	%
10–14	...	...	...	...	...	...	...	...	...	...	...	...
15–19	+1.2743	+1.9527	+1.7269	−0.1262	−0.2156	−2.2431	−0.2920	−2.7188	−3.7556	+1.6513	−0.7192	−1.5586
20–24	+0.2752	+0.5352	+0.3307	−0.8977	−0.3487	−1.9308	−0.5901	−1.8266	−1.3162	+0.3804	−0.9418	−1.1520
25–29	−0.2210	−0.1326	−0.0739	−1.1404	−0.5546	−1.7448	−1.1209	−1.5913	−1.0363	−0.1425	−1.1402	−1.1980
30–34	−0.7488	−0.6077	−0.3585	−1.6206	−0.4997	−1.2373	−1.4912	−2.0123	−1.4644	−0.5717	−1.2122	−1.3876
35–39	−0.8463	−0.8753	−0.4571	−2.2270	−1.1305	−1.3223	−1.3483	−2.2746	−3.6846	−0.7262	−1.5070	−1.9979
40–44	−1.2446	−1.0300	−0.6039	−2.7945	−1.3800	−1.5527	−1.5606	−4.2016	−5.5885	−0.9595	−1.8220	−2.8463
45 and over	−1.3563	−1.7889	−1.2208	−2.6839	−1.7416	−1.1552	−2.4402	−11.4281	−10.8766	−1.4553	−2.0052	−5.0543

* Range of years over which Average Annual Rates were calculated: Denmark 28, Sweden 20, Norway 25, Finland 22, France 20, Spain 17, Portugal 18, Italy 15, Japan 15.

† Confinement Rates.

‡ Rates for earliest period of comparison are for live and still births.

§ Rates for latest year of comparison are approximate, based on census age distribution 6 years earlier and also include infants born alive who died before registration.

‖ Life expectancy for base year is slightly below the imposed limit (i.e., E_0 = 52.8).

¶ Rates for earliest year of comparison are estimated.

able and useful from two points of view. In the first place, since the assumptions behind the projections are based on historical statistics, they may give us some idea of the order of magnitude of the demographic variables. Second, since the projections are based on different assumptions, we can make comparisons between different projections that shed some light on the nature of the population hurdle to development.

The twelve projections are described in table 14–6. For special reasons the last two projections[8] will be treated separately later. The first ten projections are in three groups which we designate, for want of better terms, as: (1) the economic stagnation projections, (2) the economic growth-constant fertility projections, and (3) the economic growth-fertility-decline projections. Projections 1*a* and 1*b* are based on the assumption that there are no changes in mortality or fertility over the 55-year projection period. The implied underlying condition behind these two projections is that the rate of economic expansion is sufficient only to maintain the initial level of living but not sufficiently great to affect those factors that determine mortality rates.

We can impute to the eight "economic growth" projections (projections 2*a* to 5, inclusive) the general notion that a sustained improvement in economic conditions leads to a sustained improvement in life expectancy and a related systematic decline in mortality rates. Strictly speaking, projections 2*a*, 2*b*, 3*a*, etc., show the demographic consequences of a 22-year increase in life expectancy over the 55-year period given the various fertility assumptions. Nothing need necessarily be assumed about the underlying economic or other changes that can bring about such an improvement in life expectancy. Clearly our interests go beyond the point of making projections for their own sake. Therefore, it is of interest to consider whether a 20-year increase in life expectancy over a 50-year period is a relatively large or a relatively small increase in life expectancy for a country undergoing development. The figures given in table 14–7 are suggestive.

We can see in table 14–7 that Germany is the only country that had a rate of increase in life expectancy of more than 20 years over a 50-year period. Thus, the table suggests, to the extent that it can be assumed to be representative of the general situation,[9] that an increase of 20 years in life expectancy, over a 50-year period, is really a very rapid rate of

[8] The last two projections involve precipitous mortality declines similar to those experienced recently in backward economies where new and improved public health measures are employed. The significance of such changes is considered later.

[9] Representativeness cannot very well be tested because there are great gaps in the data for most countries.

TABLE 14–6. A SUMMARY DESCRIPTION OF THE TWELVE POPULATION PROJECTIONS AND THE AVERAGE ANNUAL RATES OF POPULATION GROWTH DETERMINED BY THE PROJECTIONS

Projection Number	Description	Average Annual Rate of Growth
	The Economic Stagnation Projections:	
1*a*	Constant age-specific mortality rates; *low* fertility-rates assumption held constant for the projection period.	1.25
1*b*	Constant age-specific mortality; *high* fertility-rates assumption held constant for the projection period.	1.69
	The Economic Growth-Constant Fertility Projections:	
2*a*	Declining mortality rates reflecting approximately a 2-year increase in life expectancy every 5-year period; *low* constant fertility rates.	1.98
2*b*	Declining mortality rates reflecting a 2-year increase in life expectancy every five years; *high* constant fertility.	2.43
	The Economic Growth-Declining Fertility Projections:	
3*a*	Declining mortality rates; *low* fertility-rates assumption; and *low* rate of fertility decline setting in after 30 years ($t = 30$).	1.78
3*b*	Declining mortality rates; *low* fertility rates; *medium* rate of fertility decline setting in at $t = 30$.	1.74
4*a*	Declining mortality rates; *high* fertility rates; *low* rate of fertility decline from $t = 30$.	2.21
4*b*	Declining mortality rates; *high* fertility rates; *medium* rate of fertility decline from $t = 30$.	2.17
4*c*	Declining mortality rates; *high* fertility rates; *high* rate of fertility decline from $t = 30$.	2.10
5	Declining mortality rates; *high* fertility rates; *medium* rate of fertility decline from $t = 10$.	1.68
	Precipitous Mortality-Decline Projections:	
6*a*	Fertility: same as 2*b*; mortality decline reflects 12-year increase in life expectancy in first 10-year period, and 2-year increases in life expectancy every 10-year period thereafter.	2.74
6*b*	Same as 6*a* except initial mortality declines reflect a 12-year increase in life expectancy in the second 5-year period.	2.68

increase, and that for the most part, only the most successful Western nations seem to have approached this rate of achievement. On the other hand, in view of recent improvements in medicine and public health techniques, it seems likely that countries starting their economic development today would achieve in the initial stages a much more rapid *rate* of increase in life expectancy as compared with those countries whose development took place in the past. More on this point later.

TABLE 14–7. Increases in Life Expectancy at Birth for Males for Selected Countries

Country	Approximate Dates Covered	Length of Period	Increase in Life Expectancy Over Period	Beginning and Ending Life Expectancy Over Period
Australia	1885–1935	50	16	47–63
Germany	1885–1935	50	23	37–60
Italy	1885–1935	50	19	35–54
Switzerland	1885–1935	50	18	43–61
New Zealand	1895–1945	50	13	55–68
United States	1905–1950	45	17	48–65
Finland	1895–1945	50	12	43–55
Austria	1875–1935	60	24	31–55
U. S. S. R.	1895–1925	30	11	31–42

Source: Abstracted from United Nations, *The Determinants and Consequences of Population Trends*, 1953, p. 54. Also from the United Nations, *Demographic Year Book*, for 1954, pp. 630 ff.

Results of the first ten projections

The results of the population projections are summarized in figure 14–3 and in tables 14–8 and 14–9. These tables reveal a number of differences among our projections. The difference in the average rate of population growth between the related low- and high-fertility projections, 1*a* and 1*b*, 2*a* and 2*b*, 3*a* and 4*a*, and 3*b* and 4*b* is in all cases approximately 0.45 of 1 per cent. For each pair of projections, the only things that differ are the fertility-rate assumptions. It is interesting that for the three types of projections, the effect of the initial difference in the fertility rate shows up to exactly the same extent in each case. In other words, beginning with a higher, rather than a lower, set of age-specific fertility rates has the same influence on the average absolute rate of population growth, almost regardless of subsequent events.

The really large differences in the average rates of population growth are accounted for by two types of phenomena: (1) the difference between a sustained decline in mortality as against no decline in mortality and (2) the difference between no decline in fertility rates as

TABLE 14–8. PROJECTED POPULATION PATTERNS

Time Period	Total Populations for Projections											
	1*a*	1*b*	2*a*	2*b*	3*a*	3*b*	4*a*	4*b*	4*c*	5*a*	6*a*	6*b*
t_0	1,000,000	1,000,000	1,000,000	1,000,000	1,000,000	1,000,000	1,000,000	1,000,000	1,000,000	1,000,000	1,000,000	1,000,000
t_5	1,075,103	1,105,819	1,078,103	1,105,819	1,078,103	1,078,103	1,105,819	1,105,819	1,105,819	1,105,819	1,136,249	1,105,819
t_{10}	1,157,007	1,211,885	1,172,194	1,225,862	1,172,194	1,172,194	1,225,862	1,225,862	1,225,862	1,225,862	1,303,651	1,270,768
t_{15}	1,242,677	1,323,197	1,282,729	1,364,882	1,282,729	1,282,729	1,364,882	1,364,882	1,364,882	1,348,304	1,485,500	1,449,826
t_{20}	1,330,037	1,437,529	1,408,872	1,522,569	1,408,872	1,408,872	1,522,569	1,522,569	1,522,569	1,473,210	1,689,909	1,649,061
t_{25}	1,416,444	1,557,407	1,549,600	1,703,695	1,549,600	1,549,600	1,703,695	1,703,695	1,703,695	1,602,978	1,919,533	1,869,821
t_{30}	1,502,545	1,688,320	1,709,049	1,920,052	1,709,049	1,709,049	1,920,052	1,920,052	1,920,052	1,744,754	2,196,137	2,135,332
t_{35}	1,590,698	1,831,545	1,890,305	2,177,439	1,874,168	1,869,923	2,157,172	2,152,081	2,143,558	1,895,885	2,518,874	2,446,957
t_{40}	1,682,404	1,986,344	2,099,876	2,482,761	2,049,801	2,037,308	2,418,383	2,403,088	2,379,005	2,052,393	2,899,687	2,816,797
t_{45}	1,778,746	2,152,042	2,341,888	2,840,514	2,236,827	2,211,911	2,703,050	2,671,644	2,624,512	2,207,105	3,332,936	3,238,327
t_{50}	1,879,112	2,328,571	2,620,164	3,257,953	2,436,065	2,394,017	3,011,754	2,957,474	2,879,878	2,356,380	3,838,048	3,728,744
t_{55}	1,982,666	2,518,004	2,938,664	3,747,141	2,641,959	2,577,435	3,344,615	3,259,027	3,143,756	2,500,064	4,417,880	4,290,089

against the early onset of fertility decline. For example, the differences in the average rates of growth between projections 2*b* and 1*b* is 0.74 of 1 per cent (see table 14–6), which is accounted for by the fact that in 2*b* we assume declining mortality rates. The largest difference among the high-fertility (but gradual-mortality-decline) projections is between

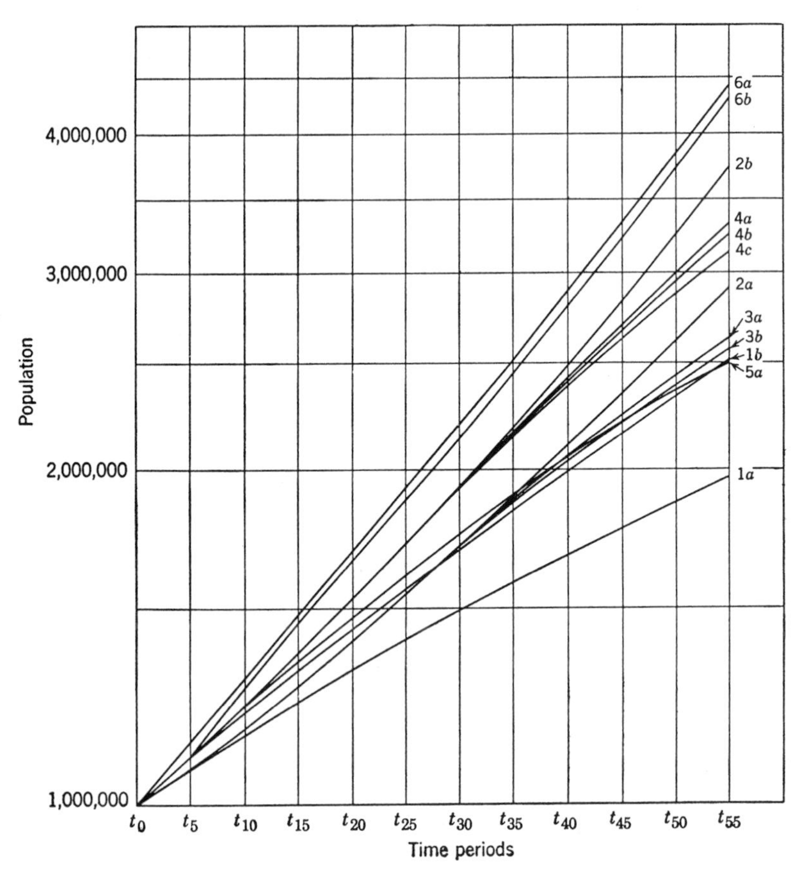

FIGURE 14–3. The pattern of total population growth for the population projections.

projection 2*b* and projection 5. Their average annual rates of growth differ by 0.75 of 1 per cent. This last difference is accounted for by the fact that in projection 5 we assume that the medium rate of fertility decline sets in 10 years after our projection period begins.

Although mortality decline is important, its significance must not be exaggerated. It accounts for only one-third of the rate of population growth. In absolute figures mortality decline adds no more than 0.8

TABLE 14–9. ANNUAL RATES OF POPULATION GROWTH FOR PROJECTIONS

(Rates in Per Cent)

Time Periods	1*a*	1*b*	2*a*	2*b*	3*a*	3*b*	4*a*	4*b*	4*c*	5*a*	6*a*	6*b*
t_0–t_5	1.52	2.03	1.52	2.03	1.52	1.52	2.03	2.03	2.03	2.03	2.59	2.03
t_5–t_{10}	1.48	1.85	1.69	2.08	1.69	1.69	2.08	2.08	2.08	2.08	2.79	2.82
t_{10}–t_{15}	1.44	1.77	1.82	2.17	1.82	1.82	2.17	2.17	2.17	1.92	2.65	2.67
t_{15}–t_{20}	1.37	1.67	1.89	2.21	1.89	1.89	2.21	2.21	2.21	1.79	2.61	2.61
t_{20}–t_{25}	1.27	1.61	1.92	2.27	1.92	1.92	2.27	2.27	2.27	1.70	2.58	2.54
t_{25}–t_{30}	1.19	1.63	1.98	2.42	1.98	1.98	2.42	2.42	2.42	1.71	2.73	2.69
t_{30}–t_{35}	1.15	1.64	2.04	2.55	1.86	1.82	2.36	2.31	2.23	1.68	2.78	2.76
t_{35}–t_{40}	1.13	1.64	2.13	2.66	1.81	1.73	2.31	2.23	2.11	1.60	2.86	2.86
t_{40}–t_{45}	1.12	1.62	2.21	2.73	1.76	1.66	2.25	2.14	1.98	1.46	2.82	2.83
t_{45}–t_{50}	1.10	1.59	2.27	2.78	1.72	1.59	2.19	2.05	1.87	1.32	2.86	2.86
t_{50}–t_{55}	1.08	1.58	2.32	2.84	1.64	1.49	2.12	1.96	1.77	1.19	2.85	2.84

of 1 per cent to the average population growth rate in the most extreme case in our gradual-mortality-decline projections. The important fact to remember is that at the stage that many underdeveloped areas are at today, the existing rate of population growth is likely to be quite large even if mortality decline does not occur. For example, projection 1*a*, reflecting the situation of the stagnant economy under the low fertility-rate assumption, yields a rate of population growth of 1.25 per cent.

Our computations further suggest that the really effective means of keeping the rate of growth within bounds is the early inception of fertility decline. *A priori* one might suppose the rate of fertility decline to be as important as the time at which the decline sets in. But to the extent that our statistics are representative of the general situation, it seems that the variations in the long-run, average rates of fertility decline are, on the whole, not so different between countries as to account for very much of the differences in the rates of population growth. Thus if our sample of average fertility-decline rates is not unrepresentative, it appears that the significant determinant of the *long-run, average* population growth rate is *how soon* fertility decline sets in after the mortality decline begins.

Projections 1*a* and 1*b*, reflecting the stagnant economy, show patterns of population growth that decrease at decreasing rates. This is due to the fact that the representative age distribution with which we began is not a stable[10] distribution; actually our age distribution represents a younger population than the relevant stable population. This last assertion reflects the fact that the underdeveloped economies from which we derived our representative age distribution had unstable age structures at the time that their expectation of life was somewhere around 40 years.

For projections 2*a* and 2*b* we find that the rates of population growth are steadily increasing, but at decreasing rates. The increasing rates are explained by our assumptions of constant fertility and declining mortality rates. But the decrease in the rate of growth reflects, in part, the fact that the initial age distribution is young as compared with the stable age distribution.

---

[10] The notion of a stable age distribution (or of a "stable population") is used in the sense in which Alfred Lotka and succeeding demographers have used the term. A stable population is one in which the proportion in each age group remains the same, period after period. Lotka has shown that for every set of age-specific fertility rates and mortality rates, a stable population exists, and it is one that will be approached asymptotically as a result of applying period after period the same set of fertility and mortality rates. See Louis I. Dublin, Alfred J. Lotka, and Mortimer Spiegelman, *Length of Life,* New York, the Ronald Press, 1949, Chapter 12.

Some special significance may be attached to the maximum rates of population growth and to the points at which they occur. If we consider population growth as a hurdle to the development of densely populated areas, then, broadly speaking, the maximum rates in the growth patterns may be rough indications of how high the hurdles are likely to become. In our projections the maximum rates occur just prior to the point where the fertility decline begins. That is, the maximum rates of population growth do not depend on the *rates* of fertility decline (compare projections 4*a*, 4*b*, 4*c*, and 5) but only on the *points* at which the declines start.[11] Of special interest is the fact that the earlier the fertility decline sets in (compare projection 4*b* with 5), the lower the maximum rate of population growth. Conversely, the larger the time gap between the onset of mortality decline and the onset of fertility decline, the larger the maximum rate of population growth.

It may be argued that the maximum rates shown in table 14–9 do not really represent the maximum population hurdle to development since (apart from projections 1*a* and 1*b*) they all assume that during the projection period life expectancy increases at a uniform rate. But there is no need for a uniform increase in life expectancy in order to achieve sustained growth. At some point we may wish for a slackening in the improvement in life expectancy in order to diminish the population hurdle. What are the consequences to population growth of such a reduction of the extent of the mortality decline? The results given in table 14–10 are quite suggestive in this regard. The extreme degree of slackening in life expectancy improvement is to have no improvement whatsoever. In column 3 of table 14–10 we show what the annual rates of population growth would be during the relevant maximum growth periods if during those periods there was a complete cessation in mortality decline; column 4 indicates the actual maximum rates of growth for the relevant periods. By comparing the figures in the two columns, it can be seen that the reduction in the rate of population growth that can be achieved by stopping life expectancy improvement is exceedingly small for a 5-year period.

It is clear that the lower the rate of overall life expectancy improvement, the lower the maximum population hurdle. For example, consider projections 1*b* and 2*b*. In projection 1*b* we have the extreme of zero life-expectancy improvement during the projection period, whereas in 2*b* we assume a 22-year improvement in life expectancy

---

[11] This result may, in part, be due to the fact that in our computations we work with discrete units and with long-period, average rates of fertility decline.

over the 55-year period which, as we have shown previously, is an exceedingly rapid improvement. Yet it is of interest to observe that the maximum rates of population growth in these extreme cases are not exceptionally wide apart. The maximum rate for projection 1*b* is approximately 2.03 per cent per year, and for projection 2*b* it is about 2.84 per cent. Hence, even if we assume a lower rate of life expectancy improvement, say a 1-year increase in life expectancy every 5 years, the maximum rate of population growth for the high fertility assumption would still be of an order of about 2.5 per cent per annum.

TABLE 14–10. RECOMPUTATION OF MAXIMUM POPULATION HURDLES ON THE ASSUMPTION OF A CESSATION IN THE IMPROVEMENT IN THE CHANCES OF SURVIVAL

(1) Population Projection	(2) Time Period of Maximum 5-Year Rate of Population Growth	(3) Recomputed Annual Rate of Growth, %	(4) Previous Rate of Growth, %	(5) Column (4) minus Column (3)
2*a*	t_{50}–t_{55}	2.25	2.32	.07
2*b*	t_{50}–t_{55}	2.77	2.84	.07
3*a*	t_{25}–t_{30}	1.85	1.98	.13
3*b*	t_{25}–t_{30}	1.85	1.98	.13
4*a*	t_{25}–t_{30}	2.29	2.42	.13
4*b*	t_{25}–t_{30}	2.29	2.42	.13
4*c*	t_{25}–t_{30}	2.29	2.42	.13
5	t_{5}–t_{10}	1.84	2.08	.24

The significance of a maximum rate of population growth can perhaps best be seen if we relate it to the incremental capital-output ratio, since the product of the two tells us the rate of investment necessary to maintain the current level of per capita output. Let us suppose that the incremental capital-output ratio is 4 to 1. (We shall see later that this is not at all an unreasonable ratio to expect. Indeed, it may be on the low side.) If the maximum rate of population growth is 2.5 per cent, it is implied that the net investment rate must be *above* 10 per cent of the national income in order to continue per capita income growth during the year of maximum population growth.

The precipitous mortality-decline projections

In recent years considerable attention has been drawn to the fact that some underdeveloped areas have achieved rapid decreases in mortality without substantial (or any) increases in per capita income. These achievements are usually attributed to chemical and medical discoveries and to improvements in public health techniques,[12] for example, malaria control. It is clear from the empirical evidence that there are circumstances nowadays under which rapid increases in life expectancy can occur prior to or during the very early stages of sustained economic development. The figures in table 14–11 are suggestive of the magnitudes that may be involved.

TABLE 14–11. LIFE EXPECTANCY INCREASES FOR SELECTED COUNTRIES AFFECTED BY MALARIA CONTROL AND OTHER PUBLIC-HEALTH MEASURES

Country	Year	Male Life Expectancy at Birth	Year	Male Life Expectancy at Birth	Gain in Years of Life Expectancy	Time Period of Gain
Mauritius	1942–46	32.25	1950–52	49.8	17.5	7
Chile	1940	37.9	1952	49.8	11.9	12
Ceylon	1945–47	46.8	1952	57.6	10.8	6
Japan	1946	42.6	1953	61.9	19.3	7
Portugal	1939–42	48.6	1949–52	55.5	6.9	10

Source: United Nations Statistical Yearbook, 1955.

In view of the above we computed projections 6*a* and 6*b* (see table 14–12) on the basis of assumptions that are in conformity with the sort of rapid mortality-decline experience that took place in some areas. For projection 6*a* we assumed that over the first 10-year period, life expectancy increased by 12 years. For projection 6*b* we assumed that the 12-year improvement in life expectancy took place during the second 5-year period. In both cases the rest of the life expectancy improvement is stretched out for the remainder of the 55-year projection period so that the total improvement is the same as in the other mortality-decline projections (projections 2*a* to 5*a*). The other assump-

[12] See, for example, "Malaria: A World Problem," *Chronicle of the World Health Organization,* Vol. 9 (February-March 1955). It is sometimes also suggested that malaria control increases fertility rates. Some countries (for example, British Guiana, Mauritius, Venezuela) have had rising birth rates during a period (1946–1952) when they were affected by malaria control. But other areas (for example, Ceylon, Sardinia, Cyprus), at least equally affected by malaria control during the same period, did not show any rise in their fertility rates. The weight of technical opinion in the medical and public health fields seems definitely against the view that malaria control increases birth rates. See one of the classic articles in this field by W. A. P. Shaffner, "Two Subjects Relating to the Epidemiology of Malaria," *Journal of the Malaria Institute of India,* Vol. 1 (September 1938), pp. 221–256. In addition see the various articles abstracted in the *Tropical Diseases Bulletin,* Vol. 50, No. 7 (July 1953), Vol. 49, 1952, pp. 220 ff., and Vol. 38, 1941, pp. 410 ff.

tions employed are the same as those used for projection 2*b*. Therefore, the summary results of these projections, given in table 14–12, are compared with those of projection 2*b*. The results suggest that under the circumstances indicated, and in the absence of fertility decline, very high rates of population growth are achieved almost at the outset, and these high growth rates are maintained throughout.

TABLE 14–12. ANNUAL RATES OF POPULATION GROWTH

	Projection		
Time Periods	2*b*	6*a*	6*b*
t_0–t_5	2.03	2.59	2.03
t_5–t_{10}	2.08	2.79	2.82
t_{10}–t_{15}	2.17	2.65	2.67
t_{15}–t_{20}	2.21	2.61	2.61
t_{20}–t_{25}	2.27	2.58	2.54
t_{25}–t_{30}	2.42	2.73	2.69
t_{30}–t_{35}	2.55	2.78	2.76
t_{35}–t_{40}	2.66	2.86	2.86
t_{40}–t_{45}	2.73	2.82	2.83
t_{45}–t_{50}	2.78	2.86	2.86
t_{50}–t_{55}	2.84	2.85	2.84

What are the implications that flow from the possibility that under some circumstances rapid mortality declines can be achieved through recently perfected public health techniques at low cost and prior to the onset of sustained development? Does this mean that all calculations based on the historical tendency of economic development *preceding* mortality decline are meaningless? The answer depends on whether or not the lower mortality rates achieved by the new public health measures can be sustained and, if so, what it takes to sustain them. Certain possibilities come to mind, and these are, perhaps, worthy of consideration.

First, it is clear that such cheaply achieved low mortality rates cannot be sustained independently of at least some economic expansion in the aggregate sense. Rapid mortality declines must mean a rapid expansion of the population and an equal, or almost equal, expansion in aggregate output in order to feed and otherwise maintain the expanding population. That is, even if declines in mortality precede development, some economic expansion in the aggregate sense must occur if these lower mortality rates are to be maintained.

Second, it may be that such low mortality rates achieved in this way cannot be maintained in another sense. That is to say, even if national output expands sufficiently to maintain the previous level of per capita income, mortality rates may still rise after some period of time. Those people who are saved from malaria and other endemic diseases may only be saved to succumb at a somewhat later date from malnutrition or from some of the other unpleasant concomitants of low per capita income levels. We do not know enough at present to assess to what extent this last possibility may or may not be true.

Third, there is the obvious possibility that the improved public health techniques do raise the expectation of life for given levels of per capita income. This means that such measures lower the subsistence equilibrium income level. But at the same time, and by the same token, the rate of population growth is increased for a given level of per capita income, and the magnitude of the population obstacle to development increases accordingly. The implication of all this, in the language of the previous chapters, is that whereas the new subsistence equilibrium income level is lower than before, the new critical minimum effort level must be higher than previously.

Population Growth, Income Growth, and Investment Requirements

Our next step is to connect the various patterns of population growth with related consistent patterns of national income growth. To do so we correlated life expectancy with per capita income and computed for the various projections the patterns and rates of national income growth required to support the growing populations at the rising income levels implied by the correlation and by the postulated rate of growth in life expectancy. Although the evidence suggests that there is some connection between life expectancy and the level of per capita income, the relation is certainly not a unique or perfect one. This is to be expected. Sanitary habits, the state of medical knowledge, and hygienic and other discoveries do play their part. Furthermore, out of a given income the amount spent on nutrition, public health, and other factors that determine the health and vitality of the group can, in principle, vary to a considerable degree. Nevertheless, the size of the correlation coefficient ($r = .71$) suggests that the historical relationship[13] between the two variables is not without significance.

---

[13] Of what significance this "historical relationship" is for present-day backward economies is most difficult to say. At best it is probably suggestive only of what the orders of magnitude were in the past. We do not know enough to say how this relationship would turn out for the "precipitous mortality-decline" countries. However, compare the interesting article by E. Dunsdorfs, "Average Expectation of Life as an Index of Civilization," *Weltwirtschaftliches Archiv*, Vol. 74, 1955, pp. 267–282.

In figure 14–4 we present the scatter diagram relating expectation of life and per capita income as measured by the International Units computed by Colin Clark. The regression line is based on the equation

$$\log Y = 0.9252 + 0.0251X$$

where X is the expectation of life at birth and Y is income per head measured in International Units.[14]

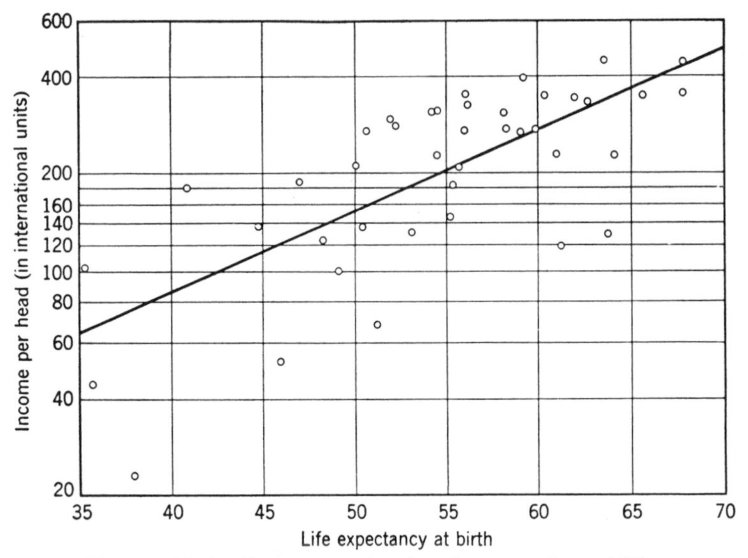

FIGURE 14–4. Income per head and expectation of life.

Every observation used in our regression involves an expectation of life for a country at a given time and the income per man at that time. For the income levels per head we based our calculations on Colin Clark's calculations found in *The Conditions of Economic Progress,* Second Edition, and on related demographic data found in a number of sources. It is unfortunate that for many countries there are no data published that would enable one to make a simultaneous estimate of their expectation of life and income level. We used those countries for which the requisite data were readily available, although we excluded certain countries, such as, Canada, Australia, and New Zealand, that could not possibly have been subject to any population pressure in the early stages of development and in which the expectation of life seems much less related to their per capita income level and

[14] Colin Clark's computations are in terms of income per head of the occupied population inclusive of both those at work and those unemployed. We recomputed Clark's data on the basis of income per head of total population. See appendix 6.

much more to the state of medical knowledge and to the health and selectivity of immigrants. These countries, both on *a priori* grounds and in fact, seem to operate on quite a different income per head—life expectancy relationship.

On the basis of this correlation we computed for each projection an index of required national income growth and the related annual *rates* of national income growth required to support the growing population at the rate of growth in income per head implied by the correlation. Underlying our computations is the simplifying assumption that the proportion of the labor force employed remains constant throughout. We shall have something to say later on this point. Our computations were made as follows: For every life expectancy there is a related income per head (of occupied population). Setting our initial (for life expectancy = 40) income per head at 100, we obtain indices of income per head for the range of life expectancies considered. From our population projections we obtained indices of population growth. For each 5-year time point and for each projection, the product of the index of income per head and the index of population growth give us an index of required national income growth. From this last we compute the annual rates of required national income growth for each 5-year interval. The results are summarized in table 14–13.

Looking at the figures for projections 2*a* to 5*a*, we observe that for almost all of the projections it takes about a 3 to 5 per cent (and in a few cases more than 5 per cent) annual growth in national income to support the growing population and a rate of national income growth consistent with the assumed rate of improvement in life expectancy. Of course, a given improvement in life expectancy can probably be achieved at a lower rate of increase in income than that implied by our correlation by allocating, to the extent possible, more income to public- and private-health measures. Roughly speaking, our computations suggest those increases in national income growth required on the basis of the average historical distribution of income between mortality-reducing and non-mortality-reducing expenditures. Here again the numbers are only suggestive of the order of magnitude. The absolute magnitudes of the figures in table 14–13 must not be taken very seriously. After all, both the data used and the nature of the computations are of too rough and ready a character to give us anything more than a broad picture.[15]

[15] Apart from the intrinsic difficulties of obtaining reliable internationally comparative indices of income per head and apart from the differences in quality of the basic statistics utilized, there may be a significant but unmeasurable bias in our calculations due to the fact that an undue proportion of our income data comes from European countries. It is mostly for these countries that data are available.

TABLE 14–13. Annual Rates of Required National Income Growth for the Twelve Projections

Time Period	1*a*	1*b*	2*a*	2*b*	3*a*	3*b*	4*a*	4*b*	4*c*	5*a*	6*a*	6*b*
t_0–t_5	1.52	2.03	3.89	4.40	3.89	3.89	4.40	4.40	4.40	4.40	5.06	4.40
t_5–t_{10}	1.48	1.85	4.11	4.56	4.11	4.11	4.56	4.56	4.56	4.56	5.08	5.23
t_{10}–t_{15}	1.44	1.77	4.22	4.48	4.22	4.22	4.48	4.48	4.48	4.27	5.07	5.08
t_{15}–t_{20}	1.37	1.67	4.24	4.63	4.24	4.24	4.63	4.63	4.63	4.14	5.08	5.03
t_{20}–t_{25}	1.27	1.61	4.26	4.67	4.26	4.26	4.67	4.67	4.67	4.10	4.92	4.98
t_{25}–t_{30}	1.19	1.63	4.38	4.84	4.38	4.38	4.84	4.84	4.84	4.12	5.17	5.08
t_{30}–t_{35}	1.15	1.64	4.44	4.94	4.29	4.24	4.73	4.68	4.60	4.01	5.20	5.14
t_{35}–t_{40}	1.13	1.64	4.51	5.05	4.18	4.07	4.73	4.63	4.51	3.99	5.24	5.27
t_{40}–t_{45}	1.12	1.62	4.61	5.12	4.12	4.05	4.63	4.54	4.36	3.86	5.24	5.24
t_{45}–t_{50}	1.10	1.59	4.66	5.20	4.12	3.98	4.60	4.42	4.27	3.68	5.28	5.27
t_{50}–t_{55}	1.08	1.58	4.71	5.24	4.00	3.86	4.50	4.36	4.15	3.55	5.26	5.25
Index of Required National Income Growth at t_{50} ($t_0 = 100$)	188	233	834	1037	776	762	959	941	917	750	1222	1187

Capital Output Ratios and Required Rates of Investment

To obtain some idea of how easy or difficult it might be to achieve some of the rates of national income growth indicated in table 14–13, we might look at various pieces of statistical evidence. First we might look at the data presented by Raymond Goldsmith[16] on the actual

TABLE 14–14. GROWTH RATES OF REAL NATIONAL PRODUCT OF "ADVANCED" COUNTRIES, 1860–1950

(Per Cent Per Year)

Country	Aggregate Real Product			Product Per Head		
	1860–1913*	1913/38	1938/50	1860–1913	1913/38	1938/50
(1) United States	4.3	2.0	5.7	2.3	.9	4.2
(2) Canada	...	1.7†	5.9	...	.2	4.0
(3) Australia	3.7	2.1	2.6	1.7	.4	1.1
(4) New Zealand	...	...	3.3‡	...	...	2.4
(5) United Kingdom	2.4	1.0	1.6	1.5	.8	1.2
(6) France	1.1	1.1	0.2	.9	.9	.0
(7) Germany	2.4	0.7	2.3§	1.5	.5	.7
(8) Netherlands	2.3	2.1	1.8	.8	.6	.6
(9) Belgium	2.2	1.0	.6	1.4	.6	.3
(10) Switzerland	2.6	1.6	2.1	1.4	1.2	1.1
(11) Sweden	2.0	1.9	2.5	1.3	1.4	1.7
(12) Norway	2.3	1.9	3.0	1.6	1.2	2.1
(13) Denmark	2.8	2.1	2.2	1.8	.8	1.2

* First period starts other than 1860: United States 1869/78; Australia 1886; United Kingdom 1870; Netherlands 1900; Belgium 1846; Switzerland 1890; Sweden 1870; Norway 1891; Denmark 1870.

† 1911 instead of 1913.

‡ 1938/39 to 1947/48.

§ From 1936 to 1952.

Source: Goldsmith, *op. cit.*, p. 115.

growth rates of a number of countries that, for the most part, did develop successfully during the period 1860–1950. (See table 14–14.) It is of interest that most of the actual growth rates in aggregate real product shown in table 14–14, especially those rates in the first period when population growth must have been most rapid, fall between the extreme rates of "required" national income growth shown in table 14–13, that is, between the rates for projections 1*a* and 1*b* that assume

[16] Raymond Goldsmith, "Financial Structure and Economic Growth in Advanced Countries," *Capital Formation and Economic Growth,* A Conference of the Universities, National Bureau Committee for Economic Research (NBER), Princeton, Princeton University Press, 1955, p. 115.

no per capita income growth and those for projections 2*a* to 5*a* that assume rather rapid rates of per capita income growth.

Second, the significance of the required annual rates of national income growth can be seen from another viewpoint if we combine these rates with incremental capital-output ratios and compare the results with usual rates of net investment in various countries. The product of the required national income growth rate and the incremental capital-output ratio yields the required rate of net investment necessary to achieve the desired growth.

TABLE 14–15. ESTIMATES OF INCREMENTAL CAPITAL-OUTPUT RATIOS FOR SELECTED COUNTRIES

Country	Period Considered	Incremental Capital-Output Ratio	Source Note
United States	1879–1929	3.0	*a*
Sweden	1896–1929	3.3	*a*
Australia	1913–1938	3.9	*a*
Canada	1911–1939	4.2	*a*
Great Britain	1865–1909	5.9	*a*
Japan	1913–1939	6.1	*a*
Netherlands	1913–1939	7.4	*a*
France	1852–1913	7.4	*a*
United States (Kuznets	1899–1944		
10-year averages)	Low Figure	2.76	*b*
	High Figure	4.03	*b*
Mexico	1940–1950	2.11	*c*
	1940–1945	1.54	*c*
	1946–1950	2.75	*c*
British Guiana	1943–1951	3.5	*d*
Ceylon	1953–1959	4.0	*e*

Sources: a. Figures computed by E. E. Hagen in "The Incremental Capital-Output Ratio," unpublished paper, December 1953. Hagen notes, however, that later data indicate the possibility of wide margins of error in the ratios. The computations are based on figures found in Colin Clark, *Conditions of Economic Progress*, 2nd Edition, London, Macmillan and Company, Ltd., 1951.

b. These are ratios of net fixed capital plus inventories to net national product. These and other computations are presented in Evsey D. Domar, "Interrelations Between Capital and Output in the American Economy," *International Social Science Bulletin*, Vol. VI, No. 2, (1954), p. 204.

c. These are ratios of gross domestic investment to net investment found in Table 26, p. 204 of *The Economic Development of Mexico*, Report of the Combined Mexican Working Party, I.B.R.D., Baltimore, Johns Hopkins University Press, 1953.

d. The Economic Development of British Guiana, I.B.R.D., Baltimore, Johns Hopkins Press, 1953, pp. 89–90.

e. This is "a conservative figure" based on very little data used as a means of evaluating a proposed six-year development plan. *The Economic Development of Ceylon*, I.B.R.D., Baltimore, The Johns Hopkins Press, 1953, p. 104.

But what are likely and reasonable capital-output ratios? To this end consider the data presented in table 14–15. It appears, from table 14–15, that capital-output ratios have varied somewhat from time to time and considerably from area to area. Also, the quality of the data varies greatly from place to place. If one has to guess it would seem that a ratio of 3 to 1 is probably low for most underdeveloped areas and that one of 5 to 1 is probably not too high. Indeed, it would be somewhat surprising if the incremental capital-output ratios were no higher for present-day densely populated backward economies than they were for the United States in the past. Dr. Hans Singer of the United Nations, in presenting some numerical models of development based on what he considers to be realistic assumptions, uses an incremental capital-output ratio of 4 to 1 in agriculture and 6 to 1 in industry. The higher industry ratio is explained, in part, by the necessary social overhead costs involved in moving labor from the countryside to urban industrial centers.[17] Singer's guess is probably no worse than that of anyone else in this matter.

TABLE 14–16. REQUIRED RATE OF NET INVESTMENT FOR SELECTED PROJECTIONS

Projection Number	Assuming a Capital-Output Ratio of 3 to 1						Assuming a Capital-Output Ratio of 5 to 1					
	1*b*	2*b*	3*b*	4*b*	5*a*	6*a*	1*b*	2*b*	3*b*	4*b*	5*a*	6*a*
t_0–t_5	6.09	13.20	11.67	13.20	13.20	15.15	10.15	22.00	19.45	22.00	22.00	25.30
Minimum Rate	4.74	13.20	11.58	13.08	10.65	14.76	7.90	22.00	19.30	21.80	17.75	24.60
Maximum Rate	6.09	15.72	13.14	14.52	13.68	15.84	10.15	26.20	21.90	24.20	22.80	26.40
t_{50}–t_{55}	4.74	15.72	11.58	13.08	10.65	15.78	7.90	26.20	19.30	21.80	17.75	26.30

Suppose that we adopt 3 to 1 as a low incremental capital-output ratio and 5 to 1 as a high one. What do such ratios imply about the investment rates required to achieve various points in our projections? (It is left to the reader to determine to what extent such assumptions are reasonable.) Table 14–16 summarizes the different required investment rates at important selected points.

For the rather rapid rate of development implied by projections 2*a* to 5*a* we need a rate of net investment that varies from a low of about

[17] H. W. Singer, "The Mechanics of Economic Development," *Indian Economic Review,* August 1952, pp. 1–18.

11 per cent to a high of over 26 per cent per year. If we suppose that 5 to 1 is the more realistic ratio, we need, in the high fertility case, a more than 10 per cent rate of investment to get underway and a more than 19 per cent rate of net investment to get started on the development pattern implied in our projections. There is little need to go

TABLE 14–17. PROPORTIONS OF NET DOMESTIC CAPITAL FORMATION TO NET NATIONAL PRODUCT

Country	1938	1947–1952[a]
1. United States	2.2	11.6
2. Canada	4.5	15.0
3. France	[b]	9.2[c,d]
4. Italy	11.3	13.1[f]
5. Ireland	6.7	12.0
6. Netherlands	1.7	15.7[f]
7. Norway	6.9	16.0
8. Austria	[b]	15.3[e]
9. Finland	[b]	22.6[e]
10. Australia	17.0	26.8
11. New Zealand	13.6	18.7
12. Philippines	[b]	6.8
13. Southern Rhodesia	[b]	44.9
14. Chile	8.8[g]	10.3[h]
15. Honduras	3.1	8.4
16. Mexico	3.9[i]	7.5[h]
17. Peru	[b]	10.9

a. Percentages of totals for the period.
b. No data.
c. Data for 1949–1952.
d. Unadjusted for depreciation on government capital.
e. Data for 1948–1952.
f. Data for 1947–1951.
g. Data for 1940.
h. Data for 1947–1950.
i. Data for 1939.

Source: Abstracted from Simon Kuznets, "International Differences in Capital Formation and Financing," in Goldsmith, *op. cit.*, p. 60.

on to discuss all possible cases since these are apparent from the tables presented. In any event, it is clear that in any specific case the incremental capital-output ratio is a crucial element in determining the possibilities of generating sustained development.

Given the required rates of net investment in table 14–16, what can we say about them? Are they realistic and achievable rates, impossible rates, or are they rates that are almost always likely to occur?[18] The data collected by Simon Kuznets,[19] some of which we present in abbreviated form in table 14–17, on actual rates of domestic net investment for various countries are suggestive in this connection. (See also Appendix 7.)

For most present-day underdeveloped countries reliable data on their rates of net capital formation are simply unobtainable. We can only guess that the rates are probably quite low. On this point Singer[20] seems to feel that it is probable that in most densely populated backward economies the rate of net investment is less than 6 per cent. It is most difficult to say how accurate this guess is.

TABLE 14–18. LABOR FORCE AVAILABILITY

Per Cent of Total Population in Age Group 15 to 65

	Population Projection											
Time Period	1*a* %	1*b* %	2*a* %	2*b* %	3*a* %	3*b* %	4*a* %	4*b* %	4*c* %	5*a* %	6*a* %	6*b* %
t_0	57.80	57.80	57.80	57.80	57.80	57.80	57.80	57.80	57.80	57.80	57.80	57.80
t_{20}	58.54	55.83	57.48	54.68	57.48	57.48	54.68	54.68	54.68	56.51	54.00	53.77
t_{40}	59.56	56.42	57.63	54.49	59.04	59.04	55.94	55.94	55.94	61.39	53.97	54.04
t_{55}	59.38	56.85	57.12	54.45	61.74	62.83	59.18	60.29	61.78	65.25	54.53	54.45

Another aspect to consider, one that we have mentioned only in passing, is the changing age pattern of a population as a country develops and its relation to the burden of dependency and to labor force availability. It seems reasonable that the greater the burden of dependency, that is, the smaller the proportion in the working age group, the greater the hurdle to development, other things being equal. Some ratios derived from our projections suggest the changing nature of these proportions under alternate circumstances. Assuming ages 15 to 65 to be our working age group, we note in table 14–18 some of the circumstances under which labor force availability increases and those under which it decreases.

[18] On this aspect of the problem see the recent article by W. W. Rostow, "The Take-Off into Self-Sustained Growth," *Economic Journal,* March 1956, pp. 33–38. Unfortunately this article came out too late to be considered adequately in this book.

[19] Simon Kuznets, "International Differences in Capital Formation and Financing," in Goldsmith, *op. cit.,* pp. 60 ff.

[20] Singer, *op. cit.*

In the long run the changes in fertility rates are the most significant influences, whereas in the short run mortality rate changes may be the most important. Looking at the results for projections 2*a* and 2*b*, we note that the effect of sustained mortality decline is to reduce the proportion in the working age group, even in the long run. But when fertility decline does take place, the longer the period of fertility decline, the greater the proportion in the working age group. (However, we must keep in mind all along that there is a tendency for the age at which people enter the work force to rise as per capita income increases.)

Consider especially the results for projection 5*a*. In the short run, the impact of declining infant mortality rates is likely to be the most important influence. Thus, in the early years (to t_{20}) the proportion in the work ages decreases, and the burden of dependency increases, despite the fact that fertility rates decline. But eventually the fertility effect predominates, and the proportion in the work force increases significantly by the end of our projection period. Therefore, to the extent that the burden of dependency is a hurdle to growth, to that extent the hurdle is greatest in the early periods.

What we can conclude from the preceding investigations is, at best, of a rather vague nature. The computations and data presented seem to suggest the probability that some of the rates of net investment needed to generate sustained development do not occur usually in many of the underdeveloped economies. On the other hand, the data on actual rates of investment for many countries suggest that even some of the higher rates of required net investment shown in table 14–16 may be achieved in some economic environments (that is, they are not *impossible* rates), although the investment effort required *may* have to be larger than that obtained by normally stimulated voluntary savings. But all of this is extremely tentative. And the difficulty of saying anything firm about the capital-output ratios that apply increases still more the tentative nature of our conclusions.

Maintaining a High Mortality Pattern versus Potential Fertility Decline

Before closing this chapter we should consider briefly one of the great issues that may face those interested in the determination of policies that foster development, an issue on which our calculations may throw some light. Should a country, in its efforts to foster development, try to prevent increases in the rate of population growth by attempting to maintain initial mortality rates, or should it permit improvements in life expectancy consistent with some desired rate of per capita income growth? At first blush, surely, we might expect that it would be easier for a country to achieve a certain pattern of per capita income growth if it held down life expectancy, and in that way prevented increases in the rate of population growth. But some of our computations, the results of which are presented in table 14–19, suggest that this need not be the case, or at least that there may be some circumstances under which it is not the case.

Consider the problem of a country trying to achieve that pattern of per capita income growth assumed in projections 2*a* to 6*b*. Suppose that mortality and fertility rates are maintained at their initial level, as they are in projection 1*b*, but that per capita income grows according to the same pattern as in projections 2*a* to 6*b*. What does this imply about the required rates of per capita income growth? The results of the necessary computations are shown in column 2 in table 14–19.

TABLE 14–19. Required Rates of National Income Growth for a Given Pattern of per Capita Income Growth for Selected Projections

	Projection			
Time Period	1*b*	2*b*	4*b*	5*a*
(1)	(2)	(3)	(4)	(5)
t_0	...	...	...	...
t_5	4.40	4.40	4.40	4.40
t_{10}	4.29	4.56	4.56	4.56
t_{15}	4.10	4.48	4.48	4.27
t_{20}	4.04	4.63	4.63	4.14
t_{25}	4.05	4.67	4.67	4.10
t_{30}	3.99	4.84	4.84	4.12
t_{35}	4.04	4.94	4.68	4.01
t_{40}	4.03	5.05	4.63	3.99
t_{45}	3.97	5.12	4.54	3.86
t_{50}	3.97	5.20	4.42	3.68
t_{55}	3.96	5.24	4.36	3.55

The other columns indicating the required growth rates for selected projections are repeated below in order to facilitate comparison. Compare columns 2 and 5. It turns out that after 35 years (t_{35}) the required national income growth rates are lower for projection 5*a* than they are when mortality and fertility are kept at their initial levels. The reader may recall that in projections 2*a* to 5*a* mortality rates are assumed to fall at a rather rapid, though steady pace, and that in projection 5*a* the rate of fertility decline starts quite early. On the whole, a comparison between columns 2 and 5 suggests the possibility that if, as we have argued in an earlier chapter, sustained fertility decline depends on the prior experience of steady (but not precipitous) mortality decline,[21] and if the tempo of change induces the onset of fertility decline at an early enough stage in the process, the required rates of national income growth and the related rates of required investment may in the long run be smaller than when mortality rates are kept at their initial high levels.

This possibility is not one that we might *necessarily* expect *a priori.* If we assume that sustained fertility decline sets in at some point there is no reason for us to expect an eventual decline in the rate of population growth. In principle, mortality decline can proceed at a more rapid rate than fertility decline. Even if fertility decline is greater than mortality decline, the difference between the two may be so small that, given the lag between the fall in mortality and the onset of fertility decline, it may take centuries before the simultaneous fall in the two rates results in a rate of population growth smaller than the initial rate. But our calculations indicate that, if the "fertility-decline lag" is not very long and if our historically based rate of fertility decline is not unrepresentative, very little or nothing is to be gained by suppressing gradual, though rapid life expectancy improvements even if we consider a period of less than two generations or so. All this seems to suggest a rather optimistic view of the old Malthusian dilemma, especially since the alternative of suppressing life-expectancy improvements is certainly a cruel one.

---

[21] T. H. Marshall argued this case forcefully with respect to the industrial revolution in England in "The Population Problem during the Industrial Revolution," *Essays in Economic History* (E. M. Carus-Wilson, Editor), London, E. Arnold, 1954, pp. 306 ff. The argument is based on a statistical analysis by Udney Yule, "The Growth of Population and the Factors Which Control It," *Journal of the Royal Society of Statistics,* Vol. LXXXVIII, No. 12.

CHAPTER 15

Economic Development Theory and Investment Policies

The theory that we have developed has certain implications for investment policy. And, it turns out, these implications do not agree, in all cases, with at least some interpretations or proposed uses of the neoclassical marginal productivity principle or with other investment policies that have been proposed from time to time.[1]

The soundness of an investment policy for development purposes depends, among other things, on the meaning or objective that we imply by the word "development," and on our vision or model of the development process. We have defined development to mean sustained growth in per capita output, and it is only with this definition that our strictures against the applicability of some of the investment policies to be considered make any sense. For other objectives or other interpretations of the word "development," or other models of the development process than the one presented here, the ensuing analysis may be invalid, and the strictured investment policies may be perfectly reasonable.

The proposals that we shall examine involve considerations that are of importance in investment policy, considerations that an investment

[1] For a summary of some of these views and for the necessary citations of their proponents see A. E. Kahn, "Investment Criteria in Development," *Quarterly Journal of Economics,* Vol. LXV, February 1951, pp. 38–61.

policy should take into account. The cautions that we shall emphasize with respect to many of the "investment rules" that have been advocated by various writers are in connection with their use as the sole or major consideration; it is in that respect that they may not *always* lead to the correct answer.

Before going into specific policies we offer a brief digression on the aspect of timing in the problem of investment. This is followed by a critical consideration of a number of the investment allocation suggestions or rules that have found their way into the literature of economic development. In the final section we shall present briefly what we hope is an approach to a more adequate investment allocation policy than those that have been proposed.

Investment Timing and the Critical Minimum Effort Thesis

The aspect of timing in the investment allocation problem is related to our critical minimum effort thesis. In detail this can be a very complicated matter and we do not intend to go into it extensively here. But a few general points should be made lest we obtain the wrong impression of the nature of the critical minimum effort thesis.

In chapter 13 it was argued that for a given tempo of change, a certain minimum per capita income level has to be achieved in order for the economy to generate sustained per capita income growth. If the initial per capita income level is below this critical minimum, it can be raised to the necessary minimum by a sufficiently large injection of investment from outside the economy. Does our critical minimum effort thesis imply that the injection has to take place all at once, or may it be advisable to divide the effort into a series of smaller injections that take place over a number of time periods? Certainly the critical minimum effort thesis does not imply that the requisite effort must, of necessity, be made all at once. Indeed, it is our purpose to show that there are circumstances under which more than one injection of investment of a smaller aggregate size is as good as or superior to a single injection of larger size.

The general argument depends on the notion that there usually are per capita income levels, lower than the critical minimum, that will generate, on their own, per capita income growth for a number of time periods, although beyond some point the per capita income path will descend toward the equilibrium level. By taking advantage of the rising part of the per capita income path we can, through a series of investment injections (each injection taking place prior to the time when the per capita income path would turn down if left alone), reach the critical minimum per capita income level at lower total cost than with a single large injection of additional capital.[2] The basic idea is illustrated in figure 15–1.

Figure 15–1 is divided into three areas bounded by the broken lines *E, F,* and M^*. Our basic suppositions are these: If the per capita income level is in Area I the per capita income path generated is one that descends gradually toward the equilibrium level *E*. At the other extreme, per capita income paths that start in Area III lead to sustained per capita income growth. But per capita income paths that *start* in Area II at first rise (but never to MM^*) and then decline toward the equilibrium level. (In our illustration the lines MM^* and *F* rise gradually to the right to indicate the possibility of considering this problem in the more complicated case in which the obstacles to growth increase over time; we need not go into this aspect of the problem here.)

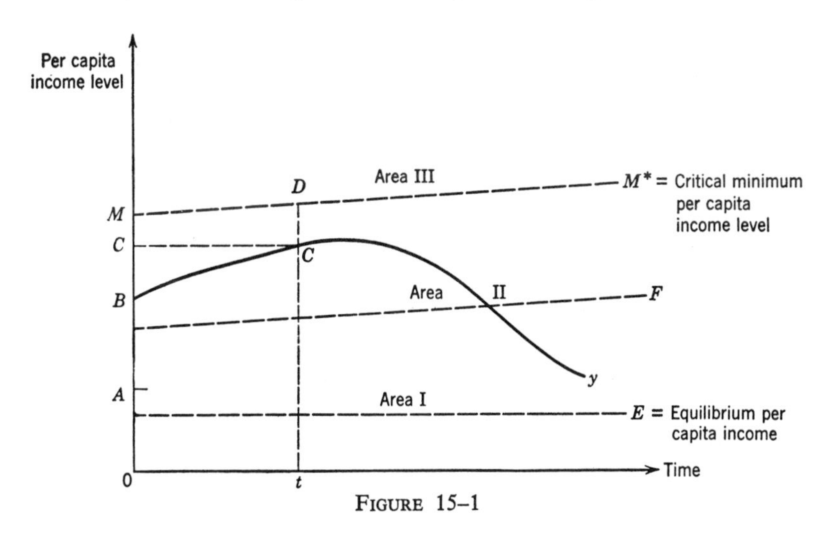

FIGURE 15–1

Suppose that the beginning per capita income level is *OA*. With an eye on figure 15–1 consider these alternatives: (1) We can at the outset inject enough investment into the system to raise the per capita income level to *OM*, the minimum necessary to generate sustained growth; or (2) we can perform our injections in two stages. For example, we can at the outset raise the per capita income level to *OB*. This will generate the income path *y* in figure 15–1, and at time *t* the per capita income level will have risen to *OC*. At that point (*t*) we could inject enough investment to raise the per capita income level by *CD*. The second injection

[2] This question is analyzed in a more formal manner in H. Leibenstein's *A Theory of Economic-Demographic Development,* Princeton, Princeton University Press, 1954, pp. 70–75.

raises the per capita income level to the critical minimum necessary for sustained growth. Let us suppose, for the sake of illustration, that the amount of investment required is always proportional to the extent to which it raises the per capita income. From figure 15–1, as drawn, we observe that $AB + CD$ is less than AM. This means that if the incremental capital requirements are in proportion to the extent to which per capita incomes are raised, the total effort (in terms of investment) required to reach the critical minimum level is less under the two-stage technique than under the single large investment effort. Intuitively, it seems reasonable to believe that there are probably many sets of circumstances under which series of smaller efforts, optimally spaced, are less costly than larger single efforts.

We can extend the foregoing type of reasoning to the possibility of three small injections of investment and to four still smaller injections, and so on. But this process cannot be carried on indefinitely. There are important, limiting factors in the question of what minimum size a single investment injection can be if the injection is to be effective. The problem is, of course, much more complicated than in our illustration. There are many more influences other than the initial level of per capita income that determine the generated income growth paths.

Consider, on the one hand, that there may be an advantage to a *series* of investment injections rather than a large, single effort in that a sensible investment program usually requires a certain sequence of events. Some types of capital construction may have to occur before other kinds are either possible or effective. For example, it may be necessary first to dig and deepen canals before a water transportation system can come into effect, which in turn may be a prerequisite for some types of large-scale manufacturing. From this point of view a *series* of investment injections is to be preferred.

On the other hand, consider some of the factors that limit the minimum size of an investment injection. First, if we return to figure 15–1 and to the assumptions behind it, we see that the initial investment injection must be at least large enough to push the per capita income level into Area II. Otherwise, the income path is a descending one from the outset, and we cannot take advantage of the self-generated growth that takes place in Area II. Second, there are often indivisibilities involved in various types of capital goods, and the injection of investment must be large enough to overcome such indivisibilities. Third, there may be certain complementarities in the production process as well as economies of scale that it would pay to take advantage of, even in a short period, by means of a sufficiently large dose of exogenous investment. Last, the tempo of change is an important determinant of the critical minimum income level, and therefore it may not pay to have any single investment injection so small that it slows unduly the tempo of change. Thus we see that while it may be less costly to have a series of smaller investment injections rather than a single larger one in order to reach the critical minimum per capita income level, there are limits to the advisable length of the series and to the consequent smallness of individual injections of investment.

The Marginal Productivity Criterion (SMP)

The criterion usually advocated as the appropriate guide for the allocation of investment funds is marginal productivity. This notion stems, of course, from the neo-classical rule that an efficient allocation is achieved by cquating the marginal productivity of any resource, including capital, in its various uses.

In the context in which the marginal productivity criterion is usually employed, that of the static equilibrium state, it is correct. In the short run, and especially if we invoke the *ceteris paribus* assumptions, the application of this criterion need not always lead to the achievement of objectives other than the maximization of national product.[3] In the long run many things may vary as a consequence of a series of investment allocations, and an allocation policy based on marginal productivity may not lead to maximization of the rate of growth of the national product. And even if it does, it may not result in maximizing the rate of growth of *per capita* output.

Some writers have added the word "social" to the marginal productivity criterion and have urged the adoption of the social marginal productivity criterion. According to this view, when we allocate investment funds we should take into account "the total net contribution of the marginal unit to national product, and not merely that portion of the contribution (or of its costs) which may accrue to the private investor. . . ."[4] When we emphasize mainly the net contribution of the marginal unit of investment to national product, then clearly the result aimed at is the maximization of the national product. Maximizing national product may or may not be the same as maximizing the *per capita* product. It depends, in part, on how the population factor is treated and affected by the investment policy.

In trying to analyze the social marginal productivity (SMP) criterion we are faced with a problem of interpretation and meaning. The fact of the matter is that nowhere is SMP or the notion of "the net contribu-

---

[3] Of course, no objection could be raised against the "marginal" part of the criterion.

[4] A. E. Kahn, *op. cit.*, pp. 39 ff.

tion to national product" completely defined. The difficulty of discussing an incompletely defined criterion is that to arguments against it there is always the possible riposte that this is not exactly what was meant by the criterion. The vagueness of the word "social" in this context, of course, compounds the difficulty. Nevertheless, we shall try to interpret this concept as best we can and see how it fares with respect to the theory we have tried to develop.

In determining the net contribution of a marginal unit of investment to national product we have to consider the present value of the output stream and the present value of the cost stream that results as a consequence of the act of investment. In evaluating the cost stream we must take into account not only private costs but also social costs (for example, smoke nuisances, water pollution, etc.). Similarly, the social evaluation of the output stream may under some circumstances differ from the value of the output stream as valued by the private entrepreneur. If we accept this interpretation of the adjective "social" in this context we may still run into difficulties in applying the SMP criterion with respect to the theory of development delineated earlier.[5] For example, how are we to choose between one allocation that leads to a larger product for a larger population and another allocation that leads to a smaller national product for a more than proportionately smaller population?

Social marginal productivity emphasizes *aggregate* output or, rather, the maximization of the output that can be attributed to the current investment effort. But it is the future *investment* stream that is significant for long-run development. SMP does not appear to take into account what happens to the final product during any period, but what happens to the final product determines, in part, the investment rate in the future. Furthermore, SMP does not take into account changes in the nature and quality of the factors of production that may, in part, be an indirect consequence of the current investment allocation. More specifically, our interpretation of the SMP criterion does not allow for the following important elements:[6] (1) the indirect effect of the investment

[5] If the adjective "social" is interpreted to take into account all the considerations mentioned in this chapter then, of course, we can under no circumstances have any quarrel with the SMP criterion. However, the literature does not clearly suggest such an interpretation.

[6] Underlying these remarks is the assumption that desired patterns of fertility, desired attitudes toward thrift and investment, desired rates of savings, and desired changes in and stimuli to the growth agents, and, most important, desired changes in mores and traditions that underlie these changes cannot be achieved easily by direct methods, wholly apart from the sequence of investment allocations that the investment policy is presumed to guide. If direct methods are presumed to be both efficient and relatively inexpensive and if they are

allocation on the expansion of the growth factors, that is, on the expansion of entrepreneurship, on the increase in the quality of the labor force, and on the expansion of skills; (2) the effect of the investment allocation on future savings habits and, therefore, on the future rate of investment; (3) the effect of the investment allocation and policy on the future consumption pattern, which, in turn, determines whether the consumption is simply on population maintenance or on the expansion of the growth agents; (4) the indirect effect of the investment allocation on the rate of population growth, which, in turn, is a consideration in determining what happens to per capita output.

The Employment Absorption Criterion

The "employment absorption" criterion is usually justified on two grounds or on some variants thereof. These are usually derived from: (1) the observation that a considerable amount of disguised unemployment exists in backward economies and (2) the belief that if the unemployed portion of the labor force could be put to work, this would then yield the greatest benefits to the economy. A related approach seems to be derived from considerations about the relationship between scarcity and productivity. Where capital is scarce, so the argument appears to run, its marginal productivity will be high while the marginal productivity of labor is low, therefore the appropriate production techniques that should be adopted are those which substitute the relatively ample labor supply for scarce capital.

The extent to which labor can be absorbed in any economic process depends on the adaptability and flexibility of the other factors of production. But the most adaptable capital stock need not maximize the addition to total output.

Suppose that we consider an economy that is *not* in a state of general equilibrium. This is certainly a likely situation for a backward economy. Under such circumstances the relative prices of capital goods will not be proportional to their productivity. Investment in two capital goods, say *A* and *B*, each costing the same amount, may, when combined with the same number of men, lead to different additions to total output. Assume

---

employed in pursuit of the development objective, the application of the marginal productivity criterion will lead to the desired outcome. Belief in the efficacy of direct action in establishing desired attitudes, traditions, and behavior patterns seems to be somewhat similar to advocating direct action in fostering the spirit of optimism during periods of economic depression. Our present knowledge of social psychology does not suggest that very much can be hoped for in this direction at present. Of course, we cannot foresee the future, and future socio-psychological discoveries may possibly change all this.

that *A*, the less flexible but more productive capital good, is twice as productive as *B* when combined with the same number of men, say, 100 men. Also let us assume that 100 men are the maximum that can be combined with *A*. It may be possible to combine 150 men with *B* and still produce less than *A* with its 100 men. Such situations are certainly conceivable. If our goal is not merely to maximize employment for its own sake, we will not choose to invest in capital good *B* rather than in *A*.

The point of the matter is that there is no reason to believe that highly productive capital is necessarily related to capital that is highly flexible and adaptable to increases in labor supply. Indeed, there is some reason to believe that the reverse is often true. It seems intuitively plausible that highly productive machines are highly specialized and, hence, are the ones that are less adaptable and flexible to changes in other factor quantities. If applied rigorously, the labor absorption criterion would never permit the introduction of labor-saving technology in "overpopulated" areas.[7] True, the effect of such investment would be to increase the excess capacity of the labor force. But the labor-displacing capital may be so productive that despite the creation of excess capacity it may still lead to greater output per head.

Nurkse's Proposal

An interesting variant of the labor absorption argument is found in a recent proposal by Ragnar Nurkse in his book *Problems of Capital Formation in Underdeveloped Areas* (pp. 32–49).

Nurkse accepts the notion that there is a great deal of concealed unemployment in underdeveloped areas. He sees this fact as a blessing in disguise with respect to the prospects for economic development. Believing that the opportunities to increase savings may be very limited, he leaps upon the excess capacity of the labor force as the means to produce the necessary capital goods needed for development.

Why not move this excess labor off the land, feed them no more than before, and put them to work building capital goods? Nurkse points out that the problem is not quite so simple as that. Some investment will be needed to pay for moving labor, to construct housing and other facilities for the workers in their new surroundings, and to increase to some extent the consumption level of the labor force left on the land. But despite this, Nurkse sees great promise for capital creation by this means. He says that "The theory of disguised unemployment is a static but nonetheless legitimate and *significant** view of the population

[7] See United Nations, *Measures for the Economic Development of Under-developed Countries,* New York, 1951, p. 7.

* Italics ours.

resources available for capital formation. Labor is the real source of wealth, and the supply of capital, we now see, can be increased by making use of unemployed labor" (p. 49).*

Since the proposal recognizes that investment for various purposes is needed in addition to labor, it really suggests two things: (1) that the investment be used in such a way as to absorb as much of the excess labor as possible and (2) that the output of the formerly excess labor less their minimum maintenance costs be used entirely for the production of capital goods. Item 1 amounts to an adoption of the employment absorption criterion, and item 2 amounts to advocacy of the maintenance of current levels of living so that the surplus is always reinvested. (The proposal is not put in quite these terms, but in reality that is what it amounts to.) The full employment of those believed to be "disguisedly" unemployed seems pointless if other investment policies yield higher growth rates, unless it be done for its own sake. The second aspect of the proposal involves essentially a plan for forced savings out of the labor of the previously disguised unemployed. For if the payment to them is to be based on their previous level of subsistence maintenance rather than on a higher level from a higher national product, this payment amounts to an imposed rate of savings on the group. It is difficult to see why *this group* and not another in the economy should be selected for this purpose. If this group is not discriminated against, this part of the proposal boils down to an assertion that economic development should be financed by forced savings with the amount of the forced saving equaling the output that results from the initial and successive injections of investment less the initial consumption level. Forced savings may be a means of obtaining the necessary investment for development, but there is no evidence to lead us to believe that the particular technique suggested by Nurkse is the best way of obtaining the forced savings, or that the amount so obtained is the optimum amount.

Investment in Agriculture

It is quite common to encounter policy recommendations that state that what is really needed in backward economies is investment in agriculture. The basis for such recommendations varies from time to time and from author to author, but, generally speaking, two sets of

---

* This section is not a critique of Nurkse's excellent, instructive, and insightful little book. Indeed, this writer found these written lectures exceedingly valuable and stimulating. All that we intend here is an examination of the implications of the proposal in the light of the previous discussion. Of course, there may be circumstances under which it would be best to put into effect Nurkse's proposal.

considerations seem to be uppermost in the minds of many writers: (1) the suggestion that efforts to increase food supply should take priority over other efforts because of the high demand and great need for additional food and (2) the suggestion (based on the *existing* distribution of resources) that the greatest marginal productivity of capital lies in agriculture.[8]

Let us examine more fully the second of the considerations. A phenomenon frequently observed in backward economies is the exceedingly primitive nature of both capital and production techniques utilized in agriculture. This observation suggests the need for investment in agricultural capital that would enable the employment of somewhat more advanced techniques, and the fact that usually over three-quarters of the population are engaged in agriculture emphasizes the pervasiveness of this need. At the same time there is often an absence or an exceedingly great scarcity of industrial entrepreneurship. Industrial enterprise involves risks that are often entirely unfamiliar to the population; also, the necessary skills for industrial undertakings, whether administrative, specialized, or general, are largely lacking at the outset; and, finally, the markets for additional agricultural goods appear to be ever present and self-evident. The markets for industrial goods may appear to be initially absent, for these are markets that have to be created. To visualize a market for some specific industrial commodities demands an effort that is not easy to achieve for it depends on an imaginative extrapolation of human wants in a changed economic environment where it is largely unknown whether the necessary changes in the economic environment will take place. All in all, it is easy to see how under such circumstances one may get the impression that the appropriate investment policy is to invest in the agricultural sector.

Yet is this the correct solution? Let us agree at the outset, for the sake of argument, that in the short run the marginal productivity of capital is greater in agriculture. Does this mean that the best investment policy would be to devote *all* the investment funds to raising agricultural productivity? Putting the question in this manner suggests the nature of the answer, that is, that our theory would suggest, given certain beliefs about some of the empirical aspects, that longer-run considerations that take into account some of the factors mentioned earlier *may* lead to quite a different investment policy if our aim be eventual sustained economic development (but not necessarily one that need exclude entirely some allocation of investment funds to agricultural pursuits).

---

[8] See for example, Kahn, *op. cit.* See also J. Viner, "The Economics of Development," in *International Trade and Economic Development,* Glencoe, Illinois, The Free Press, 1952, p. 135.

The counter argument rests on unproved and perhaps unprovable beliefs about the effects of the agricultural environment on the expansion of the growth agents and on the rate of population growth.[9] Briefly, and rather bluntly, these beliefs can be summarized as follows: Compared with the industrial, urban environment the agricultural environment will not be very effective in or conducive to the creation or expansion of an entrepreneurial class. Nor will the agricultural environment be one that is especially conducive to the creation of new skills and techniques or the expansion of such skills; nor is it likely to lead to the spread of knowledge and creation of an intellectual atmosphere that leads to technical inventions and innovations. In sum, the growth agents are more likely to be stimulated in an urban, industrial setting rather than in an agricultural environment.

In the absence of investment in other sectors of the economy the initial gain in output from investment in agriculture will be split between the owner and those who work the land. For those who work the land we can assume a marginal propensity to consume close to unity. To the extent that the small holder or tenant gets to keep a larger crop he is likely to consume that larger crop, given that the initial consumption level is close to subsistence.

The question boils down to the classical one: To what extent can we count on the landlord to save and invest productively? This is a question about which one must not be dogmatic. The answer may differ from country to country, but it is often asserted that the consumption pattern of a landed aristocracy is toward luxuries, such as jewels, foreign travel, foreign education for one's children, ceremonials and festivities of various kinds, or in durable consumption assets that add nothing to the productivity of the land.[10] Or the landlords may be interested in extending their landholdings. Competition for land increases its value, and this competition may serve as an inducement for an eventual transfer of land from the small holder to the large landowner. The small holder has a high propensity to consume and the end result will be an increase in current consumption. There is certainly little incentive to invest in labor-saving capital goods since competition from the growing labor force reduces wages to compete successfully with the labor-saving machinery. Opportunities for investment in "land-saving" capital are usually exceedingly limited since such land-savings projects as irrigation and reclama-

[9] Our argument must of necessity be based on assertions about likelihoods and probabilities in the usual case rather than in terms of effects that are definitely known.

[10] See United Nations, *Processes and Problems of Industrialization in Underdeveloped Countries,* New York, 1955, pp. 18 ff., especially p. 22.

tion are to a considerable extent once-and-for-all investments that are usually best undertaken by governments as public works. The large landowner is unlikely to reinvest his gains in the industrial sector since that sector is usually too limited at home, and furthermore he *usually* has little experience in such undertakings. Investment abroad is a possible outlet for the landlord, but this need not build up the home economy. The small landowner's time horizon is too limited, and his immediate needs are too urgent for him to invest very much in industrial pursuits. Although the picture we have just painted may represent the general case, it is probably not universally true. There may be instances when the land-owning class does produce the best industrial entrepreneurs but these are probably rare, especially since the land-owning group is usually the repository of traditional values and traditional techniques.

Last, but not least in terms of significance, we might mention the population aspect. The rural areas are usually the ones in which traditional ways are maintained the longest, and they are the last in which fertility declines set in. As a consequence, investment in agriculture will lead to a greater rate of population growth and a lower rate of per capita income growth than otherwise. For the small holdings this will mean further subdivision of the land, and even though each acre has a higher productivity than before because of the initial investment in agriculture, output *per man* eventually returns to its former subsistence level as the successive generations inherit smaller and smaller pieces of land. The same will be true of tenant farmers, because competition for land, brought about by population growth, forces up rents and causes tenants to cultivate smaller and smaller pieces of land.

But our conclusion on the basis of these arguments is not an especially strong one. It is simply this: The mere fact that it often appears that the initial marginal productivity is greater in agriculture than elsewhere does not necessarily imply that the correct investment policy is to *concentrate* on agricultural investment. It is also important to note that, by contrast, investment in industry reverses the nature of the incentives and opportunities just considered. If non-agricultural employment opportunities are created rapidly enough a gradual shortage of labor on the land will arise, the incentive for the introduction of labor-saving capital on the land will increase steadily, and at the same time the industrial sector, if it expands rapidly enough, should provide the economic climate that is conducive to the expansion of the growth agents.

Investment Allocation Policy for Development

We have argued that the shortcomings of various investment policies are due to the fact that they do not take into account the four long-run considerations mentioned on pp. 258 and 259. It follows that an adequate criterion must be one that does take them into account. We shall now indicate, on the basis of our theory and especially in view of the objective of maximizing per capita output, the outlines of a more adequate approach to the problem.

The basic consideration in allocating investment in the interest of maximizing output per head, after taking into account any welfare constraints that may be thought appropriate in the specific case, must be to choose for each unit of investment that use that will ultimately give each person, on the average, greater productive power than any other alternative. To achieve this result we must maximize (*a*) the amount

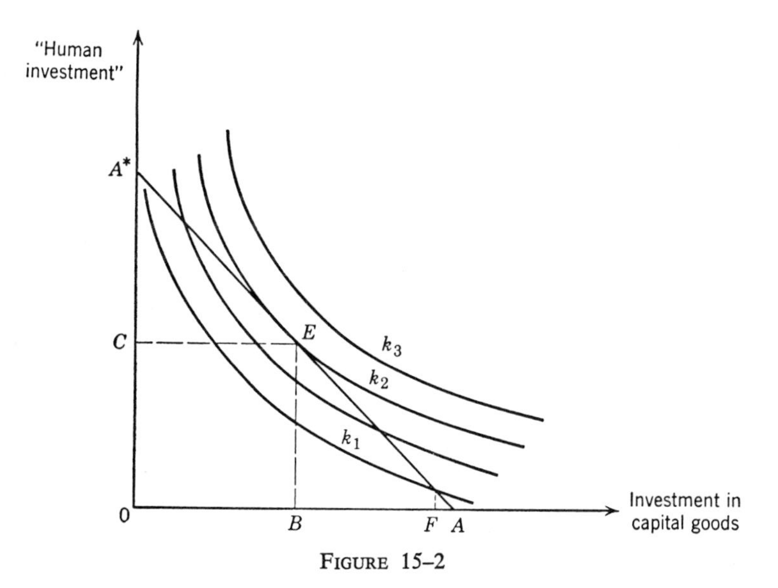

FIGURE 15–2

of capital per worker and (*b*) the quality of the population, that is, its skill, knowledge, energy, adaptability, and its perceptiveness and capacity to ferret out new economic opportunities. At any point we can conceive of a rate of substitution between investment in capital goods and "investment" (if we may use the term in this sense) in improving the quality of the population. The latter type of investment we have called "human investment." The optimum allocation between these two types of "investment" can be illustrated by the usual indifference curve type of analysis, shown in figure 15–2.

The curves marked k_1, k_2, and k_3 are three iso-product curves. The curve k_1 relates different amounts of funds for "human investment" and different amounts of investment in capital goods required to produce a given quantity of product, say, 1,000,000 units. Similarly, k_2 is the locus of combinations of expenditures on the two types of investment that would result in a greater quantity of output, say, 2,000,000 units; and so on. The given "investment fund" is OA ($= OA^*$). The graph shows that output would be greater if the "investment fund," OA, were not invested only in capital goods, but if OB were invested in capital goods and OC ($= BA$) were allocated to "human investment." For example, if OF were invested in capital goods, output would be only 1,000,000 units rather than 2,000,000.

In actuality a great deal of what we have called "human investment" will not be used directly and consciously with the intent of increasing national output. Much of it must, of course, depend upon the expenditure patterns of the income recipients. This line of reasoning suggests that an appropriate investment policy must take into account not only the magnitude of the net output stream that flows from an investment allocation but also what *happens* to that output stream. The net output stream can be viewed as being distributed among (1) capital goods accumulation, (2) "human investment," (3) "luxury" consumption,[11] and (4) "maintenance" consumption for the present population and for increases in population. This distribution will determine the extent to which the productive capacity (per head) of the population grows during the period. The greater the expenditure on capital goods accumulation and "human investment" and the less the "expenditure on population growth" and on luxury consumption, the greater the growth in productive capacity per head. And we add to this that accretion in the productive qualities of the work force that arise as a by-product of a given pattern of productive activities but which are otherwise costless.

Let us now use the term "general investment" for the aggregate of investment in both capital goods and what we have called "human investment," and we shall use the term "general capital" for the sum of physical wealth and the *learned* productive capacities of the population. The objective of development under our definition is to maximize the "general capital" per head. The growth of the "general capital" per head depends on (1) the amount of *net* "general *re*investment" year by year that is generated by the initial investment allocation both directly and indirectly and (2) the increase in the size of the population, which will also be influenced, in part, by the investment allocation. We must therefore take into account not only the increase in output that results

[11] By "luxury" consumption we are not using the word in its usual sense, but simply as consumption expenditure above and beyond pure maintenance needs that are not devoted to "human investment."

directly from an increase in capital but also the sum of all subsequent "general *re*investments" divided by the size of the population at the related time points.

Given our objective, the value that is to be placed on the allocation of a unit of investment to a specific use depends on a direct component (the net value added to the output stream of the industry employing that unit of capital, other things being equal) and on an indirect component. The magnitude of the direct component is the capitalized value of the net addition to the output stream attributed to the unit of investment in the specific use divided by population size. To this we add the contribution of the indirect components, which, in terms of the addition to the "general capital" per head, include the following: (1) the amount of reinvestment in physical capital that results from the additional output stream created by the unit of investment and (2) the amount of "human investment" that takes place period after period that would not have occurred had it not been for the output stream created by that unit of investment, or that results as a by-product of the initial allocation of investment to this particular use, or as a by-product of the resulting output stream. (This last, for example, would include such indirect effects as an increase in skills [an addition to the "human capital" stock] acquired as a result of work experience made possible by allocating investment in this particular use.) Finally, since our focus is on the *per capita* results we must take into account the population size at every time point and especially consider, and keep in the foreground, the induced increase (or change) in the population that would not have taken place in the absence of that unit of investment.

In sum, to the direct value (per capita) of the initial unit of investment we must add (for each period) the value of the indirect contributions just mentioned, divided by the population size (for that period). In this way we obtain the stream of additions to the "general capital" stock (per head) that can be attributed to the allocation of the unit of investment to the particular use. Let us call this stream the "general reinvestment" stream per capita; and keep in mind that this is inclusive of the *direct* capitalized value of the investment in the particular use.

The amount of general reinvestment per capita may differ from year to year. In general, different investment allocations will yield different time patterns of general reinvestment. It seems reasonable to assume that perspective growth closer to the present is to be preferred to growth later, other things being equal, and therefore some discounting procedure would probably be appropriate in the evaluation of alternative general reinvestment per capita streams. The appropriate rate of discount would depend on the extent to which earlier accretions to the general capital stock (per capita) were preferred to later ones.

The marginal principle, as a principle of allocation, can (and indeed must) be applied here as well as anywhere else, but it is *not* the usual marginal productivity principle. The principle suggested by the foregoing discussion is that the best allocation of investment is achieved by equating at the margin the discounted value of the general reinvestment stream in the various uses to which the investment is put. What we have in mind is that the marginal unit of capital leads to a general reinvestment stream[12] per capita whose discounted value is equal to the discounted value of the general reinvestment stream per capita at the margin in every other use. Obviously, it is not the marginal aspect that is unique to our criterion but rather what it is that is to be valued at the margin.

It must be admitted that our criterion is a more difficult one to apply since it takes into account more considerations than the other criteria mentioned. But this is simply the nature of the problem.

One final point. The application of our criterion makes sense only as long as our objective is to maximize the rate of per capita income growth. But endless growth for its own sake does not make too much sense. At some point the populace may become more concerned with enjoying the fruits of its development than maintaining or maximizing the rate of development. At this point the criterion has to be tempered by another consideration, namely, the value of current consumption to the community. How to choose between current "luxury" consumption and growth is a difficult question of welfare economics. But this goes beyond our immediate concern, which is limited to problems of development rather than the much broader problem of general welfare.

[12] To handle the fact that this is a stream that goes on into the indefinite future we have to use some discounting procedure and obtain the discounted value of the stream. This problem exists both under the marginal productivity approach and under our approach, or any other approach that considers the possibility of uneven output streams.

APPENDIX 1

The "Representative Population" (p. 221) was derived from the eighteen age distributions listed below. Listed here are the countries, the year of the age distribution, and the source used for obtaining the data. A sample of the "raw" data showing three age distributions for Egypt (1937), India and Burma (1931), and Bulgaria (1900) follow the complete listing.

Country	Date	Source
Austria	1900	*Annuaire international de statistique*, published by L'Office Permanent de L'Institut International de Statistique, Vol. I, La Haye, 1916, p. 106.
Bavaria	1900	*Ibid.*, p. 105.
Bulgaria	1900	*Ibid.*, p. 108.
Chile	1930	*Inter-American Statistical Yearbook*, under the auspices of the Argentine Commission of High International Studies, Raul C. Migone, Director, New York, The Macmillan Co., 1940, pp. 58–59.
Chile	1940	*Demographic Yearbook, 1949–1950*, Statistical Office of the United Nations, New York, 1951, p. 123.
Costa Rica	1927	*Ibid.*, p. 113.
Egypt	1927	*Statistical Yearbook of the League of Nations, 1938–1939*, League of Nations Economic Intelligence Service, Geneva, 1939. (Series of League of Nations Publications, II, Economic and Financial, 1939, II A,9.), p. 24.
Egypt	1937	*Demographic Yearbook, 1949–1950*, United Nations, *op. cit.*, p. 104.
Guatemala	1940	*Ibid.*, p. 115.
India	1901	*Annuaire international de statistique, op. cit.*, Vol. V, p. 67.
India	1911	*Ibid.*, p. 67.
India (including Burma)	1931	*Demographic Yearbook, 1949–1950*, United Nations, *op. cit.*, p. 127.

Country	Date	Source
Jamaica	1911	*Census of Jamaica and Its Dependencies*, Kingston Government Printing Office, 1912.
Jamaica	1921	*Ibid.*, 1922.
Mauritius	1944	*Demographic Yearbook, 1949–1950*, United Nations, *op. cit.*, p. 108.
Mexico	1930	*Inter-American Statistical Yearbook, op. cit.*, pp. 56–57.
Mexico	1940	*Demographic Yearbook, 1949–1950*, United Nations, *op. cit.*, p. 116.
Union of South Africa	1936	*Ibid.*, p. 105.

Age Distribution Table for Bulgaria (1900), Egypt (1937), and India and Burma (1931)

Age Group	Bulgaria (1900)		Egypt (1937)		India and Burma (1931)	
	M	F	M	F	M	F
0–4	14.5	14.7	12.9	13.7	14.7	16.0
5–9	12.9	13.3	13.9	13.9	13.3	12.8
10–14	12.5	12.5	13.0	11.0	12.0	11.2
15–19	10.9	11.0	9.0	8.0	8.9	9.4
20–24	7.2	7.2	6.8	7.1	9.0	9.8
25–29	6.3	6.7	7.7	8.7	8.6	8.7
30–34	5.7	6.0	7.0	8.0	7.9	7.6
35–39	5.7	5.1	7.5	6.8	6.4	6.0
40–44	4.3	4.6	6.0	5.9	5.5	5.1
45–49	4.3	3.9	4.3	3.9	4.2	3.9
50–54	3.4	4.0	4.1	4.2	3.3	3.1
55–59	3.6	2.9	1.8	1.7	2.3	2.3
60–64	3.4	3.2	2.5	2.9	1.8	1.9
65–69	2.0	1.5	0.9	0.9	0.9	0.9
70–74	1.6	1.6	1.3	1.5	. . .	. . .
75–79	0.6	0.6	0.3	0.4	1.2	1.3
80–84	0.6	0.7	0.5	0.7	. . .	. . .
85–	0.5	0.5	0.3	0.4	. . .	. . .
Unknown	0.0	0.0	0.2	0.3	. . .	. . .

Sources: See previous listing.

APPENDIX 2

Figures 14–1, 14–2 and table 14–2 show the relationship between life expectancy and age-specific mortality rates. The figures and the table are based on eighty-nine observations from thirty-nine countries. The following list gives the country, the dates, and the sources for the life expectancy and age-specific mortality rate data.

Country	Dates of Life Expectancy Data	Sources of Life Expectancy Data	Dates for Age-Specific Mortality Rates	Sources of Age-Specific Mortality Rates
Australia	1920–1922	1	1920–1922	1
	1932–1934	1	1932–1934	1
	1946–1948	2	1947	2
Belgium	1928–1932	1	1930–1932	1
British Honduras	1944–1948	2	1946	2
Bulgaria	1925–1928	1	1925–1928	1
Canada	1930–1932	1	1930–1932	1
	1940–1942	4	1941	2
	1945	2	1945	2
	1947	2	1947	2
Chile	1930	2	1930–1932	1
	1940	2	1940	2
Czechoslovakia	1929–1932	1	1930–1932	1
Denmark	1911–1915	1	1911–1915	1
	1921–1925	1	1921–1925	1
	1931–1935	1	1931–1935	1
	1936–1940	5	1936–1940	5
	1941–1945	2	1945	2
Egypt	1936–1938	4	1937	2
England and Wales	1871–1880	3	1871–1880	6
	1910–1912	1	1910–1912	1
	1920–1922	1	1920–1922	1
	1930–1932	1	1930–1932	1
	1937	1	1937	1
	1948	2	1948	5
	1949	5	1949	2
	1950	5	1950	5

Country	Dates of Life Expectancy Data	Sources of of Life Expectancy Data	Dates for Age-Specific Mortality Rates	Sources of Age-Specific Mortality Rates
Estonia	1932–1934	1	1933–1935	1
Finland	1931–1935	1	1931–1935	1
	1931–1940	2	1937	2
	1941–1945	2	1943	2
France	1877–1881	3	1877–1881	6
	1920–1923	1	1920–1922	1
	1928–1933	1	1930–1932	1
	1933–1938	2	1936	2
	1946–1948	2	1947	2
	1948	5	1946–1949	5
Germany	1924–1926	1	1924–1926	1
	1932–1934	1	1932–1934	1
German Federal Republic	1946–1947	2	1947	5
Greece	1928	1	1927–1929	1
Hungary	1930–1931	1	1930–1931	1
Iceland	1931–1940	2	1940	2
Ireland	1925–1927	1	1925–1927	1
	1935–1937	2	1936	2
	1940–1942	2	1941	2
Israel	1949	5	1949	5
	1950	5	1950	5
Italy	1930–1932	1	1930–1932	1
	1936	2	1936	2 (est.)
Jamaica	1945–1947	1	1946	1
Japan	1921–1925	1	1924–1926	1
	1926–1930	1	1929–1931	1
	1935–1936	1	1934–1936	1
	1947	2	1947	2
Latvia	1934–1936	1	1934–1936	1
Luxemburg	1946–1948	2	1947	2
Mexico	1940	2	1940	2
Netherlands	1931–1940	1	1936–1937	1
	1947–1949	2	1948	2
New Zealand	1911–1915	1	1911	1
	1921–1922	1	1920–1922	1
	1934–1938	2	1936	2
Northern Ireland	1936–1938	2	1937	2
Portugal	1939–1942	2	1940	2
Scotland	1930–1932	1	1930–1932	1
	1948	2	1948	2
Spain	1930–1931	2	1929–1931	1
Sweden	1921–1925	1	1921–1925	1
	1926–1930	1	1926–1930	1
	1929–1932	1	1929–1932	1
	1931–1935	1	1931–1935	1
	1931–1940	2	1936	2

Country	Dates of Life Expectancy Data	Sources of Life Expectancy Data	Dates for Age-Specific Mortality Rates	Sources of Age-Specific Mortality Rates
Sweden	1941–1945	2	1943	2
Switzerland	1876–1881	3	1876–1881	6
	1910–1911	1	1911	1
	1920–1921	1	1920–1922	1
	1933–1937	2	1937	2
	1939–1944	2	1941	2
Thailand	1947	5	1947	2
Trinidad	1947–1949	2	1948	2
Union of South Africa (European population)	1920–1922	1	1920–1921	1
	1935–1937	4	1936	2
	1940	1	1940	1
	1945–1947	2	1946	2
United States (Whites)	1929–1931	1	1929–1931	1
	1934–1936	1	1934–1936	1
	1930–1939	1	1937	1
(All)	1931–1941	2	1940	2

Sources: (1) *Statistical Yearbook, 1939–40,* League of Nations, Geneva, 1940, for life-expectancy data, pp. 66–68; for age-specific mortality rate data, pp. 58–62. (2) *Demographic Yearbook, 1951,* United Nations Statistical Office, New York, 1951, for life-expectancy data, pp. 526–539; for age-specific mortality rate data, pp. 288–319. (3) Louis I. Dublin, Alfred J. Lotka, and Mortimer Spiegelman, *Length of Life, A Study of the Life Table* (Revised Edition), New York, The Ronald Press Company, 1949, pp. 324–363. (4) *Statistical Yearbook, 1949–1950,* United Nations Statistical Office, New York, 1950, pp. 54–63. (5) *Demographic Yearbook, 1953,* United Nations Statistical Office, New York, 1953, for life-expectancy data, pp. 324–341; for age-specific mortality rate data, pp. 176–213. (6) *Allegemeines Statistiches Archiv, III,* George von Mayr (Editor), Tübingen, 1894, pp. 59 and 65.

APPENDIX 3

SOURCES FOR AGE-SPECIFIC FERTILITY RATE DATA FOR TABLES 14–3 AND 14–4

Country	Date	Source Reference*
Chile	1940	5
	1930–1932	4
Sweden	1841–1850	1
	1861–1870	1
	1851–1860	1
	1816–1840	1
Bulgaria	1925–1928	4
	1901–1905	3
Austria	1906–1910	2
	1901–1905	2
	1895–1900	2
Japan	1930	4
	1925	4
Finland	1891–1900	3
	1886–1890	3
Germany	1891–1900	3
	1881–1890	3
Mexico	1929–1931	7
Hungary	1900–1901	2
European RSFSR	1926–1927	3
European Russia	1896–1897	3

* Numbers refer to sources listed at the end of Appendix 4.

APPENDIX 4

Sources for Age-Specific Rates of Fertility Decline for Table 14–5

Country	Date	Source Reference
Denmark	1878–1884	3
	1885–1894	3
	1895–1900	3
	1901–1905	3
Sweden	1886–1890	3
	1891–1895	3
	1896–1900	3
	1901–1905	3
	1906–1910	3
Norway	1881–1885	3
	1889–1892	3
	1899–1905	3
Finland	1911–1920	3
	1921–1922	4
	1921–1930	3
	1930–1932	4
France	1908–1913	3
	1914–1919	3
	1920–1923	3
	1925–1927	3
Spain	1930–1931	6
	1940–1941	6
	1946	6
Portugal	1930–1931	3
	1940	5
	1947	5

SOURCES FOR AGE-SPECIFIC RATES OF FERTILITY DECLINE FOR TABLE 14–5 (*Continued*)

Country	Date	Source Reference
Italy	1922	2
	1931	3
	1936	5
Japan	1937	4
	1947	5
	1951	5

Sources: (1) Robert René Kuczynski, *The Balance of Births and Deaths*, Vol. 1, New York, The Macmillan Co., 1928–1931. (2) Robert René Kuczynski, *The Balance of Births and Deaths*, Vol. 2, New York, The Macmillan Co., 1928–1931. (3) Robert René Kuczynski, *The Measurement of Population Growth: Methods and Results*, London, Sidgwick & Jackson, Ltd., 1935. (4) League of Nations, *Statistical Yearbook of the League of Nations*, 1942/44. Geneva, 1945. (5) United Nations, Statistical Office, *Demographic Yearbook*, 1948 and 1955, Lake Success, New York. (6) World Health Organization, *Annual Epidemiological and Vital Statistics*, 1939–1951. Geneva. (7) Institut International de Statistique, *Aperçu de la démographie des divers pays du monde*, 1929–1936, La Haye, 1939.

APPENDIX 5

Population Projection Method

The technique of projection employed to compute the twelve population sequences given in table 14–8 is usually known as the component projection method. The method requires the following data: The initial population for each 5-year age group for each sex; mortality rates for each 5-year age group (in order to compute the proportions out of each 5-year age group that survive to enter the next age group); and the fertility rates for women in the eight 5-year age groups from 10 to 50 (in order to compute the births that occur during a 5-year period).

Computations for each projection are carried out in two stages. In stage I we compute the survival rates for each age and sex group, apply these survival rates to the initial population, and obtain the surviving population five years later. We do the same for successive 5-year periods after the male and female births, and the male and female populations aged 0 to 5, have been computed for that 5-year period. In stage II we compute the births for a given 5-year period, and the population aged 0 to 5 at the end of that 5-year period. The formulas used and the related methodological details are as follows:[1]

Stage I: Computation of Population Aged 5 to 90

(1) *Computation of the surviving population*

(1.1) Let $P^m(a, t)$ = the male population in age group a, at time t. $a = 5, 10, 15, \ldots, 90$, to signify the age groups

[1] The author is indebted to some unpublished materials by R. Dorfman for some aspects of the method here employed.

in the first 5 years of life, the second 5 years, and so on. $t = 0, 5, 10, \ldots, 55$.

(1.2) $P^f(a, t)$ = female population in age group a, at time t.

(1.3) Let $S^m(a, e)$ = the proportion of the male population in age group a that survives the 5-year period. The survival rate is related to a given expectation of life at birth e. (See below.)

(1.4) $S^f(a, e)$ = same as above for the female population.

(1.5) Now, $P^m(a, t)S^m(a, e) = P^m(a + 5, t + 5)$,

(1.6) and, $P^f(a, t)S^f(a, e) = P^f(a + 5, t + 5)$, for all a, t, and e.

Formulas 1.5 and 1.6 enable us to project the surviving population for each age group and each sex from $t = 0$ to $t = 5$, from $t = 5$ to $t = 10$ and so on, for all a, and for any given sequence of e's.

(2) Computation of 5-year survival rates

$$(2.1) \quad s^m(a, e) = 1 - d^m(a, e),$$

where $d^m(a, e)$ is the proportion of the male population in age group a at the beginning of the year that dies during that year. The death rate $d^m(a, e)$ is obtained from the regression equation between age-specific mortality rates and life expectancy at birth for age group a for males. That is, $s^m(a, e)$ is the proportion of the male population in age group a that survives one year.

(Note. The original data on mortality rates sometimes came in terms of age-specific death rates where the denominator in the death rate was for the mid-year population. In those cases where the differences were of significance these rates were adjusted to death rates where the population in the denominator was as at the beginning of the year and these were used in the computation of the least square regression equations for each age group.)

In a similar manner, 1-year survival rates (age-specific) are obtained for the female population by the formula,

$$(2.2) \qquad s^f(a, e) = 1 - d^f(a, e),$$

for all a and e.

The computation of the proportion of the males surviving 5 years in age group a for a given e, $S^m(a, e)$, is given by

$$(2.3) \qquad S^m(a, e) = [s^m(a, e)]^{2\frac{1}{2}}[s^m(a + 5, e)]^{2\frac{1}{2}},$$

for the male population, for all the 5-year age groups other than 0–5, 80–85, and 85–90 (exclusive of the upper bound).

Similarly for the female population survival rates for 5 years are given by

$$(2.4) \qquad S^f(a, e) = [s^f(a, e)]^{2\frac{1}{2}}[s^f(a + 5, e)]^{2\frac{1}{2}}$$

For the age groups above age eighty, which involve an exceedingly small proportion of any population, graphical methods were employed in determining the survival rates S^m_{85}, S^m_{90}, and S^f_{85} and S^f_{90}.

(3) Computation of the 5-year survival rates S^m_5 and S^f_5

Computation of the survival rates S^m_5 and S^f_5 requires special treatment since the death rate for the first year of life is usually very different from that of the succeeding 4 years. The method used was to obtain the ratios, P^m_{10}/P^m_5 and P^f_{10}/P^f_5, under the assumption that total births year by year are the same for the 10-year period. These ratios of the populations in the first two 5-year age groups (separately for each sex) yield approximations of the first 5-year survival rates. Omitting the symbols for each sex (m and f), and omitting e for the given life expectancy, we have the equation:

$$(3.1) \qquad P_5 = 1 + s_1 + s_1 s_5 + s_1 s_5{}^2 + s_1 s_5{}^3,$$

where s_1 is the proportion surviving 1 year in the first year of life, and s_5 is the proportion surviving 1 year for those in the age group 1–5 (exclusive of those aged 5). P_5 is the population in the first 5-year age group.

Following similar reasoning we have as the population in the next age group:

$$(3.2) \quad P_{10} = s_1 s_5{}^4 + s_1 s_5{}^4 s_{10} + s_1 s_5{}^4 s_{10}{}^2 + s_1 s_5{}^4 s_{10}{}^3 + s_1 s_5{}^4 s_{10}{}^4,$$

where P_{10} is the population in the age group 5 to 10.

And finally:

$$(3.3) \qquad S_5 = \frac{P_{10}}{P_5}.$$

Of course, these have to be computed separately for each sex.

Stage II: Computation of Births and Population Aged 0 to 5

We begin with a set of birth rates, $b_{15}, b_{20}, \ldots, b_{45}$, where b_{15} is the proportion of women aged 15–20 that give birth during one year; similarly for b_{20}, b_{25}, and so on.

Next, we compute the number of women-years of exposure to the risks $b_{15}, b_{20}, \ldots$, etc. In general notation we seek to determine the women-years of exposure to b_a over the 5-year projection period, where $a = 15, 20, 25, \ldots, 45$.

(4) Computation of number of women subject to risk b_a

We write w_{15}, w_{20}, $w_{25}, \ldots,$ w_{50}, for number of women in age groups 10–15, 15–20, 20–25, . . . , 45–50, respectively, at time t. Assuming that women are evenly distributed over the 5-year age group interval, only half the women aged 10–15 are exposed during a 5-year period to the birth rate b_{15}, and only half the women 15–20 are exposed during a 5-year period to b_{15}. Also, *not* all women survive the 5-year period.

The proportion of women in age group a who die over a 5-year period is given by D_a^f where

$$(4.1) \qquad D_a^f = 1 - S_a^f.$$

On the average the women exposed to the 5-year death rate D_a^f remain in the age group a approximately 2½ years over a 5-year period. Most surviving women enter the next age interval at some point during the 5-year period.

Therefore, the women-years of exposure to b_a by women in age group a over a 5-year period is given by $\frac{5}{2}(w_a - \frac{1}{2}D_a^f\, w_a)$; and similarly, the women-years of exposure to b_a by women in age group $a + 5$ is given by $\frac{5}{2}(w_{a+5} - \frac{1}{2}D_{a+5}^f\, w_{a+5})$.

Total women-years of exposure to b_a is therefore

$$(4.2) \qquad W_a = \tfrac{5}{2}(w_a - \tfrac{1}{2}D_a^f w_a + w_{a+5} - \tfrac{1}{2}D_{a+5}^f w_{a+5})$$

where W_a is the total women-years of exposure to b_a.

For example:

$$(4.3) \qquad W_{15} = \tfrac{5}{2}(w_{15} - \tfrac{1}{2}D_{15}^f w_{15} + w_{20} - \tfrac{1}{2}D_{20}^f w_{20}).$$

In equation (4.3) two groups of women are involved, those that start in the 10–15 age group, and those in the 15–20 age group at the outset.

It follows that:

$$(4.4) \quad B = \sum_a W_a b_a = \text{total number of children born over the 5-year period.}$$

(5) Computation of male and female population aged 0 to 5

Usually, approximately 53 of every 100 babies will be male. Also, not all babies survive the first 5-year period. Therefore, the male population in the age group 0–5, at $t = 5$ years hence, is given by

$$(5.1) \qquad P^m(5, t + 5) = .53B - \tfrac{1}{2}D_5^m(.53B),$$

where $D_5^m = 1 - S_5^m$.

And similarly the female population aged 0–5, at the end of the 5-year period is given by

$$(5.2) \qquad P^f(5, t + 5) = .47B - \tfrac{1}{2}D_5^f(.47B),$$

where $D_5^f = 1 - S_5^f$.

Adding the male and female population in that age group we obtain the total population in that age group at the end of the 5-year period.

APPENDIX 6

The data for figure 14–4 show the correlation between life expectancy and per capita income. The table on the following pages gives the dates for the life expectancy, the male life expectancy, the date of the national income data, the national income in international units where per capita figures were not available, the population date, the population, and the per capita income for twenty-two countries and forty-one observations. Explanatory notes and the sources for the population data follow. (From a larger original list of observations many were not used because of lack of life expectancy data, national income data, or because the dates of the two were not close enough.)

Country	Male Life Expectancy Date	Male Life Expectancy at Birth	National Income Date	National Income in International Units	Population Date	Population	Per Capita National Income in International Units	Population Source
Belgium	1928–32	56.02	1930	2,840,000,000	1930	8,092,000	351	1
	1946–49	62.00	1947	2,916,000,000	1947	8,512,195	343	1
Bulgaria	1925–28	45.92	1929	...	1929	5,766,000	52[b]	2
Chile	1930	35.4	1928	...	1930	4,287,445	102[b]	3
Czechoslovakia	1929–32	51.92	1929	4,100,000,000	1930	13,964,000	294	4
Denmark	1911–15	56.2	1913	922,000,000[e]	1913	2,830,000	326	5
	1921–25	60.3	1925	1,188,000,000	1925	3,434,555	346	6
Denmark[c]	1936–40	63.5	1938	1,703,000,000	1938	3,777,000	451	7
	1946–50	67.8	1947	1,836,000,000	1947	4,123,600	445	6
Egypt	1936–38	35.65	1936	...	1936	15,801,000	44[b]	8
Estonia	1932–34	53.12	1928	146,000,000	1928	1,115,747	131	9
Finland	1931–40	54.45	1936	814,000,000	1936	3,612,400	225	10
France	1877–81	40.83	1870–79	6,560,000,000	1876	36,905,788	178	11
	1920–23	52.19	1921	10,990,000,000	1921	39,209,518	280	12
	1928–33	54.30	1931	13,060,000,000	1931	41,834,923	312	13
Germany	1924–26	55.97	1925	17,300,000,000	1925	63,166,000	274	4[d]
	1932–34	59.86	1933	18,340,000,000	1933	66,000,000	278	14
Greece	1930	49.09	1929	630,000,000	1929	6,315,000	100	15
Hungary	1930–31	48.27	1930–31	1,084,000,000	1930	8,649,000	125	4
Ireland (Republic)	1935–37	58.20	1936	928,092,000[f]	1936	2,968,420	313	16
	1940–42	59.01	1941	807,696,000[f]	1941	2,992,034	270	16
Ireland	1925–27	57.37	1926	819,392,000[f]	1926	2,971,992	276	16
Italy	1935–37	55.19	1938	6,420,000,000	1938	43,979,000	146	17
Jamaica	1945–47	51.25	1942	...	...	...	68[b]	..

Country	Male Life Expectancy Date	Male Life Expectancy at Birth	National Income Date	National Income in International Units[a]	Popula-tion Date	Population	Per Capita National Income in International Units	Popula-tion Source
Japan	1926–30	44.82	1928	8,500,000,000	1928	62,070,000	137	18
	1935–36	46.92	1936	13,030,000,000	1936	69,590,000	187	18
	1947	50.06	1944	15,500,000,000	1944	73,800,000	210	18
Latvia	1934–36	55.39	1936	358,000,000	1936	1,958,324	183	19
Mexico	1940	37.92	1940	. . .	1940	19,653,552	23[b]	20
Netherlands	1931–40	65.7	1935	2,977,000,000	1935	8,433,000	353	4
Norway	1891–95	50.41	1891	270,000,000	1890	2,000,917	135	21
	1911–15	55.62	1913	515,000,000[g]	1913	2,462,350	209	21
Norway	1921–25	60.98	1923	623,000,000[g]	1923	2,731,619	228	22
	1931–32	64.1	1932	649,000,000[g]	1932	2,841,529	228	23
	1945–48	67.8	1947	1,135,000,000[g]	1947	3,165,011	359	23
Switzerland	1910–11	50.65	1913	1,057,000,000	1913	3,863,964	274	24
	1920–21	54.48	1924	1,232,000,000	1924	3,917,800	314	24
	1929–32	59.17	1930	1,615,000,000	1930	4,051,000	399	4
	1939–44	62.68	1942	1,443,000,000	1942	4,302,200	335	25
Sweden	1926–30	61.19	1928	. . .	1928	6,105,190	118[h]	26
	1931–40	63.76	1936	. . .	1936	6,266,888	129[h]	27

Explanatory Notes:

(*a*) All figures for national income in International Units are derived from Colin Clark, *Conditions of Economic Progress* (2nd Ed.), London, MacMillan and Co., Ltd., 1951.

(*b*) For Bulgaria, Chile, Egypt, Jamaica, and Mexico, Clark, *op. cit.*, gives the figures for per capita incomes in U. S. dollars (1939 purchasing power). These figures were changed into International Units by the following method:

(1) United States national income in international units in 1939—55.6 billion
United States national income in dollars at current (1939) prices—72.5 billion

∴ United States national income in international units is .767 of United States' national income in 1939 (at 1939 prices).

(2) Deflate the national-income-per-capita-in-1939-purchasing-power figures to international units by multiplying the former figure by .767.

Note: The national income figures for the United States in 1939 are found in *The Survey of Current Business*, July, 1947 Supplement, p. 20.

Clark used the United States national income figures deflated to a 1929 price index and converted them into international units. For the above computation the national income figure of 1939 was used at current (1939) prices because the per capita figures for the other nations are based on 1939 United States dollars.

(*c*) Excluding Faroe Islands.
(*d*) *De jure* population, territory of 1937.
(*e*) Net national product (Clark, *op. cit.*, p. 106).
(*f*) Clark, *op. cit.*, pp. 60–61, gives the net national product of Eire in international unit figures with allowance made for farm (home) consumption. These figures were changed into international units without allowance for farm consumption by the following method:

(1) Given, net national product with allowance in the Irish monetary unit of measure.
(2) Given, net national product without allowance in the Irish monetary unit of measure.
(3) Difference, that is, (1) − (2) is divided into (1), that is, (3)/(1) for the desired ratio.
(4) Given, net national product with allowance in international units.
(5) The ratio obtained, that is, (3)/(1) is multiplied by (4) to yield the amount "allowed for."
(6) The amount "allowed for," that is, (5), is subtracted from the net national product with allowance figure, that is, (4).

(*g*) "Produced National Income" (see Clark, *op. cit.*, p. 103).
(*h*) These figures are given in Clark, *op. cit.*, pp. 108–109, as "real income per head, arbitrary units adjusted for international comparisons."
The figure for 1936 was arrived at by the following method:
(1) Given, "real product per head, occupied population in international unit per year" for the years through 1936.
(2) Given, "real income per head, arbitrary units adjusted for international comparisons" for the years excepting 1936.
(3) The fairly constant ratio, (2)/(1), was multiplied by the "real product per head, occupied population in international units per year" figure for 1936 to yield the approximate desired figure.

Sources for Population Data:

(1) *Annuaire statistique de la Belgique et du Congo Belge, année, 1953,* Tome 74, Royaume de Belgique, Institut National de Statistique, p. 32. (2) *Annuaire statistique du Royaume de Bulgarie, 1931*, Sofia, Imprimerie de l'état, 1931, Table 1, p. 16. (3) *Anuario DIC, 1946*, Chile, Dirección general informaciones y cultura, Santiago, p. 476. (4) *Demographic Yearbook, 1954*, Statistical Office of the United Nations, New York, 1954, p. 118. (5) *Statistisk aarbok, 1913*, Udgivit af det Statistiske department, Kobenhaven, 1913, Table 4, p. 3. (6) *Ibid.*, 1954, Table 6, p. 5. (7) *Ibid.*, 1939, Table 15, p. 23. (8) *Annuaire statistique, 1949–1950 et 1950–1951*, Département de la Statistique et du Recensement, Imprimerie Nationale, Le Caire, 1953, p. 24. (9) *Estonie de 1920–1930, résumé retrospectif*, Bureau Central de Statistique de L'Estonie, Tallinn, 1931, Table 31, p. 25. (10) *Annuaire statistique de Finlande*, Nouvelle Série, 1952. Publication du Bureau Central de Statistique, Table 6, p. 5. (11) *Résultats statistiques du recensement général de la population*, effectué le 4 Mars 1906. Tome 1-première partie, Statistique Générale de la France, Ministère de Travail et de la Prévoyance Sociale, Paris, Imprimerie Nationale, 1908, p. 28. (12) *Ibid.*, 1921, p. 9. (13) *Annuaire statistique, 1932*, Statistique Générale de la France, Paris, Imprimerie Nationale, 1933, p. 3. (14) *Statistisches Jahrbuch für die Bundesrepublik Deutschland, 1955*, Heransegeber: Statistisches Bundesamt, Wiesbaden; W. Kohlhammer, Stuttgart-Köln. (15) *Annuaire statistique de la Grèce, 1930,* Statistique Générale de la Grèce, Athènes, Imprimerie Nationale, 1930, Table 2, pp. 23–24. (16) *Statistical Abstract of Ireland, 1953,* Central Statistical Office, Dublin, 1954, Table 10, p. 23. (17) *Annuario statistico italiano, anno, 1954*, Instituto Centrale di Statistica del Regno d'Italia, Roma, Table 22, p. 25. (18) *Japan Statistical Year Book, 1954*, Bureau of Statistics, Office of the Prime Minister, p. 11. (19) *Annuaire statistique de la Lettonie, pour l'année 1937/1938*, Bureau de Statistique de l'Etat, 1938, Table 6, p. 6, and Table 14, p. 13. (20) *Anuario estadístico de los Estados Unidos mexicanos, 1943–1945*, Secretaría de Economía, Dirección General de Estadística, México, 1950, p. 19. (21) *Statistisk aarbok for kongeriket Norge, 1914*, Utgit av det Statistike Centralbyraa, Kristiania, 1915, Table 2, p. 2. (22) *Ibid.*, 1924, Table 4, p. 2. (23) *Statistisk aarbok for Norge, 1954*, Statistike Centralbyraa, Oslo, Table 4, p. 5. (24) *Annuaire statistique de la Suisse, 1925*, Publié par le Bureau Fédéral de Statistique, Berne, 1926, p. 10. (25) *Ibid.*, 1943, p. 16. (26) *Statistisk arsbok för Sverige, 1924*, Uttgiven av Statistiska Centralbyrin, Stockholm, 1924, Table 8, p. 5. (27) *Ibid.*, 1937, Table 4, p. 4.

APPENDIX 7

NET CAPITAL FORMATION AS A PERCENTAGE OF NATIONAL INCOME

(Computed from Adjoining Tables from United Nations, Statistical Office, *Monthly Bulletin of Statistics*, October, 1954)

Country	1938	1948	1949	1950	1951	1952	1953
Australia	19.1	23.2	28.9	29.9	...	19.8	24.2
Brazil	...	8.9	10.5	11.8	14.7	...	...
Burma	8.0	12.7	2.9	3.8	8.0	14.1	15.7
Chile	...	16.4	16.1	14.0	...	...	...
Cuba	...	7.3	6.7	7.4	7.0	13.3	...
Denmark	8.7	9.2	11.3	15.3	13.1	11.2	...
France	1.9	8.3	15.1	12.5	14.8	9.3	...
Honduras	4.5	10.7	11.0	9.9	13.1	14.9	...
Ireland	7.4	12.5	10.3	13.0	16.4	10.0	...
Netherlands	1.9	15.0	15.2	21.9	16.7	6.5	11.9
Norway	13.2	24.5	25.2	21.4	22.7	21.6	23.1
Peru	...	6.3	4.2	8.5	16.5	16.5	...
Philippines	...	7.2	4.8	4.2	8.5	7.1	...
*Puerto Rico	...	11.5	8.2	10.9	14.0	8.5	...

*Net private capital formation (including public enterprises) as a percentage.

Author Index

Subject Index